Volume 2 Topics 9-16

Authors

Randall I. Charles
Professor Emeritus
Department of Mathematics
San Jose State University
San Jose, California

Janet H. Caldwell
Professor of Mathematics
Rowan University
Glassboro, New Jersey

Juanita Copley
Professor Emerita, College of Education
University of Houston
Houston, Texas

Warren Crown
Professor Emeritus of Mathematics
Education
Graduate School of Education
Rutgers University
New Brunswick, New Jersey

Francis (Skip) Fennell
L. Stanley Bowlsbey Professor
of Education and Graduate and
Professional Studies
McDaniel College
Westminster, Maryland

Stuart J. Murphy
Visual Learning Specialist
Boston, Massachusetts

Kay B. Sammons
Coordinator of Elementary Mathematics
Howard County Public Schools
Ellicott City, Maryland

Jane F. Schielack
Professor of Mathematics
Associate Dean for Assessment and
Pre K-12 Education, College of Science
Texas A&M University
College Station, Texas

Mathematicians

Roger Howe
Professor of Mathematics
Yale University
New Haven, Connecticut

Gary Lippman
Professor of Mathematics and Computer
Science
California State University East Bay
Hayward, California

SAVVAS
LEARNING COMPANY

Contributing Authors

Zachary Champagne
District Facilitator, Duval County Public Schools
Florida Center for Research in Science,
Technology, Engineering, and Mathematics
(FCR-STEM)
Jacksonville, Florida

Jonathan A. Wray
Mathematics Instructional Facilitator
Howard County Public Schools
Ellicott City, Maryland

ELL Consultants

Janice Corona
Retired Administrator
Dallas ISD, Multi-Lingual Department
Dallas, Texas

Jim Cummins
Professor
The University of Toronto
Toronto, Canada

Texas Reviewers

Theresa Bathe
Teacher
Fort Bend ISD

Chrissy Beltran
School Wide Project Coordinator
Ysleta ISD

Renee Cutright
Teacher
Amarillo ISD

Sharon Grimm
Teacher
Houston ISD

Esmeralda Herrera
Teacher
San Antonio ISD

Sherry Johnson
Teacher
Round Rock ISD

Elvia Lopez
Teacher
Denton ISD

Antoinese Pride
Instructional Coach
Dallas ISD

Joanna Ratliff
Teacher
Keller ISD

Courtney Jo Ridehuber
Teacher
Mansfield ISD

Nannie D. Scurlock-McKnight
Mathematics Specialist
A.W. Brown Fellowship-Leadership Academy
Dallas, TX

Brian Sinclair
Math Instructional Specialist
Fort Worth ISD

ISBN-13: 978-0-328-76727-4
ISBN-10:   0-328-76727-1
16 2021

Look for these digital resources in every lesson!

Digital Resources

🏴 Go to SavvasTexas.com

 Solve
Solve & Share problems plus math tools

 Tools
Math Tools to help you understand

 Learn
Visual Learning Animation Plus with animation, interaction, and math tools

 Check
Quick Check for each lesson

 Glossary
Animated Glossary in English and Spanish

 Games
Math Games to help you learn

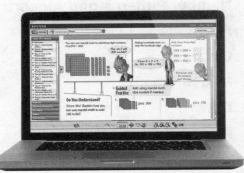

eText
The pages in your book online

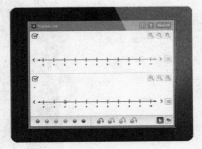

SavvasTexas.com
Everything you need for math anytime, anywhere

Contents

Key

Number and Operations

Algebraic Reasoning

Geometry and Measurement

Data Analysis

Personal Financial Literacy

Mathematical Process Standards are found in all lessons.

Digital Resources at SavvasTexas.com

Solve Learn Glossary

Check Tools Games

And remember, the pages in your book are also online!

TOPIC 1 — Addition Strategies

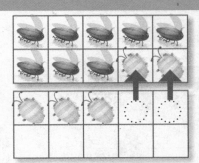

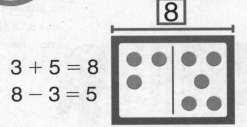

Hi, I'm Marta. This shows how you can use ten-frames to make a 10.

TEKS 2.1A, 2.1B, 2.1C, 2.1D, 2.1E, 2.1F, 2.1G, 2.4, 2.4A

TOPIC 2 — Subtraction Strategies

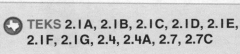

$$3 + 5 = 8$$
$$8 - 3 = 5$$

Hi, I'm Jackson. This shows a way to use counters to solve $8 - 3$.

TEKS 2.1A, 2.1B, 2.1C, 2.1D, 2.1E, 2.1F, 2.1G, 2.4, 2.4A, 2.7, 2.7C

TOPIC 3 — Numbers to 1,200

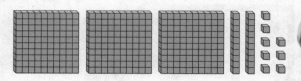

Hi, I'm Emily. This shows the number 328 using models.

⭐ TEKS 2.1A, 2.1B, 2.1C, 2.1D, 2.1E, 2.1F, 2.1G, 2.2, 2.2A, 2.2B

TOPIC 4 — Comparing and Ordering to 1,200

387

407   389

407

least ____, ____, ____ greatest

Hi, I'm Carlos. This shows how to compare and order numbers using place value.

⭐ TEKS 2.1A, 2.1B, 2.1C, 2.1D, 2.1E, 2.1F, 2.1G, 2.2, 2.2C, 2.2D, 2.2E, 2.2F, 2.7, 2.7B

TOPIC 5 — Exploring Addition and Subtraction

Hi, I'm Jada. This shows how you can add on a hundred chart.

$54 + 18 = 72$

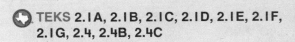

51	52	53	54	55	56	57	58	59	60
61	62	63	64	65	66	67	68	69	70
71	72	73	74	75	76	77	78	79	80

TEKS 2.1A, 2.1B, 2.1C, 2.1D, 2.1E, 2.1F, 2.1G, 2.4, 2.4B, 2.4C

TOPIC 6 — Adding 2-Digit Numbers

Hi, I'm Daniel. This shows how to model a 2-digit addition problem.

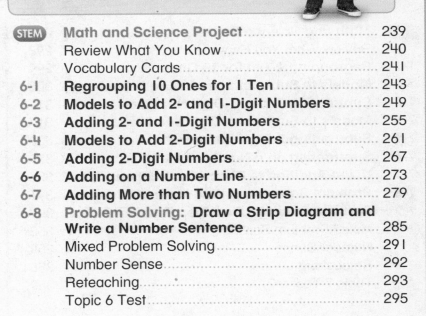

TEKS 2.1A, 2.1B, 2.1C, 2.1D, 2.1E, 2.1F, 2.1G, 2.2F, 2.4B, 2.4C, 2.9C

TOPIC 7 — Subtracting 2-Digit Numbers

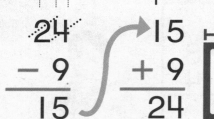

Hi, it's Marta again. This shows how you can use addition to check subtraction.

1 14
2̶4̶
− 9
‾‾‾‾
15

1
15
+ 9
‾‾‾‾
24

24
9 | 15

🔲 TEKS 2.1A, 2.1B, 2.1C, 2.1D, 2.1E, 2.1F, 2.1G, 2.2F, 2.4, 2.4B, 2.4C, 2.4D, 2.9C

TOPIC 8 — 3-Digit Addition and Subtraction

Hi, I'm Alex. This shows how you can count on to find a missing part.

100 100 10 10
440, 540, 640, 650, 660

You counted on 220.

$440 + \underline{220} = 660$

🔲 TEKS 2.1A, 2.1B, 2.1C, 2.1D, 2.1E, 2.1F, 2.1G, 2.4C, 2.4D

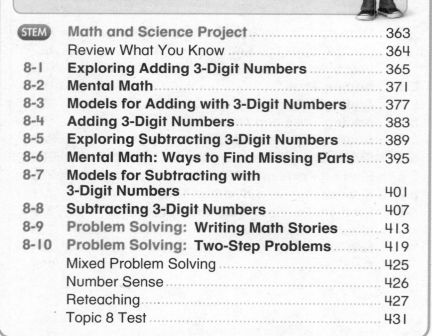

TOPIC 9
Meanings of Multiplication and Division

$8 \div 2 = ?$

Day 1 **Day 2** **Day 3** **Day 4**

$8 - 2 = 6$ $6 - 2 = 4$ $4 - 2 = 2$ $2 - 2 = 0$

Hi, it's Jada again. This shows division as repeated subtraction.

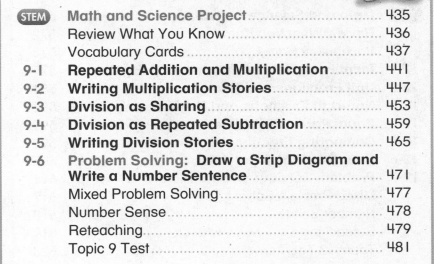

TEKS 2.1, 2.1A, 2.1B, 2.1C, 2.1D, 2.1E, 2.1F, 2.1G, 2.6, 2.6A, 2.6B

TOPIC 10
Money

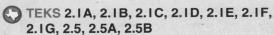

$50¢$ $75¢$ $85¢$ $90¢$ $91¢$

Hi, it's Carlos again. This shows how to count on to find the total amount of money.

TEKS 2.1A, 2.1B, 2.1C, 2.1D, 2.1E, 2.1F, 2.1G, 2.5, 2.5A, 2.5B

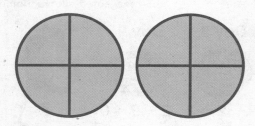

| TOPIC 11 | Number Patterns and Algebra |

110	120	130	140	150	160
210	220	230	240	250	260
310	320	330	340	350	360
410	420	430	440	450	460
510	520	530	540	550	560
610	620	630	640	650	660

Hi, it's Emily again. This shows numbers that are 100 more as you read down each column.

TEKS 2.1A, 2.1B, 2.1C, 2.1D, 2.1E, 2.1F, 2.1G, 2.2C, 2.7, 2.7A, 2.7B, 2.7C

| TOPIC 12 | Fractions |

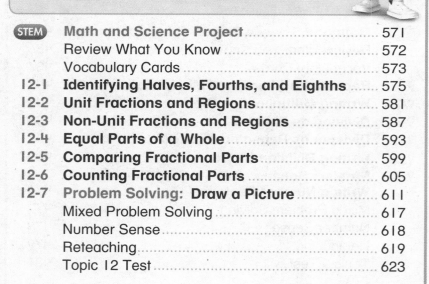

Hi, it's Jackson again. This shows that nine fourths is the same as two wholes and one fourth.

TEKS 2.1A, 2.1B, 2.1C, 2.1D, 2.1E, 2.1F, 2.1G, 2.3, 2.3A, 2.3B, 2.3C, 2.3D, 2.8E

TOPIC 13 Geometry

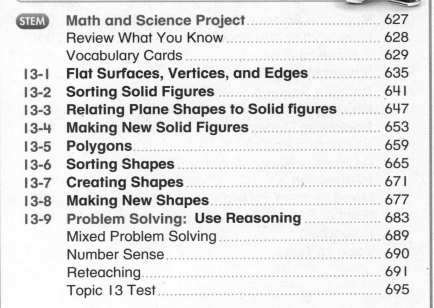

Hi, it's Marta again. This shows how you can use smaller shapes to make larger shapes.

TEKS 2.1A, 2.1B, 2.1C, 2.1D, 2.1E, 2.1F, 2.1G, 2.8, 2.8A, 2.8B, 2.8C, 2.8D, 2.8E

TOPIC 14 Measurement

Hi, it's Daniel again. This shows 8:27 on two different clocks.

TEKS 2.1A, 2.1B, 2.1C, 2.1D, 2.1E, 2.1F, 2.1G, 2.9, 2.9A, 2.9B, 2.9D, 2.9E, 2.9F, 2.9G

Volume 2

TOPIC 15 — Data

Favorite Ball Games	
Baseball	⚇⚇
Soccer	⚇⚇⚇⚇⚇⚇⚇
Tennis	⚇⚇⚇⚇

Each ⚇ = 1 student

Hi, it's Emily again. This shows a pictograph that can be used to record and compare data.

⭐ TEKS 2.1, 2.1A, 2.1B, 2.1C, 2.1D, 2.1E, 2.1F, 2.1G, 2.10, 2.10A, 2.10B, 2.10C, 2.10D

TOPIC 16 — Personal Financial Literacy

Week	Amount Joe Owes
1	$10 - $2 = $8
2	$8 - $2 = $6
3	$6 - $2 = $4
4	$4 - $2 = $2
5	$2 - $2 = $0

Hi, it's Carlos again. This shows a chart that keeps track of how much money Joe pays back each week.

⭐ TEKS 2.1A, 2.1B, 2.1C, 2.1D, 2.1E, 2.1F, 2.1G, 2.10C, 2.11, 2.11A, 2.11B, 2.11C, 2.11D, 2.11E, 2.11F

Step Up to Grade 3

These lessons help prepare you for Grade 3.

TEKS 3.1A, 3.1B, 3.1C, 3.1D, 3.1E, 3.1F, 3.1G, 3.2, 3.2A, 3.2B, 3.2D, 3.3, 3.3A, 3.3C, 3.3D, 3.4, 3.4A, 3.5A

Meanings of Multiplication and Division

Essential Question: What are different meanings of multiplication and division?

At the amusement park, a ride can make you rise, spin, or fall.

There are many different kinds of amusement park rides!

Wow! Let's do this project and learn more.

Math and Science Project: Patterns in Motion

Find Out Read about roller coasters, merry-go-rounds, or other amusement park rides. Find out the ways that riders move on the rides.

Journal: Make a Book Invent an amusement park ride, and draw a picture of it. In your book, also:

• Make up and solve multiplication and division problems about the ride.

Name _____

Review What You Know

Vocabulary

1. Circle the **addition sentence**.

$$15 + 6 = 21$$

$$12 > 5$$

$$19 - 7 = 12$$

2. Circle the **difference**.

$$14 - 5 = 9$$

3. Circle the **subtraction sentence**.

$$16 < 17$$

$$18 - 9 = 9$$

$$8 + 9 = 17$$

Writing Number Sentences

4. Write an addition sentence to solve the problem.

Craig had 15 action figures. Then he bought 3 more action figures.
How many action figures does Craig have now?

_____ + _____ = _____

_____ action figures

5. Write a subtraction sentence to solve the problem.

Fiona had 24 raisins. She ate 4 of the raisins. How many raisins does Fiona have now?

_____ − _____ = _____

_____ raisins

Using Strip Diagrams

6. Use the strip diagram to find the missing number.

$$14 + \underline{} = 29$$

My Word Cards

Study the words on the front of the card.
Complete the activity on the back.

A-Z

multiply

$3 \times 2 = 6$

$2 + 2 + 2 = 6$

times (×)

times

$7 \times 3 = 21$

product

$4 \times 2 = 8$

↑

product

multiplication sentence

$4 \times 2 = 8$

4 times 2 equals 8.

equal share

2   2   2

divide

We each get 4 peanuts!

$12 \div 3 = 4$

My Word Cards

Use what you know to complete the sentences.
Extend learning by writing your own sentence using each word.

When you multiply numbers, your answer is called the

_____.

Another word for multiply is

_____.

To _____

3 times 2 means to add 2 three times.

You _____

to separate a number of items into groups of equal size.

An _____

_____

is the same amount.

$4 \times 2 = 8$ is a

_____

_____.

My Word Cards Study the words on the front of the card. Complete the activity on the back.

A-Z

divided by (÷)

18 ÷ 3 = 6

↳ divided by

division sentence

4 ÷ 2 = 2

4 divided by 2 equals 2.

My Word Cards

Use what you know to complete the sentences.
Extend learning by writing your own sentence using each word.

$4 \div 2 = 2$ is a

_____

_____

18 _____

3 equals 6.

Name _____

Solve & Share

4 people go on a hike. Each person brings 3 oranges. How can you find how many oranges the hikers have in all? Select technology tools, counters, or paper and pencil to solve the problem. Draw what you did and explain your work.

TEKS 2.6 Connect repeated addition and subtraction to multiplication and division situations that involve equal groupings and shares. Also, 2.6A. **Mathematical Process Standards** 2.1A, 2.1C, 2.1D, 2.1F, 2.1G.

Digital Resources at SavvasTexas.com

Solve   Learn   Glossary   Check   Tools   Games

_____ total oranges

4 people are going on a hike. Each person takes 2 water bottles. How many water bottles do they take in all?

Use a model to show the problem.

You can skip count to solve.

2, 4, 6, 8

There are 8 bottles in all.

8

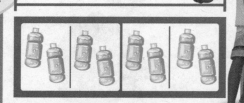

You can add to solve.

$2 + 2 + 2 + 2 = 8$

2 plus 2 plus 2 plus 2 equals 8.

The sum is 8.

Or, you can **multiply**. Write a **multiplication sentence**.

$4 \times 2 = 8$

4 **times** 2 equals 8.

The product is 8.

Do You Understand?

Show Me! Can you write $3 + 3 + 2$ as a multiplication sentence? Explain.

Guided Practice Use the model.
Complete each number sentence.

1.
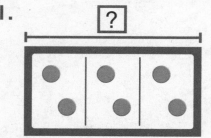

$2 + 2 + 2 = 6$

$3 \times 2 = 6$

2.
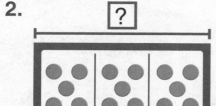

$5 + 5 + 5 = $ ____

$3 \times 5 = $ ____

Name _____

Independent Practice

Use the model. Complete each number sentence.

3.

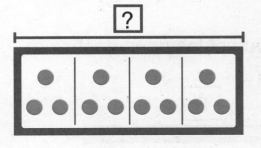

$3 + 3 + 3 + 3 =$ ___

$4 \times 3 =$ ___

4.

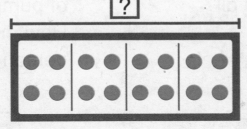

$4 + 4 + 4 + 4 =$ ___

$4 \times 4 =$ ___

5.

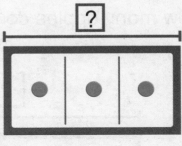

$1 + 1 + 1 =$ ___

$3 \times 1 =$ ___

6.

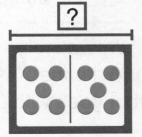

$5 + 5 =$ ___

$2 \times 5 =$ ___

7.

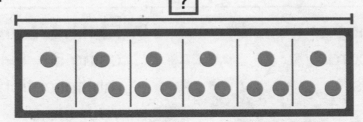

$3 + 3 + 3 + 3 + 3 + 3 =$ ___

$6 \times 3 =$ ___

8.

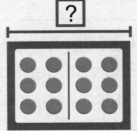

$6 + 6 =$ ___

$2 \times 6 =$ ___

9. Extend Your Thinking Write the missing numbers.

$2 + 2 + 2 + 2 + 2 =$ ___

$\square \times 2 = 10$

$9 + 9 + 9 =$ ___

$3 \times \square = 27$

$8 + 8 =$ ___

$\square \times \square = 16$

Problem Solving
Use counters to solve. Draw counters to make a model.

10. 3 people pick apples.
Each person picks 5 apples.
How many apples do they pick in all?

?

$3 \times 5 =$ _____ _____ apples

11. 4 people pick 8 pumpkins in all.
Each person picks the same number of pumpkins.
How many pumpkins does each person pick?

8

$4 \times$ _____ $= 8$ _____ pumpkins

12. 4 students go to the gift shop.
Each student buys 3 postcards.
Which sentence shows this problem?

$4 + 3 = 7$
◯

$4 \times 3 = 12$
◯

$3 \times 3 = 9$
◯

$4 + 4 + 4 + 4 = 16$
◯

13. Extend Your Thinking Write a story using $5 + 5 + 5 + 5 = 20$. Write the multiplication sentence that goes with your story.

_____

_____

_____

_____ $\times$ _____ $=$ _____

Name _____

Another Look You can add equal groups to find how many in all.
You can multiply equal groups to find how many in all.

$$2 + 2 + 2 + 2 + 2 = 10$$

$$5 \times 2 = 10$$

10 is the sum.

10 is the product.

🏠 **HOME CONNECTION**
Your child modeled repeated addition to understand multiplication.

HOME ACTIVITY Place items such as pencils or books into 3 groups, with 4 items in each group. Have your child write a repeated addition sentence and a multiplication sentence for the items.

Find the sum and the product.

1.

$$5 + 5 + 5 + 5 + 5 = \underline{\quad}$$

$$5 \times 5 = \underline{\quad}$$

2.

$$6 + 6 + 6 + 6 = \underline{\quad}$$

$$4 \times 6 = \underline{\quad}$$

3. Tony has 5 boxes.
Each box contains 6 buttons.
How many buttons does Tony have in all?

- ○ 11
- ○ 12
- ○ 24
- ○ 30

4. 2 monkeys climb a tree.
Each monkey picks 3 bananas.
Which number sentence shows this problem?

- ○ $3 + 3 + 3 = 9$
- ○ $2 \times 2 = 4$
- ○ $2 \times 3 = 6$
- ○ $3 \times 3 = 9$

Use the picture.
Write number sentences that tell how many balls are in the baskets in all.

5.

___ + ___ + ___ + ___ = ___

___ × ___ = ___

6.

___ + ___ + ___ = ___

___ × ___ = ___

7. Extend Your Thinking One student tossed 12 balls in all into baskets.

Draw a picture to show some baskets with the same number of balls in each basket.

Then write an addition sentence and a multiplication sentence to show how many balls there are in all.

Name _____

Solve & Share

Write a story for this multiplication sentence. Model your story. Then find the product.

$$2 \times 5 = \underline{\hspace{1cm}}$$

⊕ **TEKS 2.6A** Model, create, and describe contextual multiplication situations in which equivalent sets of concrete objects are joined. **Mathematical Process Standards 2.1A, 2.1E, 2.1F.**

Digital Resources at SavvasTexas.com

| Solve | Learn | Glossary | Check | Tools | Games |

_____

_____

_____

_____

Write a story for
$4 \times 3 = \underline{?}$.

You can start by drawing a picture!

I have 4 groups. There are 3 in each group.

Write a story about your picture.

Kit has 4 bags.
There are 3 apples in each bag.
How many apples does Kit have?

Solve your story.

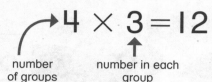

$4 \times 3 = 12$

number of groups — number in each group — number in all

Kit has 12 apples.

Do You Understand?

Show Me! How does drawing a picture help you write a multiplication story?

☆ Guided Practice ☆

Write a multiplication story for the picture. Then use counters to solve.

1. $3 \times 2 = \underline{6}$

_____

_____

2. $2 \times 5 = \underline{}$

_____

_____

Topic 9 | Lesson 2

☆ Independent ☆ Practice

Write a multiplication story for the picture. Then use counters to solve.

3.

_____

_____

_____

_____

$4 \times 4 =$ _____

4.

_____

_____

_____

_____

$2 \times 3 =$ _____

5.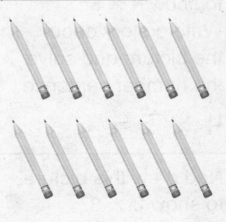

_____

_____

_____

_____

$2 \times 6 =$ _____

6. Extend Your Thinking Circle each group in the picture. Then use the picture to write a multiplication sentence.

___ $\times$ ___ = ___

___ $\times$ ___ = ___

___ $\times$ ___ = ___

7. Dina drew this picture to show 4×5. Write a story about the picture and solve the number sentence.

$4 \times 5 = \underline{\quad}$

_____

_____

_____

_____

8. Ned drew this picture to show 3×3. Write a story about the picture and solve the number sentence.

$3 \times 3 = \underline{\quad}$

_____

_____

_____

_____

9. Mr. Silva is getting snacks for his family. He puts 5 carrots on each of 3 plates. Which number sentence shows how many carrots he has?

○ $3 \times 3 = 9$

○ $2 \times 5 = 10$

○ $3 \times 5 = 15$

○ $5 + 5 = 10$

10. Extend Your Thinking Write a story for this number sentence. Then solve.

_____

_____

_____

_____

$4 \times 8 = \underline{\quad}$

Name _____

Another Look You can draw a picture and write a story to show 2 × 3.

Draw 2 fish tanks.
Draw 3 fish in each tank.
Finish the story.
Solve the problem.

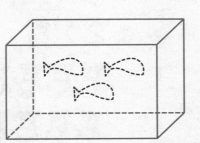 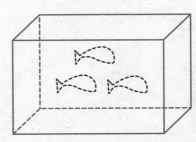

There are __2__ tanks.

There are __3__ fish in each tank.

$2 \times 3 = \underline{6}$

How many fish are there in all?

__6__ fish

🏠 **HOME CONNECTION**
Your child used models and pictures to write and solve multiplication stories.

HOME ACTIVITY Ask your child to draw a picture showing 2 × 8. Then have your child use the picture to write a multiplication story.

Draw counters in each box to model the problem.
Complete the story. Solve the problem.

1. 6 × 3

There are _____ boxes.

There are _____ counters in each box.

How many counters are there in all?

$6 \times 3 = \underline{\hspace{1cm}}$ counters in all

Write a story and find the missing number.

2. $3 \times \underline{\hspace{1cm}} = 24$

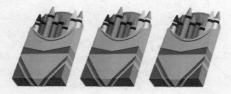

_____

_____

_____

_____

3. $2 \times \underline{\hspace{1cm}} = 12$

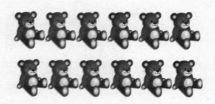

_____

_____

_____

_____

4. Liam has 9 pennies. He puts an equal number of them into each of his pockets. How many pockets does he have?

○ 2   ○ 3   ○ 6   ○ 19

5. Extend Your Thinking Choose two numbers to complete the multiplication sentence. Then write a story about your multiplication sentence.

_____

_____

_____

_____

$\underline{\hspace{1cm}} \times \underline{\hspace{1cm}} = 30$

Name _____

Solve & Share

3 students are doing an art project.
They will share 6 sheets of construction paper equally.
How many sheets of paper will each student get? Show your work.

⊕ **TEKS 2.6B** Model, create, and describe contextual division situations in which a set of concrete objects is separated into equivalent sets. **Mathematical Process Standards** 2.1A, 2.1B, 2.1C, 2.1D, 2.1F.

Digital Resources at SavvasTexas.com

Solve   Learn   Glossary   Check   Tools   Games

_____ in all   3 groups of _____

There are 8 toys.
4 dogs share them equally.
How many toys does each dog get?

Each dog will get an equal share.

Use counters to show 8 toys.

Share the counters. Make 4 equal groups.

There are 8 counters in all.

Each dog gets 2 toys.

_8_ in all

_4_ groups of _2_ toys

Do You Understand?

Show Me! Can 3 dogs share 7 toys equally? Explain.

☆ **Guided Practice** Use counters to make equal groups. Draw the groups. Write the numbers.

1. 4 toys shared by 2 friends

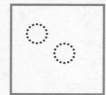

_4_ in all

_2_ groups of _2_ toys

2. 10 markers shared by 2 friends

_____ in all

_____ groups of _____ markers

Independent Practice

Use counters to make equal groups. Draw the groups. Write the numbers.

3. 18 balloons shared by 2 friends

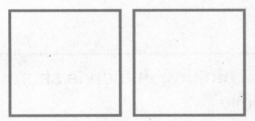

_____ in all

_____ groups of _____ balloons

4. 9 crayons shared by 3 friends

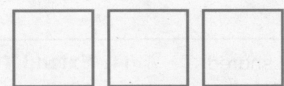

_____ in all

_____ groups of _____ crayons

5. 28 marbles shared by 4 friends

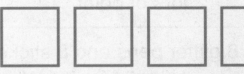

_____ in all

_____ groups of _____ marbles

Circle equal groups. Write the numbers. Use counters if you need to.

6. 24 colored pencils shared by 3 friends

_____ in all

_____ groups of _____ colored pencils

---

7. Extend Your Thinking The art teacher has 12 glue sticks. Find 5 different ways to show equal groups of glue sticks.

_____ groups of _____   _____ groups of _____

_____ groups of _____   _____ groups of _____

_____ groups of _____

8. Sara has 18 jars of paint.
She puts them in 3 rows.
Each row has an equal number of jars.
How many jars are in each row?

_____ jars of paint

9. Ray has 16 posters to give to 4 friends.
Each friend gets an equal share.
How many posters does each friend get?

_____ posters

10. 8 glitter pens and 8 stickers are shared equally by 2 friends. Which model shows the number of pens each friend gets?

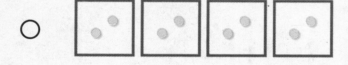

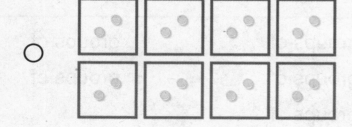

11. Extend Your Thinking 4 friends share 12 plums equally.
Then the 4 friends share 20 grapes equally.
How many more grapes than plums does each friend get?

Draw groups to help solve the problem.

_____ more grapes

Name _____

Another Look Use models to show equal shares.

5 students want to share 10 counters equally.
Draw 1 counter for each student.
Keep drawing 1 counter for each student until you
have drawn 10 counters in all.

There are __10__ counters to share equally.

There are __5__ groups of counters.

There are __2__ counters in each group.

Each student gets __2__ counters.

Each student gets the
same number of counters.
This means they get
equal shares.

🏠 **HOME CONNECTION**
Your child used counters
to model equal groups.

HOME ACTIVITY Give your
child 20 small objects, such
as pennies or buttons. Ask
your child to put the objects
into 5 equal groups and tell
how many objects are in
each group.

Draw to show equal groups.
Write how many each student gets.

1. 6 students want to share 18 counters.

Each student gets ____ counters.

Make equal groups. Write the numbers.

2. 12 books shared by 4 friends

_____ in all

_____ groups of _____ books

3. 6 apples shared by 2 friends

_____ in all

_____ groups of _____ apples

Draw boxes to show equal groups of fruit. Then write the numbers.

4. There are 12 oranges in all.

_____ groups of _____ oranges

5. There are 16 tomatoes in all.

_____ groups of _____ tomatoes

6. Tom, Tyler, Toby, Trevor, Tai, Tim, and Tamir shared 21 grapes equally. How many grapes did each boy get?

○ 1   ○ 2   ○ 3   ○ 7

7. Extend Your Thinking You have 18 pears. Find 6 different ways to show equal groups. Draw pictures to help.

_____ group of _____   _____ groups of _____

_____ groups of _____   _____ groups of _____

_____ groups of _____   _____ groups of _____

Name ______________________________

Solve & Share

I have 10 dog treats.
Suppose my dog eats 2 treats every day.
How many days can my dog eat 2 treats until there are no treats left?

Lesson 9-4
Division as Repeated Subtraction

TEKS 2.6 Connect repeated addition and subtraction to multiplication and division situations that involve equal groupings and shares. Also, 2.6B. **Mathematical Process Standards** 2.1B, 2.1C, 2.1D, 2.1F.

Digital Resources at SavvasTexas.com
Solve | Learn | Glossary | Check | Tools | Games

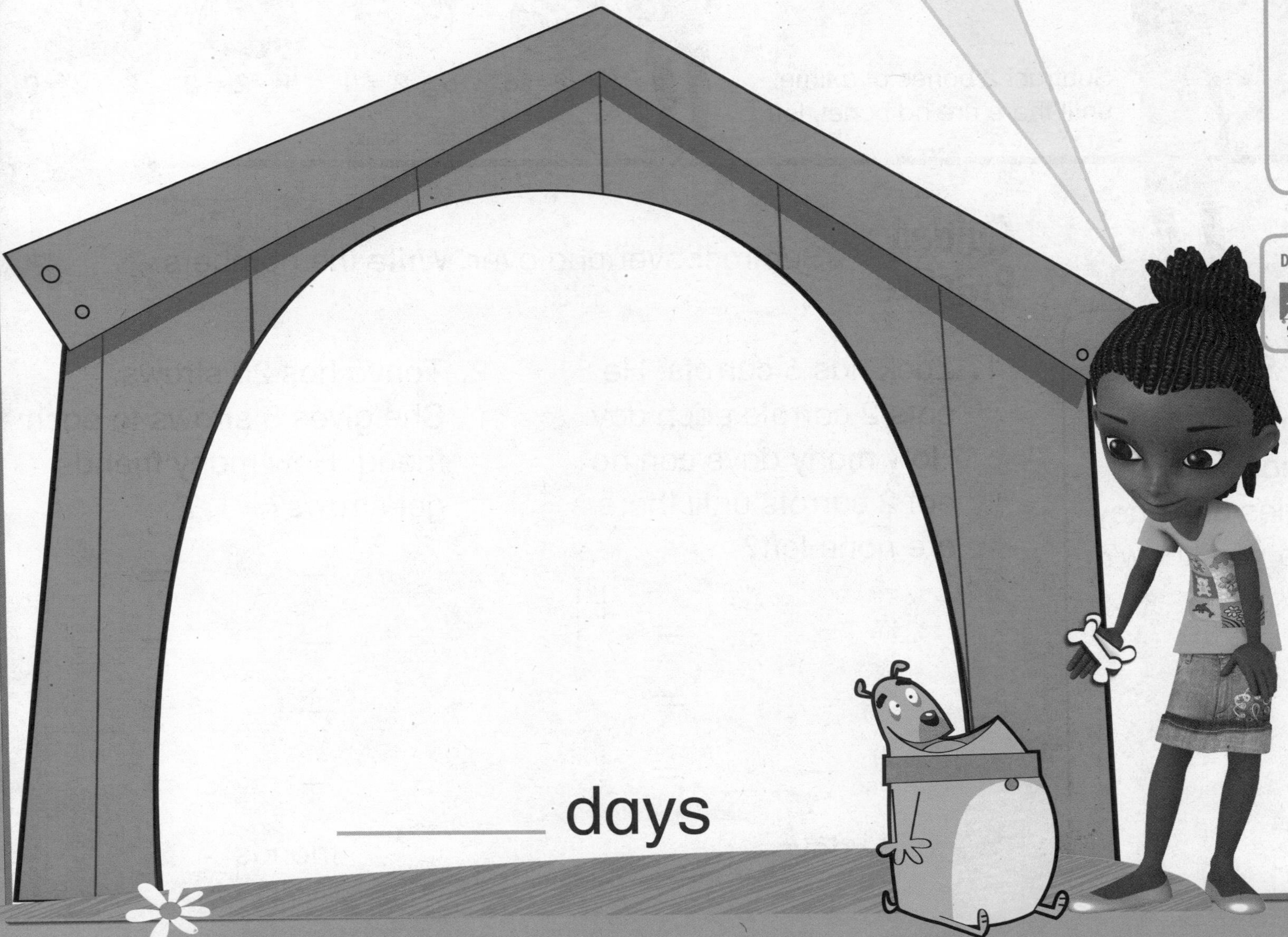

______ days

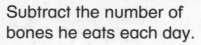

My dog has 8 bones.
He eats 2 bones each day.

How many days can he eat 2 bones until there are none left?

Subtract the number of bones he eats each day.

Start with 8.

Subtract 2 bones at a time until there are no bones left.

My dog can eat __2__ bones each day for __4__ days.

Day I	Day 2	Day 3	Day 4
$8 - 2 = 6$	$6 - 2 = 4$	$4 - 2 = 2$	$2 - 2 = 0$

Do You Understand?

Show Me! Suppose Gary has 9 cherries. How many days can he eat 3 cherries until they are gone? How do you know?

☆ Guided Practice ☆   Subtract over and over. Write the numbers.

1. Zack has 6 carrots. He eats 2 carrots each day. How many days can he eat 2 carrots until there are none left?

$$6 - 2 = 4$$
$$\_\_ - \_\_ = \_\_$$
$$\_\_ - \_\_ = 0$$

_____ days

2. Tonya has 20 straws. She gives 5 straws to each friend. How many friends get straws?

$$\_\_ - \_\_ = \_\_$$
$$\_\_ - \_\_ = \_\_$$
$$\_\_ - \_\_ = \_\_$$

_____ friends

Topic 9 | Lesson 4

Name _____

Subtract over and over. Write the numbers.

3. Molly has 12 peaches. She eats 3 each day. How many days can she eat 3 peaches until they are gone?

_____ − _____ = _____

_____ − _____ = _____

_____ − _____ = _____

_____ − _____ = _____

_____ days

4. John has $20. He spends $4 each day. How many days can he spend $4?

_____ − _____ = _____

_____ − _____ = _____

_____ − _____ = _____

_____ − _____ = _____

_____ − _____ = _____

_____ days

5. Rosa has 10 boxes of juice. She drinks 2 boxes of juice each day. How many days until the juice is gone?

_____ − _____ = _____

_____ − _____ = _____

_____ − _____ = _____

_____ − _____ = _____

_____ − _____ = _____

_____ days

Use subtraction to help solve.

6. Extend Your Thinking Marcie and Tom each have 16 apples. Marcie eats 4 apples each day. Tom eats 2 apples each day. Who will finish their apples first? How many days will it take?

_____ will finish first.

It will take _____ days.

Problem Solving
Group to subtract over and over to solve the problems below.

7. Dave has these tomatoes.
He puts 3 in each salad.
How many salads
can he make?

_____ salads

8. Sally has these ears
of corn.
She serves 2 to
each person.
How many people
can she serve?

_____ people

9. Theo has 24 peaches. He uses the
same number of peaches in each pie.
Theo did this work to find how many
pies he can make.
How many pies can he make?

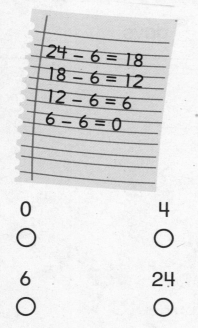

24 – 6 = 18
18 – 6 = 12
12 – 6 = 6
6 – 6 = 0

0 ○
4 ○
6 ○
24 ○

10. Extend Your Thinking Jan has 18 stamps.
Amar has 14 stamps. Each page of their
album can fit 8 stamps. How many pages
can Jan and Amar fill in all?

Draw a picture or write number sentences.

_____ pages

Name _____

Another Look Subtract equal shares over and over to solve.

Erin has 15 blueberries.
She puts 5 blueberries in
each pancake.

$$15 - 5 = 10$$
$$10 - 5 = 5$$
$$5 - 5 = 0$$

How many blueberry pancakes can
she make?

How many times did you subtract to get to 0? ___3___ times

How many blueberry pancakes can Erin make? ___3___ pancakes

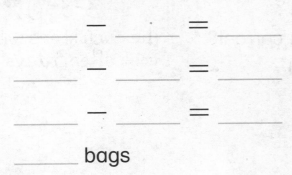

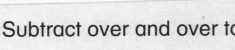
Subtract over and over to solve.

HOME CONNECTION
Your child used counters and repeated subtraction to find the number of equal groups into which a set of objects can be divided.

HOME ACTIVITY Give your child 18 coins. Ask your child to show you how to take away equal groups to answer this question: If you spend 3 coins each day, how many days can you spend the coins until there are no coins left?

1. Gina has 12 carrots and some plastic bags.
   She fills each plastic bag with 4 carrots.
   How many bags will she fill?

   ___ − ___ = ___
   ___ − ___ = ___
   ___ − ___ = ___

   _____ bags

2. Kofi has 24 grapes.
   He gives the same number of grapes
   to 6 friends.
   How many grapes does each friend get?

   ___ − ___ = ___
   ___ − ___ = ___
   ___ − ___ = ___
   ___ − ___ = ___

   _____ grapes

Subtract over and over to solve. Write the missing numbers.

3. Mia has 12 stickers.
She gives 3 stickers to each person.
How many people get stickers?

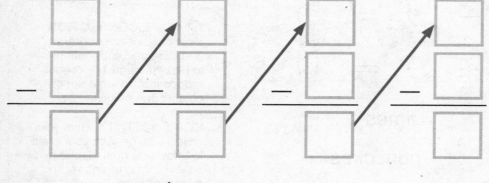

_____ people

4. Keisha has 15 stickers.
She gives 5 stickers to each person.
How many people get stickers?

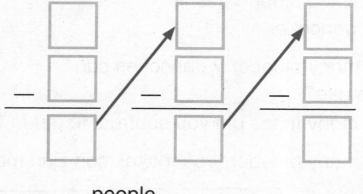

_____ people

5. ⭐ Anita had 14 apples. She and her brother ate 4 of them. Anita put the leftover apples on plates. She put 2 apples on each plate. How many plates did Anita use?

○ 2

○ 5

○ 7

○ 10

6. **Extend Your Thinking** Josh wrote this to find how many days he can use 3 cucumbers until all of his 12 cucumbers are gone.

Is Josh correct? Explain.

$12-3=9$
$9-3=6$
$6-3=3$
$3-3=0$
The cucumbers will be gone after 3 days.

_____

_____

Name _____

Solve & Share

Write a story about 8 kittens and 2 equal groups.
Then model and solve your story.

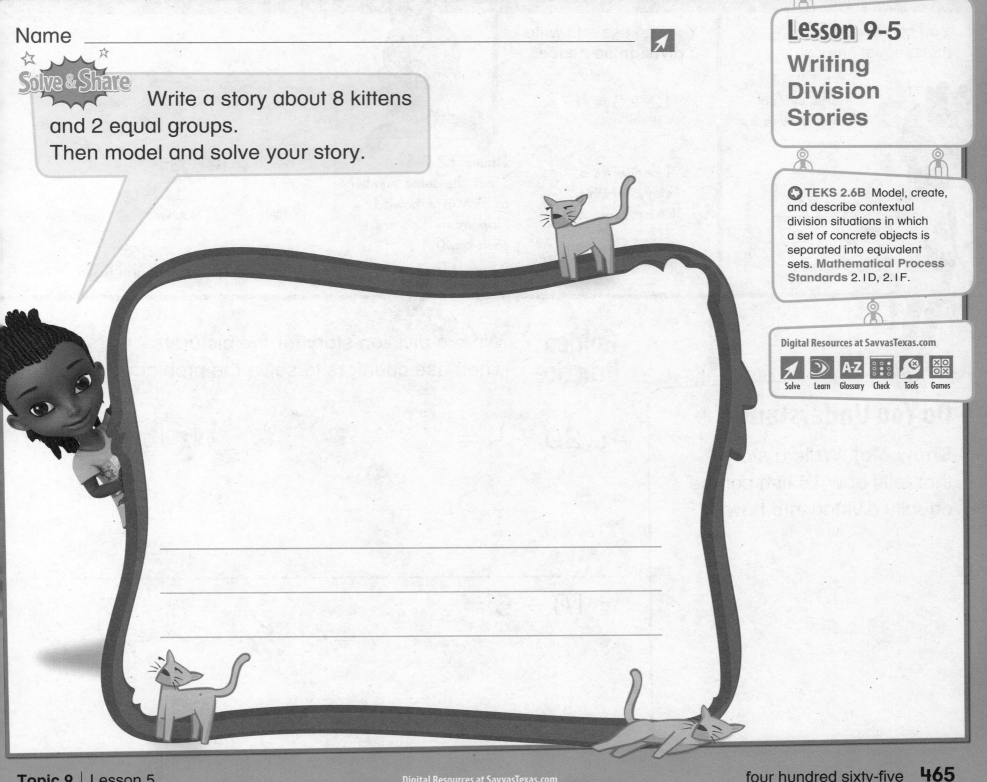

⊕ **TEKS 2.6B** Model, create, and describe contextual division situations in which a set of concrete objects is separated into equivalent sets. **Mathematical Process Standards** 2.1D, 2.1F.

Digital Resources at SavvasTexas.com

Solve Learn Glossary Check Tools Games

_____

_____

_____

You can **divide** to make equal groups.

This symbol means divided by.

$\div$

You can use $\div$ to write a **division sentence**.

$12 \div 3 = 4$

I can write a story for this division sentence.

I have 12 fish. I put the same number of fish in 3 bowls. How many fish are in each bowl?

$12 \div 3 = 4$

number in all | number of groups | number in each group

There are 4 fish in each bowl.

Do You Understand?

Show Me! Write a story that tells how 16 fish can be equally divided into bowls.

☆ **Guided Practice** ☆ Write a division story for the picture. Then use counters to solve the problem.

1. $20 \div 4 = \underline{5}$

_____

_____

2. $10 \div 5 = \underline{}$

_____

_____

466 four hundred sixty-six

Topic 9 | Lesson 5

Name _____

Write a division story for the picture. Then use counters to solve the problem.

3. $12 \div 3 =$ _____

_____

_____

_____

4. $18 \div 6 =$ _____

_____

_____

_____

Write a division story. Then use counters to solve the problem.

5. $8 \div 4 =$ _____

_____

_____

6. $15 \div 3 =$ _____

_____

_____

---

7. Extend Your Thinking Look at each story you wrote in Exercises 5 and 6.
Write what you found.

For Exercise 5:

number of equal groups _____

number in each group _____

For Exercise 6:

number of equal groups _____

number in each group _____

Problem Solving
Use counters to solve.
Draw your counters. Then write a division sentence.

8. Benito has 6 dog treats. He has 2 dogs.
He gives each dog the same number of treats.
How many treats does each dog get?

_____ ÷ _____ = _____

_____ treats

9. Carol has 16 dog treats.
She gives each of her dogs 4 treats.
How many dogs does Carol have?

_____ ÷ _____ = _____

_____ dogs

10. Which shows this story?
15 rabbits live in the forest.
5 rabbits live in each hole.
How many holes are there?

15 − 5 = 10   15 ÷ 1 = 15
   ○   ○

15 ÷ 5 = 3   15 ÷ 15 = 1
   ○   ○

11. Extend Your Thinking Write a division story about equal groups of 6. Then write a division sentence to solve your story.

_____

_____

_____

_____

Name _____

Another Look Look at the picture. Complete the story.
Then write a division sentence.

There are __10__ pilots.
An equal number of pilots fly on __5__ planes.
How many pilots are on each plane?

$$\underline{10} \div \underline{5} = \underline{2}$$

pilots   planes   pilots in each plane

10 divided by 5 is 2.

🏠 **HOME CONNECTION**
Your child wrote and solved division stories.

HOME ACTIVITY Ask your child to draw a picture and write or tell you a story for
$12 \div 2 = $ _____.

Complete the story.
Solve the division sentence.

I. A plane has 24 seats in one section.

There are __3__ seats in each row.
How many rows of seats are there?

$24 \div 3 = $ _____ rows of seats

2. A plane makes 20 trips.
It stops at _____ cities on each trip.
How many cities does the plane stop at?

$20 \div 2 = $ _____ cities

Write a division story for each problem. Then solve. Draw a picture to help.

3. 18 monkeys in 3 equal groups

_____

_____

_____

_____

_____ ÷ _____ = _____

4. 30 crackers in 5 equal groups

_____

_____

_____

_____ ÷ _____ = _____

5. Felix has 18 comic books.
He puts 14 of them into 2 piles.
Which shows how many comic books
are in each pile?

2   7
○   ○

6   9
○   ○

6. **Extend Your Thinking** Jay has 12 stamps.
He wants to put the same number
of stamps on each page of his album.
How many stamps can he put on each page?
Write division sentences to show 3 different
ways.

_____ ÷ _____ = _____ stamps

_____ ÷ _____ = _____ stamps

_____ ÷ _____ = _____ stamps

Name _____

Solve & Share

There are 12 students in a classroom. They will sit in equal groups at 4 different tables. How many students will sit at each table? Show how you know.

⭐ **TEKS 2.1D** Communicate mathematical ideas, reasoning, and their implications using multiple representations .... Also, 2.6. **Mathematical Process Standards** 2.1, 2.1B, 2.1G.

Digital Resources at SavvasTexas.com

| Solve | Learn | Glossary | Check | Tools | Games |

_____ ÷ _____ = _____

Analyze

Pat has 3 boxes. Each box has 5 marbles inside. How many marbles does Pat have in all?

Plan

I can draw a picture to show how many marbles in all.

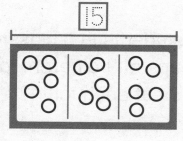

Solve and Justify

15

Evaluate

My drawing and number sentence match the problem. I can check my multiplication by adding.
$5 + 5 + 5 = 15$

$3 \times 5 = 15$

Do You Understand?

Show Me! How does a strip diagram help you solve a multiplication problem?

☆ Guided Practice ☆

Complete the strip diagram and write a number sentence to solve.

1. Mika has 16 playing cards.
   She divides the cards into 2 equal groups.
   How many cards are in each group?

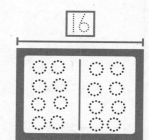

$$16 \div 2 = 8 \text{ cards}$$

2. Ray has 4 bookshelves.
   He puts 4 books on each shelf.
   How many books does Ray have in all?

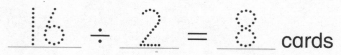

$$\underline{} \times \underline{} = \underline{} \text{ books}$$

Independent Practice   Draw a strip diagram and write a number sentence to solve.

3. Bo planted 2 gardens. There are 10 bushes in each garden. How many bushes did Bo plant in all?

_____ × _____ = _____ bushes

4. Anita has 15 baseball cards. She puts the cards in 3 equal piles. How many baseball cards are in each pile?

_____ ÷ _____ = _____ cards

5. 4 players each scored 3 points playing basketball. How many points did they score in all?

_____ × _____ = _____ points

6. **Extend Your Thinking** Write a multiplication story for the strip diagram. Then write a number sentence to solve your story.

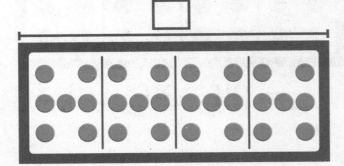

_____ ◯ _____ = _____

_____

_____

_____

Problem Solving
Draw a strip diagram and write a number sentence to solve.

7. Zach buys 9 CDs in 3 packs.
Each pack has the same number of CDs.
How many CDs are in each pack?

 _____ ◯ _____ = _____ CDs

8. Carlos makes 2 books.
Each book has 6 pages.
How many pages does Carlos make in all?

 _____ ◯ _____ = _____ pages

9. ☆ Nell has 18 toys.
She puts an equal number of toys into 2 baskets.
How many toys go into each basket?

2 ◯   4 ◯

9 ◯   18 ◯

10. Extend Your Thinking Complete the number sentences. Explain how you solved them.

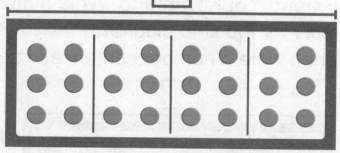

4 ◯ _____ = 24   24 ◯ 4 = _____

Topic 9 | Lesson 6

Name _____

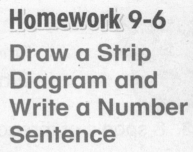
Another Look You can draw a strip diagram to solve a problem.

Fran knits 4 vests.
Each vest has 5 buttons.
How many buttons are there in all?

First, draw a strip diagram with 4 equal parts to show 4 vests.

Then, draw 5 counters in each part to show the 5 buttons.
Write the whole in the box at the top.

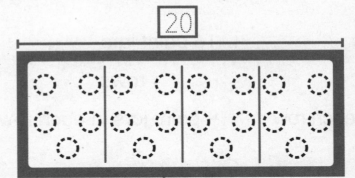

Finally, write a number sentence.

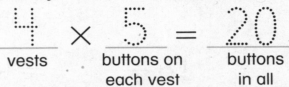

$$4 \times 5 = 20$$

vests   buttons on each vest   buttons in all

🏠 **HOME CONNECTION**
Your child drew strip diagrams to help write number sentences to solve multiplication and division problems.

HOME ACTIVITY Ask your child to draw strip diagrams that match the number sentences $2 \times 2 = 4$ and $15 \div 3 = 5$.

Draw a strip diagram and write a number sentence to solve.

1. There are 18 flowers. Each of 6 vases holds the same number of flowers. How many flowers are there in each vase?

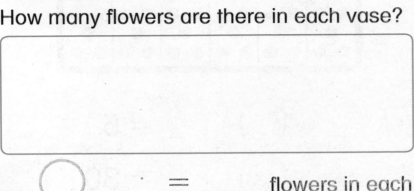

_____ ◯ _____ = _____ flowers in each

2. Casey has 2 pencil cases. He puts 7 pencils in each case. How many pencils does Casey have in all?

_____ ◯ _____ = _____ pencils

Find the number of rows for each window display at a hobby store. Draw a strip diagram and write a number sentence to solve.

3. 8 spools of thread

_____ rows

4 spools of thread in each row

$8 \div$ _____ $= 4$

4. 16 paint jars

_____ rows

4 paint jars in each row

$16 \div$ _____ $= 4$

5. 15 rolls of ribbon

_____ rows

5 rolls of ribbon in each row

$15 \div$ _____ $= 5$

---

6. The flute section of a marching band has 4 rows. It has 5 players in each row. How many people are in the flute section?

Which number sentence can you use to solve the problem?

$4 \times 4 = 16$ ○

$4 \times 5 = 20$ ○

$4 \times 6 = 24$ ○

$5 \times 5 = 25$ ○

7. Extend Your Thinking Complete the number sentences.

30

_____ ○ _____ $= 5$

_____ ○ _____ $= 30$

Name _____

 It's a new classroom! **Represent** the math to help set things up.

1. Each table can seat 4 students. Write a repeated addition sentence to show how many seats in all.

   _____

2. Write a multiplication sentence to show how many seats in all.

   _____

3. Group classroom objects to show a multiplication situation.
   Draw a picture and use words to describe the situation.
   Then, write a multiplication sentence.

   ____ × ____ = ____

4. Separate classroom objects into groups to show a division situation.
   Draw a picture and use words to describe the situation.
   Then, write a division sentence.

   ____ ÷ ____ = ____

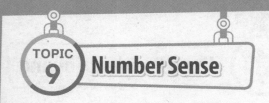

What Comes Next?

1. Write a multiplication sentence for each model.

Model	Number Sentence
● ● ● ● ● ●	___ × _3_ = ___
● ● ● ● ● ● ● ● ●	___ × ___ = ___
● ● ● ● ● ● ● ● ● ● ● ●	___ × ___ = ___
● ● ● ● ● ● ● ● ● ● ● ● ● ● ●	___ × ___ = ___

What's Wrong?

2. Jamal got this problem wrong. What was his mistake? Explain. Then solve the problem.

$$4 \times 3 = 7$$

_____

_____

_____

Code Math

3. Use the code to solve the problems.

▼ = 2	□ = 3	☆ = 4
✶ = 5	☉ = 6	◆ = 7

✶ + ☆ = ☐

☉ − □ = ☐

◆ + ☐ = 12

☉ − ▼ = ☐

Name _____

Set A

You can add or multiply to solve.

$$3 \times 2 = ?$$

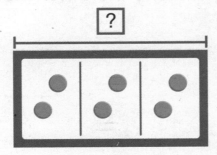

$$2 + 2 + 2 = \underline{6}$$

$$3 \times 2 = \underline{6}$$

Use the model.
Complete each number sentence.

1.

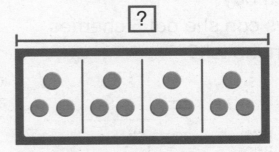

$$3 + 3 + 3 + 3 = \underline{}$$

$$4 \times 3 = \underline{}$$

Set B

You can use counters to make equal groups.

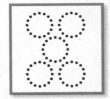

$\underline{15}$ counters in all

$\underline{3}$ groups of $\underline{5}$ counters

Use counters to make equal groups.
Draw the groups. Write the numbers.

2. 12 grapes are shared equally by 3 friends.

_____ grapes in all

_____ groups of _____ grapes

You can subtract the same number over and over to solve a story problem.

Kerry has 10 cherries.
She eats 5 each day.
How many days can she eat 5 cherries until there are none left?

$$10 - 5 = 5$$
$$5 - 5 = 0$$

__2__ days

Subtract over and over to solve.

3. Kyle has 18 blueberries. He eats 6 each day. How many days can he eat 6 blueberries until there are none left?

_____ − _____ = _____

_____ − _____ = _____

_____ − _____ = _____

_____ days

You can draw a model to help solve.

Ali has 4 packs of stamps, 2 in each pack. How many stamps does he have?

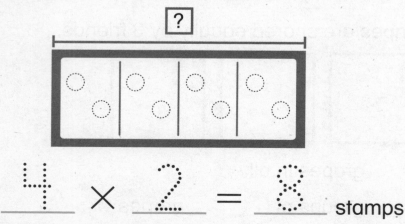

$$4 \times 2 = 8$$ stamps

Draw a model. Then solve.

4. Jana drew 3 kinds of animals, 4 of each kind. How many animals did she draw in all?

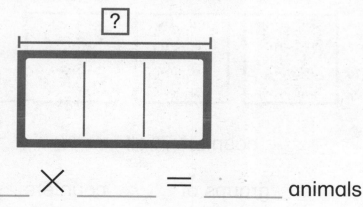

_____ × _____ = _____ animals

Name _____

Test

1. Which addition and multiplication sentences match the model?

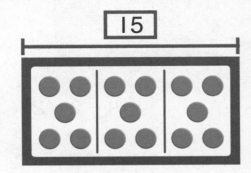

15

○ $3 + 3 + 3 = 9$; $3 \times 3 = 9$

○ $3 + 3 + 3 + 3 + 3 = 15$; $5 \times 3 = 15$

○ $3 + 5 = 8$; $3 \times 5 = 15$

○ $5 + 5 + 5 = 15$; $3 \times 5 = 15$

2. There are 8 dog treats in a bag. Fido eats 2 treats a day. How many days can Fido have treats before they are all gone?

○ 2

○ 4

○ 6

○ 12

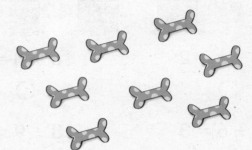

3. Which shows how 20 pennies are shared equally by 4 children?

○

○

○

○

4. Which multiplication sentence matches the picture?

○ $3 \times 5 = 15$

○ $3 \times 4 = 12$

○ $5 \times 4 = 20$

○ $6 \times 5 = 30$

5. Jeff has 18 pencils. He put the same number of pencils in each cup. Which shows how many pencils are in each cup?

$12 \div 6 = 2$
○

$16 \div 4 = 4$
○

$18 \div 6 = 3$
○

$18 \div 9 = 2$
○

6. Jorge has 4 cups. He puts 2 ice cubes in each cup. Which shows how many ice cubes in all?

$4 + 2 = 6$
○

$4 - 2 = 2$
○

$2 \times 4 = 8$
○

$2 \times 2 = 4$
○

---

7. Pedro puts his crayons in 4 equal groups. There are 3 crayons in each group. How many crayons does Pedro have? Draw a strip diagram and write a number sentence to solve.

_____ ◯ _____ = _____ crayons

8. Nikki has 24 strawberries. She needs 6 strawberries to make a smoothie. How many smoothies can she make?

Circle groups and write a number sentence to solve.

_____ ◯ _____ = _____

Nikki can make _____ smoothies.

Money

What strategies can be used to count money?

Look at all the coins! They come in so many sizes and colors.

Coins can be made using different types of metal and designs.

Wow! Let's do this project and learn more.

Math and Science Project: Coin Facts

Find Out Find a library book or other reference source about coins of the United States or about coins from other countries. Find out what coins are made of and how they are made.

Journal: Make a Book Draw pictures of at least three kinds of coins. In your book, also:

• Write labels to name each coin and the metal each is made of.

• Draw a group of pennies, nickels, dimes, and quarters. Add and record their value in cents.

Name _____

Review What You Know

Vocabulary

1. Circle the **penny**.

2. Circle the **nickel**.

3. Circle the **dime**.

Skip Counting

Write the numbers that come next.

4. 5, 10, 15, 20,

_____, _____, _____

5. 10, 20, 30,

_____, _____,

Comparing Numbers

Write >, <, or =.

6. 72 ◯ 27

49 ◯ 50

My Word Cards

Study the words on the front of the card.
Complete the activity on the back.

A-Z

dime

10 cents or 10¢

nickel

5 cents or 5¢

penny

1 cent or 1¢

quarter

25 cents or 25¢

half-dollar

50 cents or 50¢

cents

1 cent (¢)   10 cents (¢)

My Word Cards

Use what you know to complete the sentences.
Extend learning by writing your own sentence using each word.

A _____

is 1 cent or 1¢.

A _____

is 5 cents or 5¢.

A _____

is 10 cents or 10¢.

A dime is 10

_____

and a penny is 1

_____.

A _____

is 50 cents or 50¢.

A _____

is 25 cents or 25¢.

greatest value

The quarter has the greatest value.

least value

The dime has the least value.

dollar

$1.00 or 100¢

dollar bill ($)

dollar sign

$375

↑
dollar sign

decimal point

$1.25

↑
decimal point

tally mark

Ways to Show 30¢			
Quarter	Dime	Nickel	Total
I		I	30¢
	III		30¢
	II	II	30¢
	I	IIII	30¢
		ℍℍ I	30¢

My Word Cards

Use what you know to complete the sentences.
Extend learning by writing your own sentence using each word.

One _____

equals 100¢.

The coin that has the

_____

_____

is the coin that is worth the least.

The coin that has the

_____

_____

is the coin that is worth the most.

Use a _____

_____

to keep track of each piece of information in an organized list.

A _____

_____

separates dollars from cents.

A _____

_____

is a symbol used to show that a number means money.

Name _____

 Solve & Share

Look at your coins. How much money do you have?

⊕ **TEKS 2.5A** Determine the value of a collection of coins up to one dollar. Also, 2.5, 2.5B. **Mathematical Process Standards** 2.1.A, 2.1B, 2.1C, 2.1F.

Digital Resources at SavvasTexas.com

| Solve | Learn | Glossary | Check | Tools | Games |

_____ cents

dime 10¢

  nickel 5¢

  penny 1¢

  quarter 25¢

 half-dollar 50¢

Count on to find the total amount of these coins.

The total amount is **91 cents**. The cent sign is **¢**.

50¢   75¢   85¢   90¢   91¢

Do You Understand?

Show Me! What is the value of a half-dollar? How many quarters make the same amount as a half-dollar? How many dimes make the same amount?

Guided Practice ☆ Count on to find the total amount.

1.   → 86¢

   25¢   50¢   80¢   85¢   86¢

   Total Amount

2.    → 86¢

   50¢   75¢   85¢   86¢

   Total Amount

490 four hundred ninety

Topic 10 | Lesson 1

Name _____

Independent Practice

Count on to find the total amount.

3.

25¢   35¢   45¢   55¢

55¢ → **Total Amount**

4.

25¢   35¢   40¢   41¢   42¢

42¢ → **Total Amount**

5.

50¢   60¢   70¢   75¢   80¢

80¢ → **Total Amount**

6. Extend Your Thinking Draw and label the missing coin.

92¢ → **Total Amount**

7. Tori has coins that total 65¢. She counts the value of the coins: 25¢, 50¢, 60¢, 65¢. Draw and label Tori's coins.

8. Which group of coins has a value of 100¢ − 10¢?

55

90

70

90

9. Lucas has the coins shown. He will spend the coins on a gift for his brother. If he had one more nickel, which item would he have exactly enough money to buy?

41¢ 50¢ 84¢ 76¢

10. **Extend Your Thinking** Write a story about what coins you could use to buy an orange for 60¢.

Topic 10 | Lesson 1

Name _____

Another Look You can count on to find the total value of a group of coins.

 quarter   25 cents
25¢

 half-dollar   50 cents
50¢

Start with 25¢. Count on by fives.

Think: 25¢   5¢ more   5¢ more

25¢   30¢   35¢

Start with 50¢. Count on by tens.

Think: 50¢   10¢ more   10¢ more

50¢   60¢   70¢

🏠 **HOME CONNECTION**
Your child counted groups
of half-dollars, quarters,
dimes, nickels, and pennies
and found the total value.

HOME ACTIVITY Encourage
your child to take 5 coins
from a group of half-dollars,
quarters, dimes, nickels,
or pennies, find the value,
and write that amount with
a cent symbol.

Count on to find the total amount.
Use coins if you need to.

1. Start with 25¢. Count on by tens.

                  → 65¢

25¢   35¢   45¢   55¢   65   **Total Amount**

2. Start with 50¢. Count on by tens and ones.

               → 72¢

50¢   60¢   70¢   71¢   72¢   **Total Amount**

Topic 10 | Lesson 1   four hundred ninety-three   **493**

3. If one more dime is added to these coins, what will be the total amount?

28¢
○

38¢
○

45¢
○

48¢
●

4. Jamal has these coins.

He needs 85¢ to buy a toy car.
Draw another coin so that Jamal has enough money to buy the toy car.

dime

5. Extend Your Thinking Find the coins needed to buy each toy. Use the fewest number of coins possible. Write how many coins to use.

Count on as you use each coin.

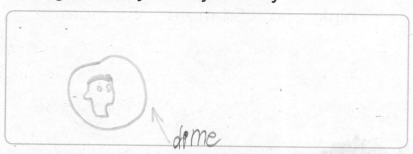				
67¢	50¢	10¢		
🐷 82¢				
🧸 46¢				

Topic 10 | Lesson 1

Name _____

Solve & Share

Choose 5 coins. Which coin is worth the least amount? Which coin is worth the greatest amount? What is the total amount of money you have?

⭐ TEKS 2.5A Determine the value of a collection of coins up to one dollar. Also, 2.5B. **Mathematical Process Standards** 2.1C, 2.1D, 2.1F.

Digital Resources at SavvasTexas.com

 Solve   Learn   **A-Z** Glossary   Check   Tools   Games

_____ greatest _____ ¢

_____ least _____ ¢

Total amount: _____ ¢

How can you find the total amount?

Start with the coin of **greatest value**.

Count on to the coin of **least value**.

Total
90¢

50¢   75¢   85¢   90¢

Do You Understand?

Show Me! Why is it a good idea to put 1 nickel, 1 penny, and 1 quarter in a different order to find the total?

Guided Practice

Draw the coins from the greatest to the least value. Count on to find the total amount. You can use coins.

1.

25¢   50¢   55¢   60¢

60¢

Total Amount

2.

50¢   75¢   80¢   81¢

81¢

Total Amount

1.29.
50

Name _____

Count on to find the total amount.

3.

50¢   60¢   65¢   66¢   The total amount is __66¢__.

4.

25¢   35¢   45¢   50¢   The total amount is __50¢__.

5.

50¢   75¢   85¢   95¢   The total amount is __95¢__.

6. Extend Your Thinking What 4 coins have a value of 20¢? Draw the coins. Label the value of each coin.

08   113/

Problem Solving Solve each problem below.

7. What is the total amount?

_____ ¢

8. Lydia has 3 coins. The total amount is 40¢. She has 1 quarter and 1 nickel. Which shows her third coin?

○   ○   ○   ○

9. Emily has 90¢. What coins could Emily have? Draw the coins.

Emily has _____

10. Extend Your Thinking Write a story about finding 75¢. Draw the coins.

_____

_____

_____

Topic 10 | Lesson 2

Name _____

Another Look To count coins, start with the coin that has the greatest value. Count on coins from the greatest to the least value.

Find the total amount.
Draw an X on the coin with the greatest value.

Think: 50¢   60¢   70¢   75¢

Start with 50¢.   50¢   60¢   70¢   75¢

🏠 **HOME CONNECTION**
Your child identified coins with the greatest and least values from a group of coins. Then your child counted coins from greatest to least value and used the cent symbol to record the total.

HOME ACTIVITY Have your child take 4 coins from a cup of mixed coins and count on to find the value. Ask your child to record the value with a cent symbol.

 Find the total amount. Draw an X on the coin with the greatest value.

1.

Start with _____.

____ ____ ____ ____

2.

Start with _____.

____ ____ ____ ____

3. Glenn had these coins. Then he lost 1 dime. What total amount did Glenn have then?

_____ ¢

4. Karen has 85¢. She has a half-dollar and a dime. Which other coin does Karen have?

  ○   ○

  ○   ○

Extend Your Thinking Circle the coins that show the correct amount.

5. Megan had 50¢. She lost 1 nickel.
Circle the 5 coins that show how much she has left.

6. Yoshi had 55¢. He gave his sister a dime.
Circle the 3 coins that show how much he has left.

7. Kayla had 60¢. She gave her brother 4 pennies.
Circle the 3 coins that show how much she has left.

Name _____

Solve & Share

The pig has a nickel, a half-dollar, and a quarter.
The cow has a quarter, a dime, and 3 pennies.
Who has the greater value of coins?
Use the symbol $>$, $<$, or $=$ to show your answer.

⭐ **TEKS 2.5A** Determine the value of a collection of coins up to one dollar. Also, 2.5B. **Mathematical Process Standards** 2.1C, 2.1E, 2.1F, 2.1G.

Digital Resources at SavvasTexas.com

Solve   Learn   Glossary   Check   Tools   Games

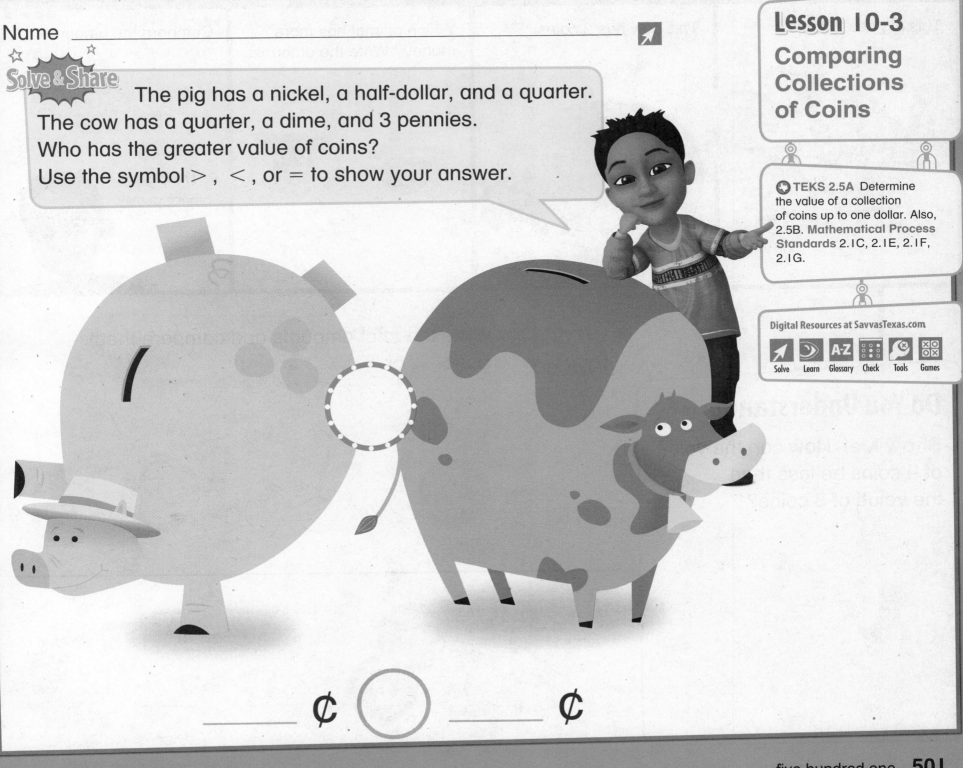

_____ ¢ ◯ _____ ¢

This pig has 2 coins.

This cow has 3 coins.

Which animal has more money? Write the amounts.

51¢ ◯ 45¢

Compare the amounts.

51¢ > 45¢

The pig has more money.

Do You Understand?

Show Me! How can the value of 4 coins be less than the value of 3 coins?

☆ Guided Practice ☆

Write the total amounts and compare them. Use >, <, or = .

1.

21¢ < 40¢

2.

_____ ◯ _____

Topic 10 | Lesson 3

Name _____

Independent ☆ Practice

Write the total amounts and compare them. Use >, <, or =.

3.  _____ ◯ _____

4.  _____ . ◯ _____

Which group of coins has the greater value?

5.  _____ ◯ _____

Extend Your Thinking Write an amount that makes the number sentence true. Then draw coins to show that amount.

6. 75¢ > _____

7. 27¢ < _____

8. Write the amounts and the correct symbol.

_____ cents   _____ cents

9. Choose the symbol that would be correct if I nickel was added to the quarter and 2 dimes.

¢   <   >   =

○   ○   ○   ○

10. Draw coins to show a value less than 55¢.

11. **Extend Your Thinking** Write the total amounts and compare.
Ann has 2 quarters.
Joe has 2 dimes and 2 nickels.
Who has more money?

_____ > _____

_____ has more money.

How much more? _____

Another Look To compare two amounts, first count on to find the value of each group of coins.

Which group has more money?
Count the coins in each group.
Compare the amounts.

> means "is greater than"
< means "is less than"
= means "is equal to"

🏠 **HOME CONNECTION**
Your child used the >, <, and = symbols to compare the values of two sets of coins.

HOME ACTIVITY Take 3 coins from a cup of mixed coins. Ask your child to also take 3 coins. Have your child order each set of coins from the greatest to the least value. Then have your child count on to find the total value. Ask your child which set of coins has the greater value.

25¢   30¢   31¢      10¢   20¢   21¢

31¢   =   21¢

Count the coins. Then compare the amounts.

1.

_____ > < = _____

_____

2.

_____ > < = _____

_____

3. ⭐ Which symbol would be correct if the picture showed only 1 quarter?

○ >

○ =

○ <

○ ¢

4. Extend Your Thinking Which group of coins has the greater value? Explain.

_____

_____

_____

---

5. Shari has 25¢.
Beth also has a coin.
Together they have more than 35¢.
Circle the coin that Beth has.

6. Ahmal has 40¢.
Maya also has a coin.
Together they have less than 60¢.
Circle the coin that Maya has.

7. Margie has 3 quarters.
Linda has a coin too.
Together they have less than 85¢.
Circle the coin that Linda has.

Name _____

Solve & Share

What is one way you can show 100¢ with coins? Use coins to model. Draw and label the coins you use.

⭐ **TEKS 2.5B** Use the cent symbol, dollar sign, and the decimal point to name the value of a collection of coins. Also, 2.5A. **Mathematical Process Standards 2.1B, 2.1F, 2.1G.**

Digital Resources at SavvasTexas.com

Solve | Learn | Glossary | Check | Tools | Games

100¢

This is 1 **dollar**.

I dollar bill

1 dollar coin

This is 1 dollar another way.

1 dollar = 100¢

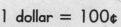

To write 1 dollar, begin with the dollar sign. You write a decimal point to separate the dollar from the cents.

$1.00

You can write other amounts in this way, too. $0.35 is 0 dollars and 35 cents.

$0.35 = 35¢

Do You Understand?

Show Me! Compare a dollar bill and a dollar coin. Is one worth more than the other? Explain.

☆ **Guided Practice** ☆ Use coins to show $1.00. Draw the coins. Write the number of coins.

1. Use only half-dollars.

_____ half-dollars = $1.00

2. Use only quarters.

_____ quarters = $1.00

3. Use only dimes.

_____ dimes = $1.00

Independent Practice

Write each total amount. Circle sets of coins that equal $1.00.

4.  → [ ]

5. → [ ]

6.  → [ ]

7.  → [ ]

Extend Your Thinking

Write each total amount. Then draw the coin that makes the set equal $1.00.

8.

$. [   ]

9.

$. [   ]

10. ⭐ Tina wants to buy a poster that costs $1.00. She has these coins.

How much more money does Tina need to make 1 dollar?

20¢ ○   25¢ ○   30¢ ○   35¢ ○

11. What amount do these coins show?

_____ cents

12. Draw coins to show 0 dollars and 72 cents.

13. **Extend Your Thinking** Ed shows 80¢ with 3 coins. One of the coins is a half-dollar. Draw and label Ed's other two coins.

Name _____

Another Look You can show $1.00 in different ways.

A dollar bill is equal to 100¢. Remember to use a dollar sign and decimal point when you write $1.00.

🏠 **HOME CONNECTION**
Your child used different coin combinations to show 100¢, or $1.00.

HOME ACTIVITY Have your child use coins to show $1.00 in more than one way.

100 pennies = 1 dollar

$100¢ = \$1.00$

Circle coins to show $1.00.
Write the number of coins.

1.

_____ dimes = 1 dollar

2.

_____ quarters = 1 dollar

3.

_____ half-dollars = 1 dollar

4. Tim found these coins in his pocket.
He wants to buy a sandwich that costs 95¢.

How much more money does he need
to make 95¢?

$0.01
○

$0.05
○

$0.15
○

$0.25
○

5. Pam has 4 coins. The coins total 100¢.
Circle the coins that Pam has.

Extend Your Thinking Each student has $1.00. Use the clue cards to complete the chart.
Write how many of each coin are needed. Write the total amount to check.

Nina has 3 of one coin and 5 of another coin.

Elena has only 1 coin.

Todd has 8 of one coin and 4 of another coin.

Roxanne has 3 coins.

Student	(dollar)	(half dollar)	(quarter)	(dime)	(nickel)	Total Amount
6. Nina						
7. Elena						
8. Todd						
9. Roxanne						

512 five hundred twelve

Name _____

Solve & Share

Suppose you want to buy a pencil that costs 35¢. How many different ways can you use your coins to make 35¢? Show each way. Tell how you know.

TEKS 2.1E Create and use representations to ... communicate mathematical ideas.
TEKS 2.5 Determine the value of coins ... to solve monetary transactions. Also, 2.5A. **Mathematical Process Standards** 2.1A, 2.1B, 2.1D, 2.1F, 2.1G.

Digital Resources at SavvasTexas.com

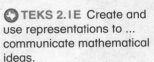

Solve   Learn   Glossary   Check   Tools   Games

Quarter	Dime	Nickel	Total Amount
			35¢
			35¢
			35¢
			35¢
			35¢
			35¢

Analyze

I have some quarters, dimes, and nickels. I want to buy a banana.

How many ways can I make 30¢?

30¢

Plan

An organized list shows different ways to make the same amount.

Tally marks record the number of coins.

Ways to Show 30¢			
Quarter	Dime	Nickel	Total
I		I	30¢
	III		30¢

Solve and Justify

Ways to Show 30¢			
Quarter	Dime	Nickel	Total
I		I	30¢
	III		30¢
	II	II	30¢
	I	IIII	30¢
		Ж I	30¢

Each way makes 30¢.

Evaluate

The list shows I can make 30¢ in five different ways using quarters, dimes, and nickels.

Do You Understand?

Show Me! How does an organized list help show different ways to make the same amount of money?

☆ **Guided Practice** ☆ Use coins. Finish each list.

1. Shira needs 50¢ to buy an eraser. She has half-dollars, quarters, and dimes. Find ways she can make 50¢.

 50¢

Half-Dollar	Quarter	Dime	Total Amount
I			50¢
	II		50¢
		Ж	50¢

2. Tony wants to buy a pencil for 55¢. He has half-dollars, quarters, and nickels. Find ways he can make 55¢.

 55¢

Half-Dollar	Quarter	Nickel	Total Amount
I		I	55¢

Topic 10 | Lesson 5

Independent Practice

Use coins. Finish each list.

3. Sue needs 70¢ to buy a marker. She has half-dollars, quarters, and dimes. Find all of the ways she can make 70¢.

Half-Dollar	Quarter	Dime	Total Amount
I		II	70¢

4. Raul wants to buy a bookmark for 14¢. He has dimes, nickels, and pennies. Find all of the ways he can make 14¢.

Dime	Nickel	Penny	Total Amount
	II	IIII	14¢

5. Mia wants to buy a notebook for 60¢. She has half-dollars, quarters, and dimes. Find all of the ways she can make 60¢.

Half-Dollar	Quarter	Dime	Total Amount
		IIII I	60¢

Extend Your Thinking What is the fewest number of coins that you could use to make each amount? You can use the tables in Exercises 3–5 to help.

6. 70¢

Number of coins: _____
Coins I would use:

_____

7. 14¢

Number of coins: _____
Coins I would use:

_____

8. 60¢

Number of coins: _____
Coins I would use:

_____

9. The top row of this list shows one way to make 37¢. Complete the other rows to show three more ways to make 37¢.

Dimes	Nickels	Pennies	Total
III	I	II	37¢
II			37¢
	III		37¢
		卌 II	37¢

10. This list shows some ways to make 28¢. Which shows the missing way to make 28¢?

○ I dime, 4 nickels, 3 pennies
○ I dime, 2 nickels, 13 pennies
○ I dime, I nickel, 13 pennies
○ I dime, I nickel, 8 pennies

Dimes	Nickels	Pennies	Total
I	III	III	28¢
I	II	卌 III	28¢
			28¢
I		卌 卌 卌 III	28¢

11. Extend Your Thinking Circle **yes** or **no**. Can you make exactly 38¢ with these coins? Explain your answer.

yes   no

Name _____

Another Look Show three ways to make 25¢.
Two ways are shown in the chart.

Use coins to help you
find another way.
Show 1 dime.
Make 1 tally mark.
How many nickels do you
need to make 15¢?

Write 3 tally marks.

Ways to Show 25¢

Quarter	Dime	Nickel	Total Amount
I			25¢
	II	I	25¢
	⋮	⋮⋮⋮	25¢

🏠 **HOME CONNECTION**
Your child made an organized list with tallies to show combinations of coins equal to 35¢.

HOME ACTIVITY Ask your child to use quarters, nickels, and dimes to show all the ways to make 40¢.

Solve each problem.

1. Show three ways to make 45¢.
   Use tally marks to record the coins.

Ways to Show 45¢

Quarter	Dime	Nickel	Total Amount
			45¢
			45¢
			45¢

2. What is the fewest number of coins that you could use to make 45¢?
   You can use the table in Exercise 1 to help.

   Number of coins: _____
   Coins I would use:

   _____

   _____

3. This list shows some ways to make 55¢.
⭐ Which shows the missing way to make 55¢?

○ I quarter, I dime, 2 nickels
○ I quarter, 2 dimes, I nickel
○ I quarter, I dime, 3 nickels
○ I quarter, 6 nickels

Quarters	Dimes	Nickels	Total
II		I	55¢
I	II	II	55¢
I	I	IIII	55¢
			55¢

An organized list can help you see patterns in money amounts.
Complete the list. Then answer the questions.

Toy Trains	Cost
I	10¢
2	
3	
4	
5	

4. What is the cost of 5 toy trains? _____

5. What is the pattern for the numbers of toy trains?

_____

6. What is the pattern for the costs of the toy trains?

_____

7. Extend Your Thinking Choose an item. How would you use an organized list to show the cost of three of that item?

_____

_____

Name _____

Hello, shoppers!
Show the math you use to buy things.

 87¢

 98¢

 55¢

 66¢

 72¢

1. You have these coins.

The total amount is _____ ¢.

_____

2. Circle one item that you have enough money to buy.

3. Write the price of the item you circled at the top of the table.
Show two different ways to make that amount. Use tally marks.

Ways to Pay _____ ¢		
Quarters	**Dimes**	**Pennies**

4. Suppose you want to buy the sunglasses. How much more money do you need?
Write a number sentence to solve.

_____ ¢ ☐ _____ ¢ = _____ ¢

5. Carla only brought nickels to the store. How many nickels does she need to buy a pencil sharpener? Explain your answer.

Add on the Values

1. Fill in the table. Start with the price.
   Count on each coin value.
   In the last row, work backward!

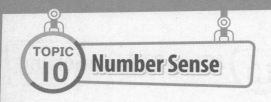

Price	+ 🪙	+ 🪙	+ 🪙
16¢	26¢	31¢	32¢
27¢			
38¢			
49¢			
			76¢

What's Wrong?

2. Nell subtracted wrong.
   Redo the problem to make it right.

$$
\begin{array}{r}
\overset{3\,7}{4\cancel{8}3} \\
-279 \\
\hline
106
\end{array}
$$

_____

Coin Riddles

3. Solve the coin riddles.

   • I have 4 coins. They total 16¢.
     What coins are they?

   • I have 4 coins. They total 70¢.
     What coins are they?

   • I have 3 coins. They total less than 25¢.
     I cannot make 15¢. But I can make 6¢.
     What are my coins?

Name _____

Set A

When you count coins, start with the coin of greatest value.

half-dollar   quarter   dime   nickel

50¢   75¢   85¢   90¢

The total is 90¢.

Draw the coins in the order of their values, from greatest to least. Count on to find the total amount.

1.

_____ _____ _____

Total Amount

Set B

You can compare the values of coins to find which amount is greater.

50¢ ⊙> 25¢

50¢ is greater than 25¢.

Compare the coins.

2.

_____ ◯ _____

3.

_____ ◯ _____

You can show the same amount
in different ways.

Circle another way to show $1.00.

Write the name of the coin
that makes this true.

4.

_____

Write another way to show 100¢.

5. _____ = 100¢

You can use an organized list to show
the same amount.

Dime	Nickel	Penny	Total
I		III	13¢
	II	III	13¢
	I	||||| II	13¢
		||||| ||||| III	13¢

There are four ways to make 13¢.

Complete the list. Use coins
if you need to.

6.

Dime	Nickel	Penny	Total
			11¢
			11¢
			11¢
			11¢

What is the total amount? Count on to find the total.

1.

7¢   33¢   35¢   70¢
○   ○   ○   ○

2.

60¢   67¢   72¢   92¢
○   ○   ○   ○

3. Mollie wants to count her 5 coins.
She wants to start with the coin
of greatest value.
Which coin should she start with?

○   dime

○   nickel

○   quarter

○   penny

4. Chen has these coins.
How much money does he have?

○ $0.85

○ $0.90

○ $0.95

○ $1.00

5. Choose the correct symbol.

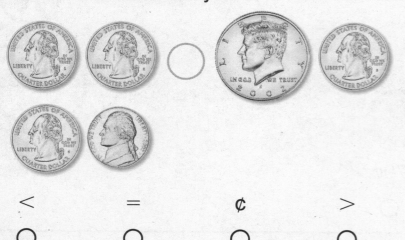

<   =   ¢   >

○   ○   ○   ○

6. Count on to find the total amount.

○ 76¢

○ 71¢

○ 66¢

○ 61¢

7. Jonah needs 35¢.
Find all of the ways he can make 35¢.
Circle the way that uses the least
number of coins.

Quarter	Dime	Nickel	Total Amount
1			35¢
1			35¢
			35¢
			35¢
			35¢
			35¢

8. Cody needs $1.00 to ride the bus.
He has only 2 quarters, 2 dimes,
and 2 pennies.
How much more money does he need?
Draw coins to show the amount.

Number Patterns and Algebra

Essential Question: What are ways to describe how different numbers are related?

Day always follows night. Night always follows day.

When it is day where I live, it is night somewhere else on Earth.

Wow! Let's do this project and learn more.

Math and Science Project: Pattern of Day and Night

Find Out Find a globe and a flashlight. Shine the flashlight on Texas. Then slowly spin the globe from left to right. How do day and night change in Texas and other places?

Journal: Make a Book Draw pictures of the globe and flashlight. In your book, also:

• Add labels to show day and night.

• Write a sentence to describe the pattern of day and night in your own words.

Review What You Know

Vocabulary

1. Circle the **tens digit**.

673

2. Circle the **hundreds digit**.

1,029

3. Circle the **doubles fact**.

$8 + 9 = 17$

$9 + 9 = 18$

Addition and Subtraction

4. There are 182 students in the first grade.
There are 156 students in the second grade.
How many students are in both grades?

_____ + _____ = _____

_____ students

5. Randy has 76 books on his bookshelf.
He gives 29 of the books to Jodi.
How many books does Randy have now?

_____ − _____ = _____

_____ books

Place Value

6. Kyle's number has 3 hundreds.
The tens digit is greater than 7 and less than 9.
The number of ones is 3 less than the tens digit.

What is Kyle's number?

_____

My Word Cards

Study the words on the front of the card.
Complete the activity on the back.

even

8 is even.

odd

9 is odd.

decrease

$$600 \longrightarrow 550$$

600 decreased by 50 is 550.

input

Input	Output
3	5
4	6
5	7

output

Input	Output
3	5
4	6
5	7

My Word Cards

Use what you know to complete the sentences.
Extend learning by writing your own sentence using each word.

When you

_____

a number, you lessen
its value.

An _____

number cannot be shown
as two equal parts using
cubes.

An _____

number can be shown
as two equal parts using
cubes.

The _____

is the number you get after
using the rule with an input.

The _____

is the number that you
start with.

Name _____

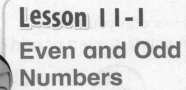

Solve & Share

Use cubes to make the numbers below. Shade all the numbers that can be shown as two equal groups of cubes.

What do you notice about the numbers you shaded?

⭐ TEKS 2.7A Determine whether a number up to 40 is even or odd using pairings of objects to represent the number. Also, 2.7. Mathematical Process Standards 2.1C, 2.1D, 2.1F, 2.1G.

Digital Resources at SavvasTexas.com

Solve Learn Glossary Check Tools Games

1	2	3	4	5	6	7	8	9	10
11	12	13	14	15	16	17	18	19	20

How can you tell if a number is **even** or **odd**?

Use cubes to find out.

8

9

An even number can be shown as two equal parts using cubes.

8 is even.
$4 + 4 = 8$

An odd number cannot be shown as two equal parts using cubes.

9 is odd.
$5 + 4 = 9$

The ones digit tells you if a number is even or odd.

18 is even.
19 is odd.

1	2	3	4	5	6	7	8	9	10
11	12	13	14	15	16	17	18	19	20

Do You Understand?

Show Me! You break apart a tower of cubes to make two equal parts, but there is one cube left over. Is the number of cubes even or odd? How do you know?

☆ Guided Practice ☆

Circle even or odd.
Then write the number sentence.

1.

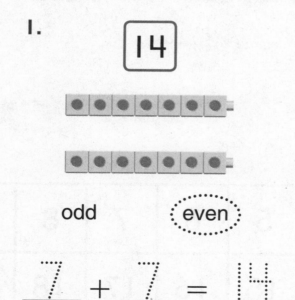

14

odd   (even)

$\underline{7} + \underline{7} = \underline{14}$

2.

19

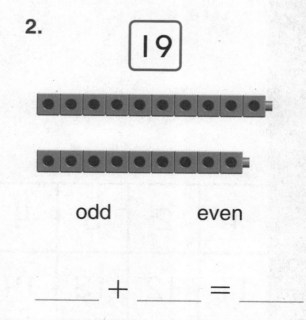

odd   even

$\underline{\quad} + \underline{\quad} = \underline{\quad}$

Topic 11 | Lesson 1

Name _____

Independent Practice

Circle even or odd. Then write the number sentence.

3. $\boxed{20}$

odd   even

___ + ___ = ___

4. $\boxed{13}$

odd   even

___ + ___ = ___

5. $\boxed{16}$

odd   even

___ + ___ = ___

6. $\boxed{17}$

odd   even

___ + ___ = ___

7. $\boxed{36}$

odd   even

___ + ___ = ___

8. $\boxed{31}$

odd   even

___ + ___ = ___

Circle true or false. Then explain your thinking.

9. Extend Your Thinking
Dave says 12 is even.
He says 21 is odd.
Is this true or false?

12   21

True   or   False

_____

_____

_____

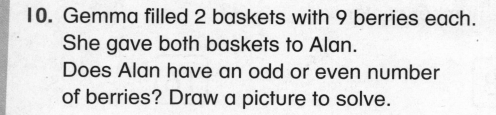

Problem Solving Solve the problems below. Use cubes to help.

10. Gemma filled 2 baskets with 9 berries each.
She gave both baskets to Alan.
Does Alan have an odd or even number
of berries? Draw a picture to solve.

_____ + _____ = _____

Alan has an _____ number of berries.

11. Tyrone puts 20 marbles in one jar.
He puts 19 marbles in another jar.
Does Tyrone have an odd or even number
of marbles? Draw a picture to solve.

_____ + _____ = _____

Tyrone has an _____ number of marbles.

12. Rosa writes an addition sentence.
The answer is an odd number less than 12.
Which addition sentence does Rosa write?

$5 + 5 = ?$ ⃝ $6 + 7 = ?$ ⃝

$8 + 8 = ?$ ⃝ $9 + 2 = ?$ ⃝

13. **Extend Your Thinking** If you add two odd
numbers, will the sum be odd or even?
Explain. Use numbers, pictures, or words.

Name _____

Another Look An **even** number can be shown as two equal parts using cubes.

An **odd** number cannot be shown as two equal parts using cubes.

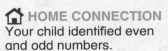 **HOME CONNECTION**
Your child identified even and odd numbers.

HOME ACTIVITY Choose a number between 1 and 40. Have your child tell if it is even or odd. If needed, he or she can use pennies to help solve.

There are 6 cubes.
Is 6 an even or odd number?
Draw lines to match the cubes.

The cubes can be shown as two equal parts.
$3 + 3 = 6$

6 is an _even_ number.

There are 7 cubes.
Is 7 an even or odd number?
Draw lines to match the cubes.

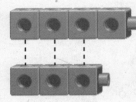
The cubes cannot be shown as two equal parts.
$4 + 3 = 7$

7 is an _odd_ number.

 Draw lines to match the cubes.
Then tell if the number is even or odd.

1.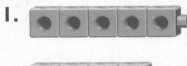

9 is an _____ number.

2.

12 is an _____ number.

3.

15 is an _____ number.

Tell if the number is odd or even. Use objects if needed. Then complete the number sentence.

4. 28 is an _____ number.

$14 + \underline{\quad} = 28$

5. 33 is an _____ number.

$17 + \underline{\quad} = 33$

6. 40 is an _____ number.

$\underline{\quad} + 20 = 40$

Circle the number to add or subtract. Complete the number sentence.

7. The sum is an **odd** number.

15   or   14

$5 + \underline{\quad} = \underline{\quad}$

8. The difference is an **odd** number.

8   or   9

$15 - \underline{\quad} = \underline{\quad}$

9. The difference is an **even** number.

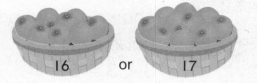

16   or   17

$31 - \underline{\quad} = \underline{\quad}$

10. Emma writes a subtraction sentence. The answer is an even number greater than 20.
Which subtraction sentence did Emma write?

$27 - 12 = ?$ ◯

$38 - 18 = ?$ ◯

$35 - 12 = ?$ ◯

$40 - 12 = ?$ ◯

11. Extend Your Thinking Shailen is adding three numbers.
He gets a sum that is an even number between 30 and 40.
Show two addition sentences Shailen could have written.

$\underline{\quad} + \underline{\quad} + \underline{\quad} = \underline{\quad}$

$\underline{\quad} + \underline{\quad} + \underline{\quad} = \underline{\quad}$

Name ______________________

Solve & Share

Complete the chart below.
Which numbers can you use to complete the sentences?

Lesson 11-2
10 More, 10 Less; 100 More, 100 Less

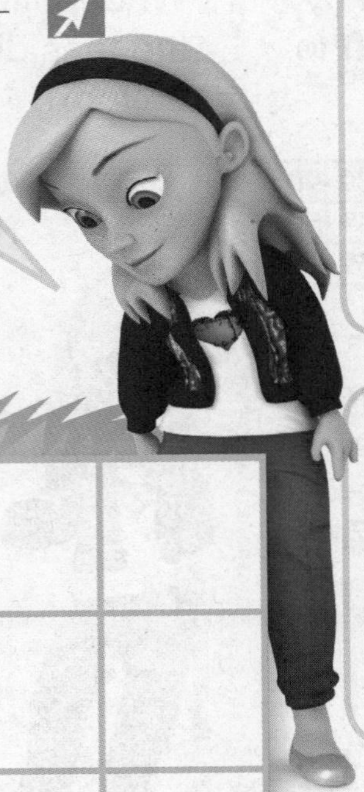

TEKS 2.7B Use an understanding of place value to determine the number that is 10 or 100 more or less than a given number up to 1,200. Also, 2.2C, 2.7. **Mathematical Process Standards** 2.1C, 2.1D, 2.1E, 2.1F.

Digital Resources at SavvasTexas.com

Solve Learn Glossary Check Tools Games

10	20	30							
110	120	130							
210									
310									
410	420	430	440	450	460	470	480	490	500

10 more than ______ is ______.

100 more than ______ is ______.

10 less than ______ is ______.

100 less than ______ is ______.

What pattern is shown by the ones digits from left to right?

31	32	33	34	35	36	37	38	39	40
41	42	43	44	45	46	47	48	49	50
51	52	53	54	55	56	57	58	59	60

The ones digits in each row go up by 1. 1 more than 36 is 37.

What pattern is shown by the tens digits from top to bottom?

The tens digits go up by 1. 10 more than 63 is 73.

43	44	45	46
53	54	55	56
63	64	65	66
73	74	75	76
83	84	85	86

What pattern is shown by the hundreds digits from top to bottom?

The hundreds digits go up by 1. 100 more than 410 is 510.

110	120	130	140	150	160
210	220	230	240	250	260
310	320	330	340	350	360
410	420	430	440	450	460
510	520	530	540	550	560
610	620	630	640	650	660

Guided Practice

Write the missing numbers.

Do You Understand?

Show Me! Describe the pattern in the tens digits from left to right in the chart.

530	540	550
630	640	650
730	740	750

1.

25	26	27
35	36	37
45	46	47

2.

250	260	270
350	360	370
450	460	470

3.

12		14
22		
	33	

4.

120		140
220		
	330	

536 five hundred thirty-six

★ Independent ★ Practice

Write the missing numbers in each chart.

5.

		38
46	48	
	58	

6.

	770	780
	870	
		980

7.

1,012	1,013	
1,022		1,024
	1,033	1,034

8.

	250	
330	350	
	450	

9.

60		
	71	72
80		

10.

		1,157
1,165	1,166	
1,175		1,177

11. Extend Your Thinking Devin and Adele are each thinking of a number.
Devin's number is the sum of 45 + 33. Devin's number is 10 less than Adele's number.
What is Adele's number? Explain how you know.

_____

_____

_____

Problem Solving Solve the problems below.

12. What pattern is shown by the tens digits from **bottom to top** in the chart below?

33	34	35	36
43	44	45	46
53	54	55	56

____

13. Ron sees a pattern in the chart below on the left. Complete the chart on the right to show another pattern.

44	45	46
54	55	56
64	65	66

	450	460
	550	

14. Which of the sentences is **NOT** correct?

168	169	170
178	179	180
188	189	190

- ○ 10 more than 178 is 188.
- ○ 10 less than 189 is 169.
- ○ 10 more than 170 is 180.
- ○ 10 less than 178 is 168.

15. Extend Your Thinking Explain why the pattern of hundreds digits from top to bottom in the chart is 7, 8, 9, 0.

710	720	730	740
810	820	830	840
910	920	930	940
1,010	1,020	1,030	1,040

____

____

____

____

____

Name _____

Another Look

Look at the top chart. Read the numbers across one row. Then read the numbers from top to bottom in one column.

11	12	13	14	15	16	17	18	19	20
21	22	23	24	25	26	27	28	29	30
31	32	33	34	35	36	37	38	39	40

The ones digits go up by ___.

The tens digits go up by ___.

Look at the bottom chart. The hundreds digits from top to bottom go up by ___.

110	111	112	113	114	115	116	117	118	119	120
210	211	212	213	214	215	216	217	218	219	220
310	311	312	313	314	315	316	317	318	319	320
410	411	412	413	414	415	416	417	418	419	420

🏠 HOME CONNECTION Your child identified number patterns on hundreds charts.

HOME ACTIVITY Draw a hundreds chart that includes a three-digit number such as 120. Ask your child to write the numbers below it and identify the pattern of 100 more.

Look at the digits.
Write the missing numbers.

1.

	77	78
86	87	
96		98

2.

470		490
570		590
		690

3.

920	930	
1,020		
	1,130	1,140

Tell which digits describe the pattern for each set of number pairs.

4. 130 ➔ 230 330 ➔ 430 530 ➔ 630

   The _____ digits go up by 1.

5. 1,132 ➔ 1,142 1,152 ➔ 1,162
   1,182 ➔ 1,192

   The _____ digits go up by 1.

6. The chart shows part of a hundreds chart.
   Write the missing numbers.

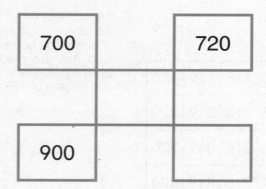

7. Which shows a pattern of 10 more in the chart below?

121	122	123
131	132	133
141	142	143

○ ones digits from top to bottom

○ tens digits from left to right

○ tens digits from top to bottom

○ hundreds digits from left to right

8. **Extend Your Thinking** Complete the sentences below. Fill in the chart to help you.

10 more than _____ is 1,070.

10 less than _____ is 1,190.

100 more than _____ is 1,080.

100 less than _____ is 1,000.

950	960			
1,050				

Name _____

Solve & Share

What pattern do you see in these numbers?
What number comes next in the pattern?

837

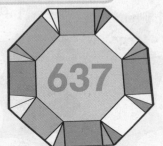
737

637

537

⭐ TEKS 2.7B Use an understanding of place value to determine the number that is 10 or 100 more or less than a given number up to 1,200. Also, 2.2C, 2.7. Mathematical Process Standards 2.1B, 2.1C, 2.1D, 2.1F.

Digital Resources at SavvasTexas.com

Solve   Learn   Glossary   Check   Tools   Games

The next number is _____.

What number comes next in the pattern?

131, 141, 151, 161, __?__

Look at the numbers. What changes? What stays the same?

The hundreds digits stay the same. The ones digits stay the same.

131, 141, 151, 161, __?__

But the tens digits change.

Look at the tens digits.

131, 141, 151, 161, __171__

The tens digits increase by 1 each time.

The numbers are 10 more each time. The next number in the pattern is 171.

171, 161, 151, 141, __131__

Now the tens digits **decrease** by 1 each time.

The numbers are 10 less each time. The next number in the pattern is 131.

Do You Understand?

Show Me! Show a number pattern that decreases by 10.

☆ Guided Practice ☆

Write the numbers that come next in the pattern. Describe the pattern.

1. 393, 493, 593, 693, __793__, __893__, __993__

The numbers increase by 100.

2. 410, 420, 430, 440, ____, ____, ____

3. 997, 897, 797, 697, ____, ____, ____

Name _____

☆
Independent
☆ **Practice**   Write the number that comes next in the pattern. Describe the pattern.

4. 567, 557, 547, 537, _____, _____, _____

_____

_____

5. 26, 126, 226, 326, _____, _____, _____

_____

_____

6. 1,131, 1,121, 1,111, 1,101, _____, _____,

_____

_____

7. 777, 787, 797, 807, _____, _____, _____

_____

_____

8. 872, 772, 672, 572, _____, _____, _____

_____

9. 602, 502, 402, 302, _____, _____, _____

_____

10. 656, 646, 636, 626, _____, _____, _____

_____

11. 13, 113, 213, 313, _____, _____, _____

_____

12. Extend Your Thinking Write the missing numbers in each pattern.

575, _____, 555, _____, 535

_____, 118, _____, _____, 418

882, _____, _____, 912, _____

> Think about whether the numbers increase or decrease.

Problem Solving   Complete the patterns to solve.

13. Maria lines up 4 number cards to make a pattern.
The first card shows the number 36.
The pattern decreases by 10.

| 36 | _____ | _____ | _____ |

What number is on the last card? _____

14. Shane lines up 4 number cards to make a pattern.
The last card shows the number 1,158.
The pattern increases by 100.

| _____ | _____ | _____ | 1,158 |

What number is on the first card? _____

15. Ken uses a pattern to make a game board.
He uses 3 numbers. All the numbers are between 110 and 150.
The numbers are 10 more each time.

Which pattern does Ken use?

90, 100, 110
○

95, 195, 295
○

130, 120, 110
○

120, 130, 140
○

16. Extend Your Thinking Arrange the numbers below to make a pattern that decreases. Then complete the sentences to describe the pattern.

897   917   877   907   927   887

____, ____, ____, ____, ____, ____

The _____ digits decrease by _____ each time.

The numbers are _____ less each time.

Name _____

Another Look Look for a pattern to find what number comes next.

240, 250, 260, 270, ?

The _tens_ digits increase by __1__.

The hundreds and ones stay the same.

The next number will be _10 more_ than 270.

240, 250, 260, 270, _280_

Think: Which digit changes? Does it increase or decrease?

🏠 **HOME CONNECTION**
Your child made number patterns that increase or decrease by 10 or 100.

HOME ACTIVITY Write a 3-digit number such as 650. Ask your child to decrease the number by 10 several times to continue the pattern.

Write the numbers that come next in the pattern. Tell which digits change and how they change.

1. 261, 271, 281, 291, _____, _____

The _____ digits _____ by _____.

2. 885, 785, 685, 585, _____, _____

The _____ digits _____ by _____.

3. 606, 706, 806, 906, _____, _____

The _____ digits _____ by _____.

4. 330, 340, 350, 360, _____, _____

The _____ digits _____ by _____.

Write the missing numbers to make a pattern. Then write **10 more, 10 less, 100 more,** or **100 less** to complete the sentence.

5. 781, _____, _____, _____, 1,181

The numbers are _____ each time.

6. 1,037, _____, _____, _____, 997

The numbers are _____ each time.

7. ⭐ Fatima is making a pattern.

_____, 999, 989, 979

Which is the missing number?

○ 1,119   ○ 1,109

○ 1,009   ○ 909

8. ⭐ Wade started a pattern. So far, he has:

116, 126, 136, _____, _____, _____

Which number could **NOT** be part of his pattern?

○ 166   ○ 164

○ 156   ○ 146

9. Extend Your Thinking Find the treasure. Follow a pattern that is 100 more each time to find the 900 gold coins.

Start at zero.

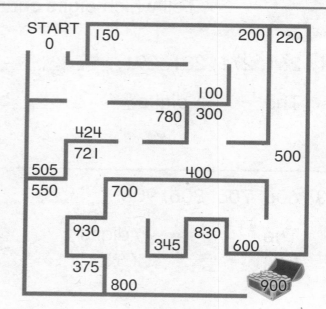

Name _____

Solve & Share

Juno has a seashell collection. Juno's mother gives her 16 new seashells. Now Juno has 43 seashells in all. How many seashells did she have to start with?

Solve the problem any way you choose.

⊕ **TEKS 2.7C** Represent and solve addition and subtraction word problems where unknowns may be any one of the terms in the problem. **Mathematical Process Standards** 2.1A, 2.1B, 2.1D, 2.1F.

Digital Resources at SavvasTexas.com

Solve   Learn   Glossary   Check   Tools   Games

Amy and Michelle dance for charity.
Amy dances first for 18 minutes.
Then Michelle dances.
For how long did Michelle dance?

Total Minutes Danced

TIMER
44
reset
min sec
start/stop

Draw a strip diagram to show what you know.

44 minutes in all

| 18 | ? |
Amy's   Michelle's
time   time

You could write two number sentences.

18 + ? = 44
or
44 − 18 = ?

Solve the subtraction sentence.

3 14
4̶ 4̶
− 18
26

Michelle danced for 26 minutes.

Do You Understand?

Show Me! How does a strip diagram help you find a missing number in an addition problem?

☆ Guided Practice ☆

Complete the strip diagram.
Write two number sentences for the diagram.
Choose one of the number sentences to solve.

1. Blake has 45 raisins.
   He eats some of the raisins.
   Then he has 16 raisins left.
   How many raisins did
   Blake eat?

45 raisins in all

| ? | 16 |
raisins eaten   raisins left

$45 − ? = 16$

$? + \underline{\quad} = \underline{\quad}$

____ raisins

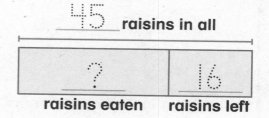
4 5
⊖ 1 6

Name _____

Complete the strip diagram and write a number sentence to solve each problem.

2. Kim and Latisha jumped rope for 37 minutes. Kim jumped rope first for 20 minutes. Latisha jumped rope the rest of the time. How many minutes did Latisha jump rope?

_____ minutes in all

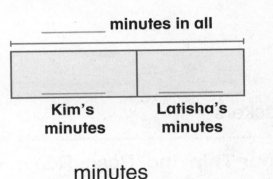

Kim's minutes   Latisha's minutes

_____ minutes

3. Sam has some action figures. He gives 19 of them to his brother. Now Sam has 12 action figures left. How many did Sam start with?

_____ action figures in all

action figures given to brother   action figures left

_____ action figures

4. **Extend Your Thinking** Phoebe wrote two number sentences for the strip diagram. Which one is easier to solve? Explain.

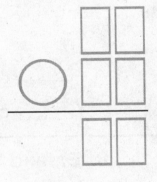

98

| ? | 59 |

$? + 59 = 98$

$98 - 59 = ?$

_____

_____

_____

Problem Solving Draw a strip diagram and write a number sentence to solve each problem.

5. Cal needs to bake a cake for 45 minutes in all. The cake has 27 minutes left to bake. How long has the cake been baking?

_____ ◯ _____ = _____

_____ minutes

6. A package contains some crackers. 24 of the crackers have triangle shapes. 56 of the crackers have square shapes. How many crackers are there in all?

_____ ◯ _____ = _____

_____ crackers

7. Tomi bought 60 eggs in all. 24 eggs are brown. The rest are white. How many white eggs did Tomi buy?

Which could you use to solve the problem?

◯ $24 + ? = 60$ or $24 + 60 = ?$

◯ $24 + ? = 60$ or $60 - 24 = ?$

◯ $60 - ? = 24$ or $24 + 60 = ?$

◯ $60 - 24 = ?$ or $24 + 60 = ?$

8. Extend Your Thinking Rosa, Roger, and Louis are sharing a bag of 70 grapes. Rosa eats 24 grapes. Roger eats 25 grapes. How many grapes are left for Louis? Explain how you solved the problem.

_____

_____

_____

_____

_____

Topic 11 | Lesson 4

Name _____

Another Look A strip diagram can help you add or subtract to find a missing number.

A jar contains 75 marbles in all. 48 are red. The rest are blue. How many marbles are blue?

The number of blue marbles is the missing number.

$$\underset{\substack{\text{red} \\ \text{marbles}}}{48} + \underset{\substack{\text{blue} \\ \text{marbles}}}{?} = \underset{\substack{\text{marbles} \\ \text{in all}}}{75}$$

$$\underset{\substack{\text{marbles} \\ \text{in all}}}{75} - \underset{\substack{\text{red} \\ \text{marbles}}}{48} = \underset{\substack{\text{blue} \\ \text{marbles}}}{27}$$

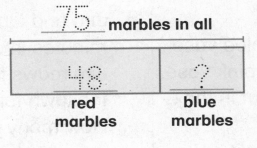

75 marbles in all

48	?
red marbles	**blue marbles**

27 blue marbles

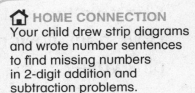

🏠 **HOME CONNECTION**
Your child drew strip diagrams and wrote number sentences to find missing numbers in 2-digit addition and subtraction problems.

HOME ACTIVITY Ask your child to draw strip diagrams that match the number sentences 52 + ? = 68 and 95 − ? = 37.

Complete the strip diagram and write a number sentence to solve the problem.

1. A box contains 64 blocks in all.
   There are 37 yellow blocks.
   The rest of the blocks are green.
   How many blocks are green?

_____ blocks in all

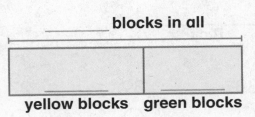

yellow blocks	**green blocks**

____ ◯ ____ = ____

_____ green blocks

Use the strip diagram to write the missing numbers in each story below. Then write a number sentence to solve.

2.

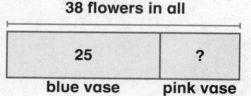

38 flowers in all

25	?
blue vase	pink vase

Mrs. Jones has _____ flowers in all.
She puts _____ of the flowers in a blue vase.
She puts the rest of the flowers in a pink vase.
How many flowers did Mrs. Jones put in the pink vase?

_____ ◯ _____ = _____ flowers

3.

72 minutes in all

?	38
Jim	Omar

Jim and Omar mow the lawn for _____ minutes in all.
Jim mows for a while. Then Omar mows the lawn for _____ minutes.
How many minutes did Jim mow the lawn?

_____ ◯ _____ = _____ minutes

---

4. ☆ Paola and Rick ate 65 blueberries in all.
Paola ate 26 blueberries.
How many blueberries did Rick eat?

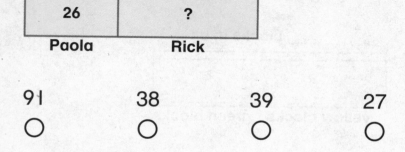

65 blueberries in all

26	?
Paola	Rick

91 ◯ 38 ◯ 39 ◯ 27 ◯

5. Extend Your Thinking Mai, Gary, and Nick walked their dog for 60 minutes in all. Mai walked the dog for 25 minutes. Nick walked the dog for 10 fewer minutes than Mai. How many minutes did Gary walk the dog? Show your work.

_____ minutes

Name _____

Solve & Share

By Thursday, the students at Franklin School had collected 535 coupons for a fundraiser.
By Friday, their total was 671 coupons.
How many coupons did students bring in on Friday?

Draw a strip diagram and then solve the problem.

⊕ TEKS 2.7C Represent and solve addition and subtraction word problems where unknowns may be any one of the terms in the problem. Mathematical Process Standards 2.1B, 2.1D, 2.1F.

Digital Resources at SavvasTexas.com

Solve   Learn   Glossary   Check   Tools   Games

268 males live in this town. How many females live there?

Welcome to our town!

Population: 532

Draw a strip diagram to show what you know.

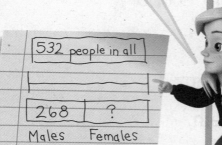

532 people in all

| 268 | ? |
| Males | Females |

You could write two number sentences.

268 + ? = 532

or

532 − 268 = ?

Solve the subtraction sentence.

$$\begin{array}{r} 4\ 12\ 12 \\ .5\overset{.}{3}\overset{.}{2}. \\ -\ 268 \\ \hline 264 \end{array}$$

264 females live in the town.

Do You Understand?

Show Me! How is finding a missing 3-digit number different from finding a missing 2-digit number?

☆ **Guided Practice** ☆ Complete the strip diagram.
Write two number sentences for the diagram.
Choose one of the number sentences to solve.

1. A movie theater sold 335 tickets in all. The theater sold 186 adult tickets. The rest of the tickets sold were child tickets.
How many child tickets did the movie theater sell?

335 tickets in all

| 186 | ? |
| adult tickets | child tickets |

186 + ? = 335

_____ − _____ = ?

_____ child tickets

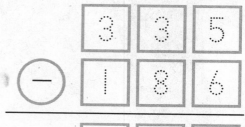

Name _____

☆ **Independent** ☆
☆ **Practice**

Complete the strip diagram and write a number sentence to solve each problem.

2. Jamal had 426 songs on his music player.
He buys some new songs.
Now he has 525 songs.
How many songs did Jamal buy?

_____ songs in all

Jamal's songs | new songs

_____ new songs

3. There are 207 students in the second grade at Lakeside School. Some of the students are girls. 105 of the students are boys.
How many of the students are girls?

_____ students in all

girls | boys

_____ girls

4. Extend Your Thinking Jack wrote two number sentences for the strip diagram. He says the missing number in both number sentences is the same. Is Jack correct? If not, explain his error and correct it.

$? - 252 = 697$

$697 - 252 = ?$

697

? | 252

_____

_____

_____

_____

5. A book has 225 pages in all. Rex read some pages. He has 115 more pages to read.
How many pages has Rex read so far?

____ ◯ ____ = ____

_____ pages

6. Kayla scored 586 points in a video game. She needs 397 more points to reach the top score.
What is the top score of the game?

____ ◯ ____ = ____

_____ points

7. Some students want to collect 500 cans for a food drive. They have collected 335 cans so far. How many more cans do the students need to collect?

Which could you use to solve the problem?

○ $? + 335 = 500$ or $? - 500 = 335$

○ $? - 335 = 500$ or $500 + 335 = ?$

○ $335 + 500 = ?$ or $500 - ? = 335$

○ $335 + ? = 500$ or $500 - 335 = ?$

8. Extend Your Thinking Judy buys blue and white tiles. 120 of the tiles are white. The rest of the tiles are blue. There are 60 more blue tiles than white tiles. How many tiles did Judy buy in all?
Explain your thinking.

_____

_____

_____

_____

Name _____

Another Look You can use what you know about finding missing numbers in 2-digit problems to find missing numbers in 3-digit problems.

Jane had some pennies in a jar.
She put 185 more pennies in the jar.
Now there are 510 pennies in the jar.
How many pennies were in the jar at the start?

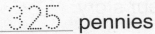
_510_ pennies in all

? | 185

pennies at the start | **pennies added**

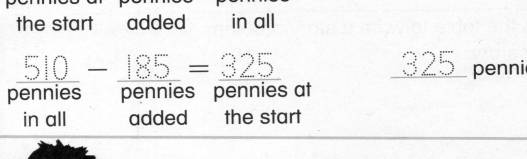

$$\underline{?} + \underline{185} = \underline{510}$$

pennies at | pennies | pennies
the start | added | in all

$$\underline{510} - \underline{185} = \underline{325}$$

pennies | pennies | pennies at
in all | added | the start

_325_ pennies

🏠 **HOME CONNECTION**
Your child drew strip diagrams and wrote number sentences to solve 3-digit addition and subtraction problems.

HOME ACTIVITY Have your child draw a strip diagram and write two number sentences for this problem: There are 450 spools of thread on sale. There are 280 spools of red thread. The rest of the spools are blue thread. How many spools of thread are blue?

 Complete the strip diagram and write a number sentence to solve the problem.

1. Shawn uses 85 blocks to build a tower.
   He has 130 blocks left.
   How many blocks did Shawn start with?

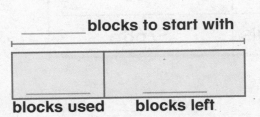
blocks to start with

blocks used | **blocks left**

_____ ◯ _____ = _____

_____ blocks

2. There are 18 empty seats on an airplane. The rest of the seats are filled. If 191 seats are filled, how many seats are on the airplane?

173 ○

209 ○

183 ○

219 ○

3. There are 622 runners in a marathon race. 259 runners have finished the race. How many runners have not finished the race? Write a number sentence to solve.

_____ ○ _____ = _____

_____ runners

4. Extend Your Thinking Use the data in the table to write a story problem. Write a number sentence to match your story. Then solve your story problem.

Toy Factory Monthly Report	
Type of Toy	Number Made
Dolls	512
Toy Trains	195
Stuffed Animals	768

_____ ○ _____ = _____

Name _____

Solve & Share

Jade had 35 boxes of cookies to sell.
She was able to sell 5 boxes at each house.
How many boxes did she have left after the fifth house? Explain.

⭐ **TEKS 2.1E** Create and use representations to organize, record, and communicate mathematical ideas. Also, 2.7, 2.7C. **Mathematical Process Standards** 2.1A, 2.1B, 2.1D, 2.1F.

Digital Resources at SavvasTexas.com

Solve   Learn   Glossary   Check   Tools   Games

Jade had _____ boxes left.

Analyze

Sara made a table to show toy prices.
What rule did she use?
What will be the sale price of the last toy?

Plan

The **input** shows the regular price.

The **output** shows the sale price.

Input	Output
$20	$15
$17	$12
$15	$10
$18	?

Solve and Justify

The output is always 5 less than the input.
So, the rule is

subtract 5 .

Input	Output
$20	$15
$17	$12
$15	$10
$18	$13

Evaluate

I found the sale price by subtracting $5 from $18.
$18 – $5 = $13

Do You Understand?

Show Me! How does a table help you see a pattern?

☆ Guided Practice ☆

Complete the table and look for a pattern.
Then use the table to solve the problems.

Input	Output
1	3
2	4
3	5
4	6

The input shows Joy's age.
The output shows Hope's age.
When Joy was 1 year old,
Hope was 3 years old.
When Joy was 2 years old,
Hope was 4 years old.

1. How old will Hope be when Joy is 8 years old? _____

2. What is the rule? _____

Topic 11 | Lesson 6

Name _____

Complete the table and look for a pattern.
Then use the table to solve the problems.

Input	Output
5	8
6	9
7	10
8	
9	
10	

The input shows Len's age. The output shows his brother's age. Len is 5 years old. His brother is 8 years old. When Len is 6, his brother will be 9.

3. What is the rule? _____

4. How old will Len's brother be when Len is 9? _____

5. How old will Len's brother be when Len is 10? _____

6. How old will Len's brother be when Len is 11? _____

Input	Output
$20	$13
$17	$10
$15	
$12	
$10	

The input shows the regular prices of shirts. The output shows the sale prices.

7. What is the sale price of the $12 shirt? _____

8. What is the sale price of the $10 shirt? _____

9. What is the rule?

_____

10. Using the rule, what is the sale price of a shirt that costs $9? _____

11. Extend Your Thinking
Think about the pattern in a table. How can you tell whether the rule is an addition rule or a subtraction rule?

_____

_____

_____

_____

Problem Solving

Use the tables to solve the problems below.

12. Frank is younger than his sister. In the table below, Frank's age is the input. His sister's age is the output.

What is the rule for the table? _____

How old will Frank be when his sister is 19 years old?

_____ years old

Input	Output
7	11
9	13
11	15
13	17
?	19

13. Students score extra points if they get a bonus question right. The input is the score. The output is the score with the bonus question.

What is the rule?

_____

If you score 85, what is your bonus question score?

_____ points

Input	Output
70	
75	80
80	85
85	
90	
95	100

14. Maya forgot to finish her table. Look at Maya's table. Which numbers did she forget?

○ Input: 6
  Output: 12

○ Input: 16
  Output: 16

○ Input: 16
  Output: 12

○ Input: 12
  Output: 11

Input	Output
9	1
11	3
?	8
18	10
20	?

15. Extend Your Thinking

Write a problem about a pattern you see in real life. Complete the table to solve the problem.

Input	Output

_____

_____

_____

Name _____

Another Look Look for a pattern in the numbers in the table. What happens to the input number to get the output number each time?

The rule is _subtract 2_.

You can use the rule to complete the table.

Input	Output
10	8
11	9
12	10
13	11
14	12
15	13

 HOME CONNECTION
Your child made and used tables and number patterns to solve problems.

HOME ACTIVITY Work with your child to make tables that show the differences in ages between siblings or friends.

Look for a pattern and complete the table. Then use the table to solve the problems.

Input	Output
$45	$35
$40	$30
$35	$25
$30	
$25	

1. Ling needs to record income during a store sale. He makes a table to show the sale prices.
What will be the sale price of an item that usually sells for $30?

$ _____

2. What will be the sale price of an item that usually sells for $25?

$ _____

3. What is the rule for this table?

_____

4. Using the rule, what would be the sale price of an object that usually sells for $15?

$ _____

Look for a pattern and complete the table. Then use the table to solve the problems.

Input	Output
20	25
21	26
22	27
25	
33	
	42

5. Tia brings oranges for her soccer team and coaches after each game. The input is the number of players. The output is the number of oranges. How many oranges will Tia bring if 25 players show up?

_____ oranges

6. How many extra oranges does Tia bring to each game?

_____ oranges

7. What is the rule for this table?

_____

8. How many oranges will Tia bring if 33 players show up?

_____ oranges

9. Tia brings 42 oranges for the team and coaches. How many players showed up?

_____ players

Input	Output
1	9
2	10
3	?
?	12
?	?

10. Misha has not completed her table. Look at Misha's table. When Misha writes 13 as the output, what is the input?

○ 3

○ 4

○ 5

○ 6

11. Extend Your Thinking Mike has a number machine. When he put 2 in, 9 came out. When he put 6 in, 13 came out.

Complete the sentences.
When the output is 12, the input is _____.

When the input is 14, the output is _____.

Mike's rule is _____.

Name _____

Patterns at work! Use **reason** to think about numbers and solve the problems.

37 24 21 9 40 25 18 32

1. Sort the odd and even numbers from the banners.

   Write the odd numbers from least to greatest. _____

   Write the even numbers from greatest to least. _____

2. Pick one odd and one even number.
   Write each one in its own box below.
   Draw a picture to show why the odd number is odd.
   Draw a picture to show why the even number is even.

Odd number _____	Even number _____

3. Find the sum of your two numbers.   Find the difference of your two numbers.

      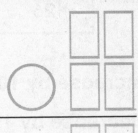

   What do you notice about the two answers?

   _____

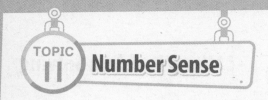

Choose the Numbers

1. Use the numbers in the box
   to make 4 different patterns.
   One number will not be used.
   Two numbers will each be used twice.

216	470	326
446	116	370
336	436	170
416	270	306
426	316	506

Increase by 10 _____

Decrease by 10 _____

Increase by 100 _____

Decrease by 100 _____

What's Wrong?

2. Nell wrote the value of these coins as
   $100¢. What did she do wrong?
   Tell how to fix Nell's mistake.

_____

_____

_____

Hundreds Chart Puzzles

3. Each puzzle was cut from a hundreds chart.
   Use number sense to fill in the missing
   numbers.

390	
	500

	20
29	

47	48

Set A

You can use the ones digit to tell if a number is even or odd.

24

The ones digit is 4.
4 is even.
So, 24 is an even number.

odd   (even)

Circle even or odd.
Use cubes if needed.

1. **19**   odd   even

2. **38**   odd   even

3. **27**   odd   even

Set B

You can use a hundreds chart to write missing numbers.
The hundreds digits go up by 1 from top to bottom.
The tens digits go up by 1 from left to right.

430	440	450	460
530	540	550	560
630	640	650	660
730	740	750	760

Look at the digits in the hundreds chart.
Write the missing numbers.

4.

860		880	
960	970		990
1,060		1,080	
	1,170		1,190

You can use a strip diagram to show what you know and help solve a problem.

Lacey studied for 55 minutes in all.
She studied math for 28 minutes.
How many minutes did she study science?

_55_ minutes in all

28	?
math	science

_27_ minutes

$$\overset{4\ \ 15}{\cancel{5}\ \cancel{5}} - 2\ 8 \over 2\ 7$$

5. Jay bought some pencils. He gives 16 pencils to Rosa. Now he has 24 pencils. How many pencils did Jay buy?

_____ pencils

given to Rosa	pencils left

○

_____ pencils

Find the rule for the pattern.

Input	Output
3	2
6	5
9	8
12	11

You subtract 1 from the input number to get the output number.

The rule is _subtract 1_.

Complete the table. Find the rule.

6.

Input	Output
1	3
2	4
3	
4	
5	

Rule: _____

7.

Input	Output
11	8
9	6
7	
5	
3	

Rule: _____

1. Which shows the missing numbers?

440	450	
	550	560
640		660

- ○ 560, 440, 540
- ○ 400, 500, 600
- ○ 460, 540, 650
- ○ 451, 549, 641

2. Willa writes an addition sentence. The sum is an even number.

Which addition sentence does Willa write?

- ○ $2 + 9 = ?$
- ○ $2 + 7 = ?$
- ○ $6 + 7 = ?$
- ○ $9 + 9 = ?$

3. Leila picked 43 apples in all.
28 of the apples are red.
The rest of the apples are green.
How many green apples did Leila pick?

43 apples in all

28	?
red apples	green apples

Which number sentences can you use to find the missing number?

- ○ $28 + 43 = ?$ or $43 - 28 = ?$
- ○ $28 + ? = 43$ or $43 - 28 = ?$
- ○ $28 + 43 = ?$ or $28 + ? = 43$
- ○ $28 + ? = 43$ or $? - 28 = 43$

4. The bookstore ships 177 books on Monday.
It ships 167 books on Tuesday.
It ships 157 on Wednesday.

If the pattern continues, how many books will the bookstore ship on Thursday?

- ○ 187
- ○ 167
- ○ 147
- ○ 57

5. Lana bought a package of beads.
She uses 210 beads to make a necklace.
There are 356 beads left in the package.

How many beads were in the package
at the start?

○ 136

○ 146

○ 556

○ 566

6. Ethan wrote the pattern below.

997, 897, 797, 697

Which list of numbers continues the pattern?

○ 597, 497, 397, 297

○ 687, 677, 667, 657

○ 707, 717, 727, 737

○ 696, 695, 694, 693

7. Complete the table.
Then write the rule.

Input	Output
4	8
7	11
10	
13	
	20

Rule: _____

8. Complete the strip diagram and solve
the problem.

Angie has 281 rocks.
She gives some rocks to Ben.
Now she has 249 rocks left.
How many rocks did Angie give to Ben?

_____ rocks in all

rocks to Ben   rocks left

_____ rocks

Fractions

How can fractions be used to name a part of a whole object?

These butterflies are breaking out of sacks called cocoons. Now they are ready to fly!

Butterflies go through many changes during their lives.

Wow! Let's do this project and learn more.

Math and Science Project: Butterfly Facts

Find Out Find a reference book about insects. Learn about the four stages of a butterfly's life. The stages are egg, larva or caterpillar, pupa, and adult.

Journal: Make a Book Draw and label pictures of the four stages of a butterfly's life. In your book, also:

• Write a sentence about the butterfly's life.

• Draw one caterpillar. Divide your picture into fourths. Decorate some fourths. Write a fraction about the parts you decorated.

Name _____

Review What You Know

Vocabulary

1. Circle the number that is **even**.

   31   24

   17

2. Circle the number that is **odd**.

   26   14

   39

3. Circle the pattern that **increases**.

   20, 30, 40, 50

   50, 40, 30, 20

Money

4. Circle the coins that make $1.00.

5. Pablo has two coins that equal $1. One coin is a half-dollar. What is the other coin Pablo has?

   _____

Mental Math

6. Add on to find the other part of 100.

   $28 + \underline{\hspace{1cm}} = 100$

My Word Cards

Study the words on the front of the card.
Complete the activity on the back.

A-Z

halves

2 equal parts

fourths

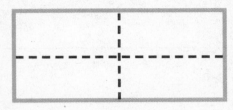

4 equal parts

eighths

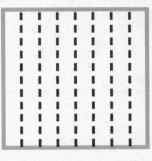

8 equal parts

equal parts

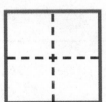

The square has
4 equal parts.

fraction

one   one   one
half   fourth   eighth

whole

Two halves make one
whole circle.

My Word Cards

Use what you know to complete the sentences.
Extend learning by writing your own sentence using each word.

When 1 whole is separated into 8 equal parts, the parts are called

_____.

When 1 whole is separated into 4 equal parts, the parts are called

_____.

When 1 whole is separated into 2 equal parts, the parts are called

_____.

You add parts to find the

_____.

A _____

names part of a whole or part of a set.

When parts of 1 whole are the same size, they are

_____

_____.

Solve & Share

Use one type of pattern block to cover this shape.
Draw lines to show how you placed the pattern blocks.
How many parts does the shape have now?
What do you notice about the parts?

⊕ **TEKS 2.3D** Identify examples and non-examples of halves, fourths, and eighths. Also, 2.3A, 2.8E. **Mathematical Process Standards 2.1D, 2.1F, 2.1G.**

Digital Resources at SavvasTexas.com

Solve   Learn   Glossary   Check   Tools   Games

_____ parts

Are these parts equal?

| 2 **equal parts** 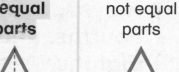 | not equal parts | 4 equal parts | not equal parts 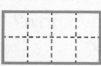 | 8 equal parts 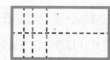 | not equal parts 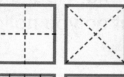 |
| These are **halves**. | These are not halves. | These are **fourths**. | These are not fourths. | These are **eighths**. | These are not eighths. |

You can show equal parts in different ways.

These all have 4 equal parts. These all show fourths.

Do You Understand?

Show Me! Does this picture show eighths? Why or why not?

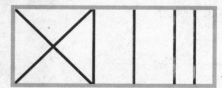

I. Circle the shapes that show halves. Put an **X** on the shapes that do **NOT** show halves.

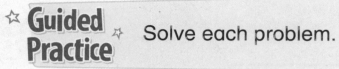

2. Circle the shapes that show fourths. Put an **X** on the shapes that do **NOT** show fourths.

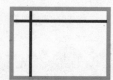

Copyright © Savvas Learning Company LLC. All Rights Reserved.

Topic 12 | Lesson 1

Independent Practice

Solve each problem.

3. Circle the shapes that show eighths. Put an **X** on the shapes that do **NOT** show eighths.

  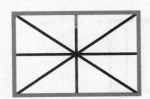 

4. Circle the shapes that show halves. Put an **X** on the shapes that do **NOT** show halves.

 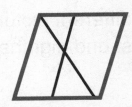  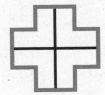

5. Circle the shapes that show fourths. Put an **X** on the shapes that do **NOT** show fourths.

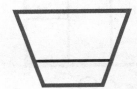 

6. **Extend Your Thinking** Draw what comes next.

7. Leon cut a sandwich into halves. Circle the shape that shows the way he cut the sandwich.

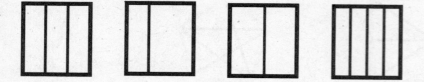

8. ⭐ Matt wants to use a flag that shows fourths. Which shows a flag that Matt should **NOT** use?

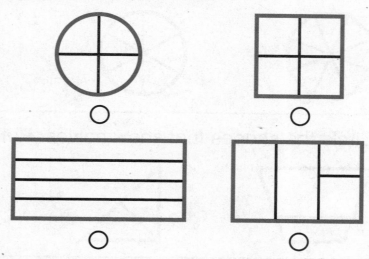

9. **Extend Your Thinking** Draw lines on the picture to solve the problem.

4 friends want to share a watermelon. How could they cut the watermelon so each friend gets an equal part?

They can cut it into _____.

10. **Extend Your Thinking** Draw and label three different pictures to show halves, fourths, and eighths.

Name _____

Another Look Equal parts are the same size.

2 equal parts

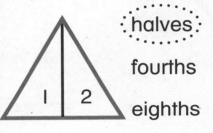

halves

fourths

eighths

4 equal parts

1	2
3	4

halves

fourths

eighths

8 equal parts

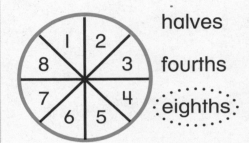

halves

fourths

eighths

🏠 **HOME CONNECTION**
Your child learned to identify equal parts (halves, fourths, and eighths) and unequal parts.

HOME ACTIVITY Draw three squares. Ask your child to draw lines in each to show halves, fourths, and eighths.

Write the number of equal parts for each shape.
Circle the correct fraction if the shape shows halves, fourths, or eighths.

1. _____ equal parts

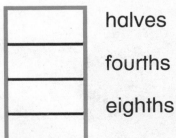

halves

fourths

eighths

2. _____ equal parts

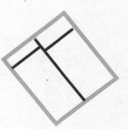

halves

fourths

eighths

3. _____ equal parts

halves

fourths

eighths

4. _____ equal parts

halves

fourths

eighths

5. Tom cut his muffin in half to share with his brother. Which picture shows how Tom cut his muffin?

6. This shape is divided into equal parts. Ryan says this shape is divided into fourths. Is he correct? Explain.

_____

_____

_____

Extend Your Thinking Divide the shapes into equal parts.

7. Two students want to share a small pizza. Draw two ways to split the pizza into halves.

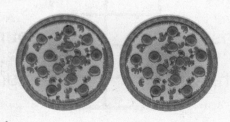

8. Eight students want to share a tray of apple crisp. Draw two ways to split the apple crisp into eighths.

9. Four students want to share an apple pie. Draw lines to split the pie into fourths.

580 five hundred eighty

Topic 12 | Lesson 1

Name ______________________

Solve & Share

How can you make these shapes match the statements below?
Compare work with a partner. Did you both solve this problem the same way? Explain.

Lesson 12-2
Unit Fractions and Regions

TEKS 2.3A Partition objects into equal parts and name the parts, including halves, fourths, and eighths, using words. Also, 2.3, 2.3D. **Mathematical Process Standards** 2.1A, 2.1B, 2.1D, 2.1F.

Digital Resources at SavvasTexas.com
Solve | Learn | Glossary | Check | Tools | Games

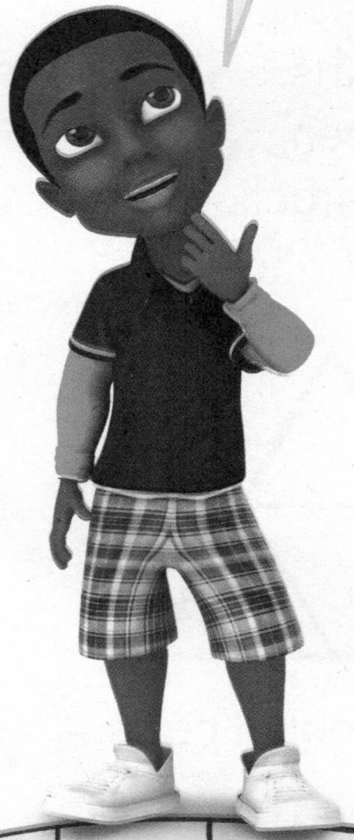

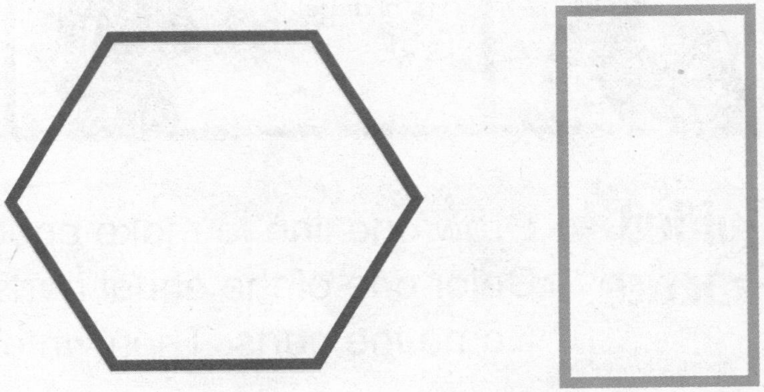

Each shape has 2 equal parts.
Each shape has 1 shaded part.

____

____

You can show equal parts of a **whole**. A **fraction** can name the equal parts.

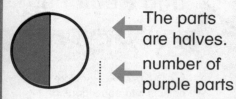

← The parts are halves.

⫶ ← number of purple parts

One half is purple.

The parts are fourths.

number of yellow parts

One fourth is yellow.

The parts are eighths.

number of orange parts

One eighth is orange.

Write the fraction.

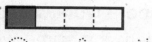

One half is red.

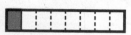

One fourth is blue.

One eighth is green.

Do You Understand?

Show Me! Ahmed will eat one eighth of a pizza. How many pieces of pizza are there? How many pieces will Ahmed eat?

Guided Practice

Draw one line to make equal parts. Color one of the equal parts green. Name the parts. Then write the fraction.

1.

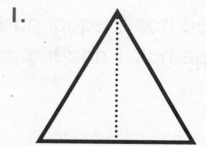

__2__ equal parts

The parts are ___halves___.

___One half___ is green.

2.

_____ equal parts

The parts are _____.

_____ is green.

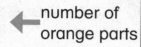

Name _____

Draw one line to make equal parts. Color one of the equal parts blue.
Name the parts. Then write the fraction.

3.

_____ equal parts

The parts are _____.

_____ is blue.

4.

_____ equal parts

The parts are _____.

_____ is blue.

5.

_____ equal parts

The parts are _____.

_____ is blue.

6.

_____ equal parts

The parts are _____.

_____ is blue.

7.

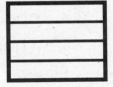

_____ equal parts

The parts are _____.

_____ is blue.

8.

_____ equal parts

The parts are _____.

_____ is blue.

9. Extend Your Thinking Write a story about 1 part of 4 equal parts.

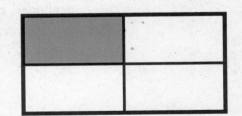

_____

_____

10. Alex cut an orange into 8 equal parts.
He ate one part.
What fraction of the orange did Alex eat?
Draw a picture to solve.

_____

11. Nina cut a pear into 2 equal parts.
She ate one part of the pear.
What fraction of the pear did
Nina **NOT** eat?

○ one eighth

○ one fourth

○ three eighths

○ one half

12. Julia shaded one equal
part of this shape.
What fraction of
the shape is shaded?

_____

Think about the
number of equal parts
and the number of
shaded parts.

13. **Extend Your Thinking** Write a story
about 1 part of 8 equal parts.
Then write the fraction in your story.

_____

_____

_____

_____

The fraction in my story is _____.

Name _____

Another Look A fraction can name one of the equal parts of a whole shape.

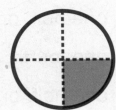

2 equal parts

halves

One half is shaded.

4 equal parts

fourths

One fourth is shaded.

8 equal parts

eighths

One eighth is shaded.

🏠 **HOME CONNECTION**
Your child divided shapes into equal parts and named the parts.

HOME ACTIVITY Draw three rectangles. Ask your child to draw lines and color the rectangles to show one half, one fourth, and one eighth.

 Color one part. Write how many equal parts. Name the parts. Then write the fraction.

1.

____ equal parts

The parts are _____.

_____ is shaded.

2.

____ equal parts

The parts are _____.

_____ is shaded.

3.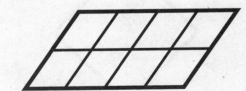

____ equal parts

The parts are _____.

_____ is shaded.

4. Luz colored one equal part of the square. What fraction of the square did she color?

_____

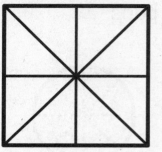

5. Maria divided one shape into 2 equal parts and another shape into 4 equal parts. She shaded 1 part of each shape. Which shows the fractions for the parts Maria shaded?

○ one half, one eighth

○ one fourth, one eighth

○ one half, one fourth

○ one eighth, one eighth

Extend Your Thinking Divide each shape into equal parts. Shade 1 part. Write a fraction for the shaded part.

6. 4 equal parts

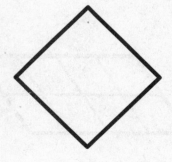

_____

7. 8 equal parts

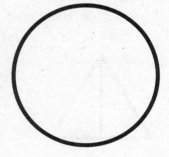

_____

8. 2 equal parts

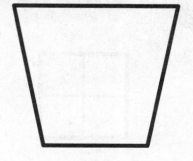

_____

Name ____________________

Solve & Share

How can you color three fourths of this shape blue? Write the number of equal parts. Write the number of blue parts.

Lesson 12-3
Non-Unit Fractions and Regions

TEKS 2.3A Partition objects into equal parts and name the parts, including halves, fourths, and eighths, using words. Also, 2.3, 2.3D. **Mathematical Process Standards** 2.1C, 2.1D, 2.1F.

Digital Resources at SavvasTexas.com

Solve Learn Glossary Check Tools Games

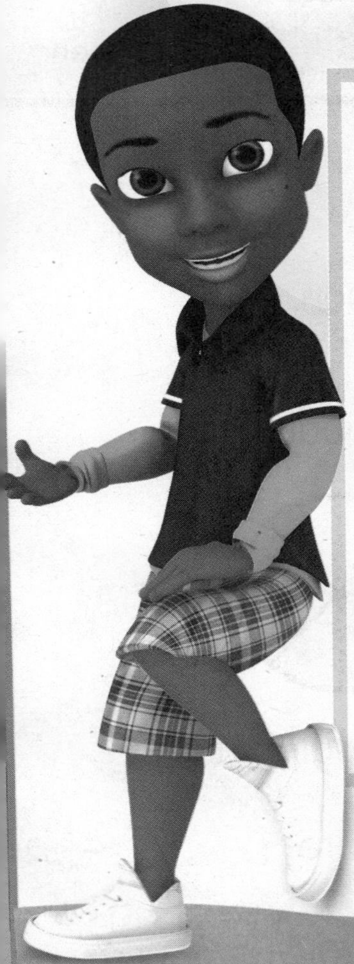

_____ equal parts

_____ blue parts

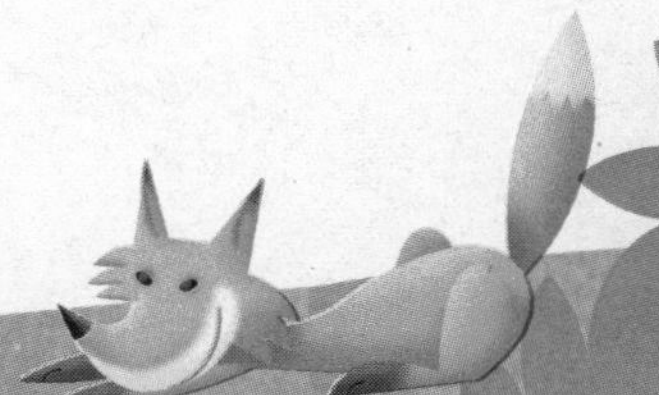

Fractions can name more than one equal part of a whole.

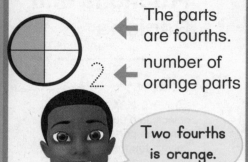

The parts are fourths.

number of orange parts

Two fourths is orange.

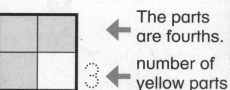

The parts are fourths.

number of yellow parts

Three fourths is yellow.

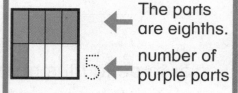

The parts are eighths.

number of purple parts

Five eighths is purple.

Write the fraction.

Two fourths is red.

Four eighths is blue.

Six eighths is green.

Do You Understand?

Show Me! Does this shape show three fourths shaded?

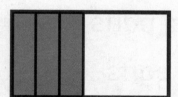

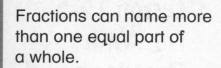

Guided Practice

Draw one line to make equal parts.
Color the equal parts blue.
Name the parts. Then write the fraction.

1. Color 4 equal parts.

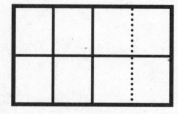

__8__ equal parts

The parts are _eighths_.

Four eighths is blue.

2. Color 5 equal parts.

_____ equal parts

The parts are _____.

_____ is blue.

Name _____

Draw one line to make equal parts. Color the equal parts blue.
Name the parts. Then write the fraction.

3. Color 3 equal
parts.

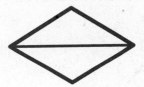

___ equal parts

The parts are

_____.

_____
is blue.

4. Color 6 equal
parts.

___ equal parts

The parts are

_____.

_____
is blue.

5. Color 2 equal
parts.

___ equal parts

The parts are

_____.

_____
is blue.

6. Color 2 equal
parts.

___ equal parts

The parts are

_____.

_____
is blue.

Extend Your Thinking Shade the last shape in each set to complete the pattern.

7.

8.

9. Ms. Fan plants her garden in 8 equal parts. She plants flowers in 2 of the parts.
Which parts of the garden do **NOT** have flowers?

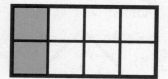

two eighths
○

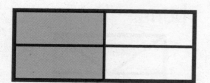

two fourths
○

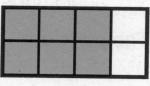

six eighths
○

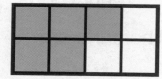

five eighths
○

10. Sheila cut a cake into 8 equal parts to share with friends.
The shaded part of the figure shows the part of the cake that was **NOT** eaten.

What part of the cake did Sheila and her friends eat?

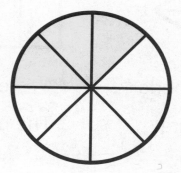

_____

11. Extend Your Thinking Write a story about more than one equal part of a shape that has 4 or 8 equal parts.
Then draw a picture to go with your story.

Think about which fraction describes the parts in your story.

_____

_____

_____

Name _____

 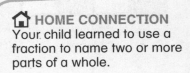
Another Look A fraction can name one, two, or more equal parts of a whole shape.

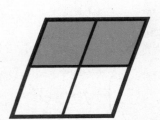

__4__ equal parts

Each part is _one fourth_.

Two fourths is shaded.

🏠 **HOME CONNECTION**
Your child learned to use a fraction to name two or more parts of a whole.

HOME ACTIVITY Draw a circle and divide it into 4 equal parts. Color 3 of the parts. Ask your child to say and write the fraction that tells what part of the circle is shaded and to explain his or her thinking.

Color the equal parts red. Name the parts. Then write the fraction.

1. Color 3 equal parts.

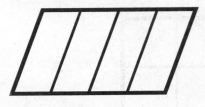

_____ equal parts

Each part is _____.

_____ is red.

2. Color 5 equal parts.

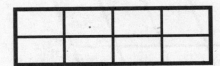

_____ equal parts

Each part is _____.

_____ is red.

3. Jill has a rug with 8 equal parts. Four eighths is white. Four eighths is blue.
Which could be Jill's rug?

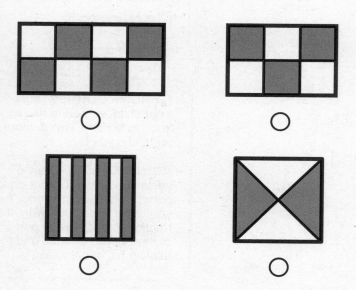

○   ○

○   ○

4. Jeff cuts a paper plate into 4 equal parts. He uses two equal parts for an art project.
Show how he cuts the plate.
Shade how much he uses, and then write that fraction.

Jeff uses _____ of the plate.

Extend Your Thinking Color the equal parts. Write the fraction for the parts you color.

5. Color one eighth yellow.
Then color another two eighths yellow.
Color the rest green.

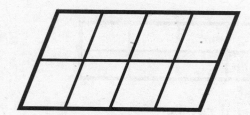

What part is green?

_____

6. Color one fourth green.
Then color another one fourth green.
Color the rest purple.

What part is purple?

_____

Topic 12 | Lesson 3

Name _____

☆ Solve & Share

Fold your paper strip into eighths.
How many eighths should you color to make the whole of your paper strip blue?

Place your paper strip in the space below and complete the sentence.

TEKS 2.3C Use concrete models to count fractional parts beyond one whole using words and recognize how many parts it takes to equal one whole. Also, 2.3, 2.3A. **Mathematical Process Standards** 2.1A, 2.1B, 2.1D, 2.1F.

Digital Resources at SavvasTexas.com

Solve Learn Glossary Check Tools Games

_____ eighths is blue.

One whole is blue.

This is 1 whole sandwich.

It can be cut into 4 equal parts.

Each part is called one fourth.

Ken eats 4 of the equal parts. What fraction did he eat?

Four fourths!

Four fourths equal one whole.

Ken ate four fourths of the sandwich. He ate the whole sandwich.

Do You Understand?

Show Me! Darnell cut an apple into two equal parts. He ate both parts. What fraction of the apple did Darnell eat? Did he eat the whole apple? Explain.

⭐ **Guided Practice** ⭐ Shade parts to show one whole. Write the fraction that equals one whole.

1.

Eight eighths equal one whole.

2.

_____ equal one whole.

Topic 12 | Lesson 4

Name _____

Cut and fold shapes to show halves, fourths, or eighths. Draw lines to show how you folded each shape. Complete the sentences.

3. Show halves.

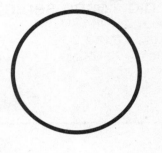

_____ equal one whole.

4. Show fourths.

_____ equal one whole.

5. Show eighths.

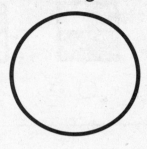

_____ equal one whole.

6. Show fourths.

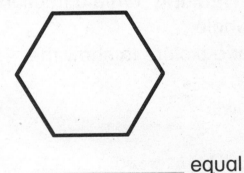

_____ equal one whole.

7. Show eighths.

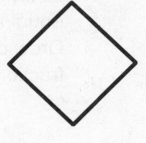

_____ equal one whole.

8. Show halves.

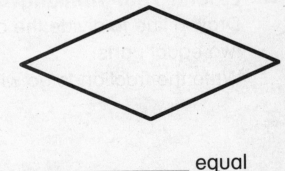

_____ equal one whole.

9. Extend Your Thinking Debbie cut a square-shaped cloth into 4 equal parts.
Then she cut each part in half.
Write a fraction for the whole cloth.

_____

10. ★ Tim cut a square casserole into four equal sections. He served the whole casserole. Which picture shows the parts Tim served?

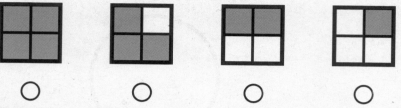

○   ○   ○   ○

11. Tasha cut a pizza into 8 equal pieces. She served LaToya, Jamie, and Paolo each 1 piece.

What part of the pizza did Tasha serve?

_____ eighths

Draw a picture to show a fraction. Name the fraction.

12. **Extend Your Thinking** Draw a circle. Draw a line to divide the circle into two equal parts. Write the fraction to go with your drawing.

13. **Extend Your Thinking** Write a fraction equal to one whole. Draw and color a picture to show the fraction.

Name _____

Another Look The whole pie is cut into equal parts. All the parts together equal **one whole**.

A whole can have different numbers of equal parts. Complete these fractions to show one whole.

🏠 **HOME CONNECTION**
Your child wrote fractions equal to one whole.

HOME ACTIVITY Draw a square. Ask your child to draw lines and color the square to show four fourths. Then ask him or her how many fourths equal one whole.

Two halves
equal one whole.

Four fourths
equal one whole.

Eight eighths
equal one whole.

Shade parts to show one whole. Write the fraction that equals one whole.

1.

_____ equal
one whole.

2.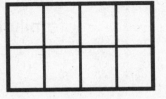

_____ equal
one whole.

3.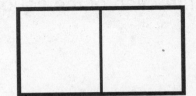

_____ equal
one whole.

4. Zeta folded a paper plate into fourths to make a spinner. Then she shaded each part. What fraction shows how much of the plate Zeta shaded?

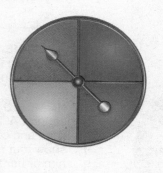

_____

5. Which shows one whole shaded?

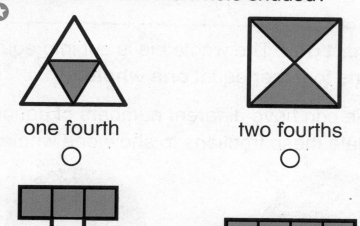

one fourth
○

two fourths
○

three fourths
○

four fourths
○

Extend Your Thinking Solve each problem. Draw pictures to help you.

6. Claire drew a square.
She divided it into two equal parts.
Claire colored the whole square.
What fraction of the square did Claire color?

7. Blake baked a pie.
He cut it into eight equal pieces.
His family ate the whole pie.
What fraction of Blake's pie did his family eat?

She colored _____ of her square.

His family ate _____ of his pie.

598 five hundred ninety-eight

Topic 12 | Lesson 4

Name _____

Solve & Share

Which fraction is larger: one half or one fourth of the same sandwich?
Divide the sandwiches.
Circle the sandwich that has larger equal parts.

★ TEKS 2.3B Explain that the more fractional parts used to make a whole, the smaller the part; and the fewer the fractional parts, the larger the part. **Mathematical Process Standards** 2.1A, 2.1D, 2.1F, 2.1G.

Digital Resources at SavvasTexas.com

Solve   Learn   Glossary   Check   Tools   Games

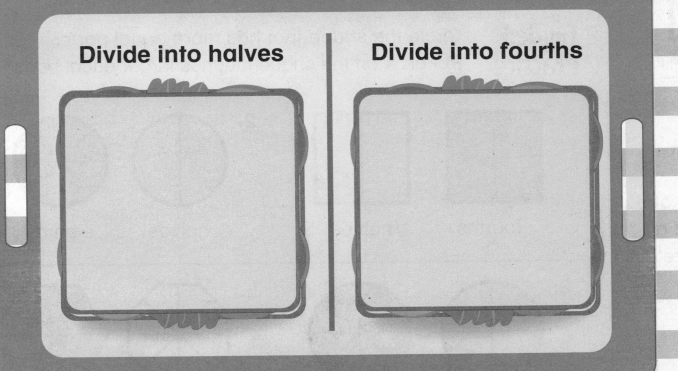

Divide into halves   **Divide into fourths**

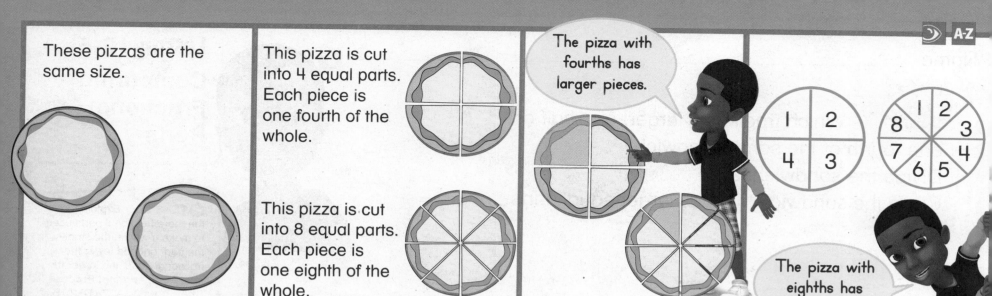

These pizzas are the same size.

This pizza is cut into 4 equal parts. Each piece is one fourth of the whole.

This pizza is cut into 8 equal parts. Each piece is one eighth of the whole.

The pizza with fourths has larger pieces.

The pizza with eighths has more pieces.

Do You Understand?

Show Me! David is very hungry. Do you think he would rather eat one half of a sandwich or one fourth of a sandwich of the same size? Explain.

☆ **Guided Practice** ☆   Circle the shape that has more equal parts.
Put an **X** on the shape that has larger equal parts.

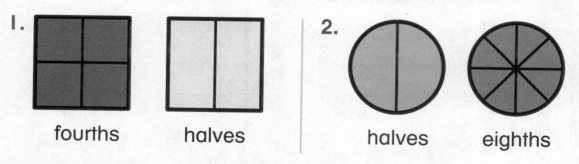

1.
fourths   halves

2.
halves   eighths

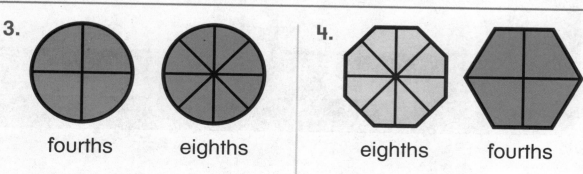

3.
fourths   eighths

4.
eighths   fourths

Topic 12 | Lesson 5

Name _____

Circle the shape that has fewer equal parts.
Put an **X** on the shape that has smaller equal parts.

5.

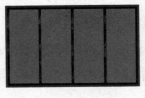 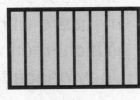

fourths   eighths

6.

fourths   halves

7.

eighths   halves

8.

eighths   fourths

Extend Your Thinking Joan is going to draw lines to divide the first square into halves, the second square into fourths, and the third square into eighths.

9. Which square will have the most equal parts?

_____

Which square will have the fewest equal parts?

_____

10. Which square will have the smallest equal parts?

_____

Which square will have the largest equal parts?

_____

Problem Solving Solve each problem.

11. Steve wants to cut a pan of cornbread into equal parts. Will the pieces be larger if he cuts the cornbread into halves or into fourths? Draw lines to show your answer.

The larger pieces will be _____.

12. Joey is making some lemonade but needs a little more water. He needs to add the smallest amount of water that he can measure with his measuring cup.
Which fraction shows the amount of water Joey needs to add to the lemonade?

○ one half

○ one eighth

○ one fourth

○ one whole

13. **Extend Your Thinking** Burke and Alisha are cutting up paper for an art project.
Their papers are the same size.
Burke uses one half of his paper.
Alisha uses two fourths of her paper.
Alisha said that they have used equal amounts of paper.

Is she correct? Explain your answer.
You can draw a picture to help.

_____

_____

_____

_____

Name _____

Another Look These rectangles are the same size.
The rectangle with more equal parts has smaller parts.
The rectangle with fewer equal parts has larger parts.

<u>8</u> equal parts

eighths

smaller equal parts

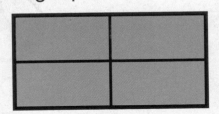

<u>4</u> equal parts

fourths

larger equal parts

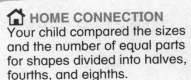 **HOME CONNECTION**
Your child compared the sizes and the number of equal parts for shapes divided into halves, fourths, and eighths.

HOME ACTIVITY Draw two circles that are the same size. Ask your child to draw lines to divide one circle into halves and one circle into fourths. Then ask your child which circle has more equal parts and which circle has larger equal parts.

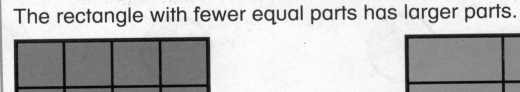 Compare the two shapes. Tell how many equal parts.
Then circle **smaller** or **larger** and **more** or **fewer** for each.

1. halves

equal parts:

smaller   larger

more   fewer

_____ equal parts

fourths

equal parts:

smaller   larger

more   fewer

_____ equal parts

2. eighths

equal parts:

smaller   larger

more   fewer

_____ equal parts

halves

equal parts:

smaller   larger

more   fewer

_____ equal parts

3. Ginny and Martha each have a pizza.
Their pizzas are the same size.
Ginny cuts her pizza into fourths.
Martha cuts her pizza into eighths.

Who has more slices? _____

Who has larger slices? _____

4. Mary is designing a flag for her team. She wants
one half of the flag to be red, one fourth of it to
be blue, and one fourth of it to be yellow.

Which shows what Mary's flag might look like?

○ ○

○ ○

Extend Your Thinking Lucas is making a quilt using squares.
Draw lines and color to show what each square on his quilt will look like.

5. Divide the square into
fourths. Shade one half
purple and two fourths
yellow.

6. Divide the square into
eighths. Shade one half
green and four eighths
blue.

7. Divide the square into
eighths. Shade two eighths
brown, two eighths orange,
and one half yellow.

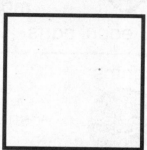

Name _____

☆ **Solve & Share**

How many one-fourth crackers can you make from two whole crackers? Show the fourths. Explain.

⭐ **TEKS 2.3C** Use concrete models to count fractional parts beyond one whole using words and recognize how many parts it takes to equal one whole. **Mathematical Process Standards** 2.1C, 2.1D, 2.1E, 2.1F.

Digital Resources at SavvasTexas.com

Solve Learn Glossary Check Tools Games

_____ **fourths**

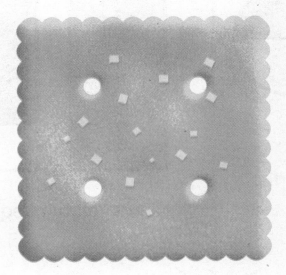 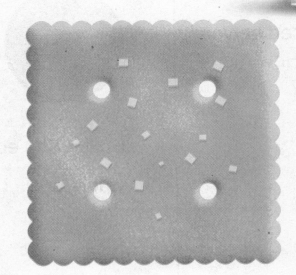

This circle is cut into four equal parts. Each part is one fourth of the circle.

Sometimes you have so many fourths that you have more than one whole!

Here are some fourths. How many one-fourth parts of a circle are there?

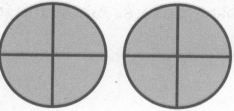

There are nine fourths.

Nine one-fourth parts make two whole circles. One fourth is left over!

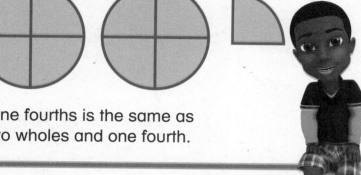

Nine fourths is the same as two wholes and one fourth.

Do You Understand?

Show Me! Ellen used halves to make 3 wholes. How many halves did she use?

1.

Six fourths equals _one_

whole and _two_ fourths.

2.

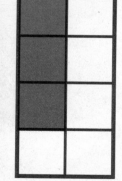

Eleven eighths equals

_____ whole and

_____ eighths.

Name _____

Cut and fold shapes to show halves, fourths, or eighths. Draw lines to show how you folded each shape. Shade the number of parts given. Complete the sentence.

3. Show fourths. Shade five fourths.

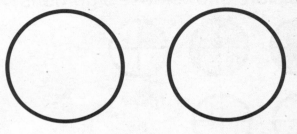

Five fourths equals _____ whole and _____ fourth.

4. Show halves. Shade five halves.

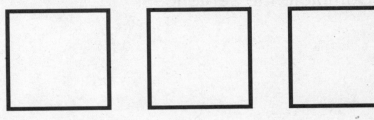

Five halves equals _____ wholes and _____ half.

5. Show eighths. Shade ten eighths.

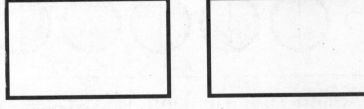

Ten eighths equals _____ whole and _____ eighths.

6. Show fourths. Shade seven fourths.

Seven fourths equals _____ whole and _____ fourths.

7. **Extend Your Thinking** Kay cuts 3 pears into fourths. Does she have enough so that she and each of her 10 friends can have a piece? Explain.

_____

_____

Problem Solving

Solve each problem.

8. Draw three of the same shape.
Draw lines to divide each shape into fourths.
Shade more than two wholes.
Complete the sentences.

I shaded _____ fourths.

This equals _____ wholes and _____ fourths.

9. José divided each of his three gardens into fourths.
He filled nine fourths with different plants.
Which picture shows José's gardens?

○ 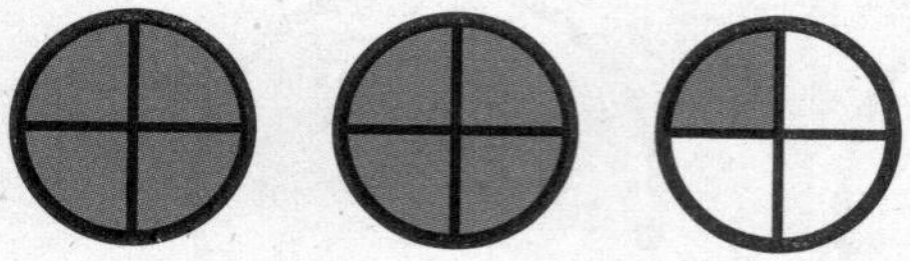

○ 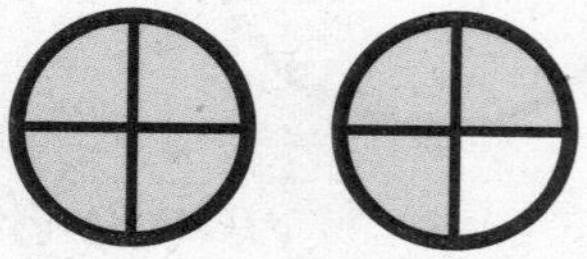

○ 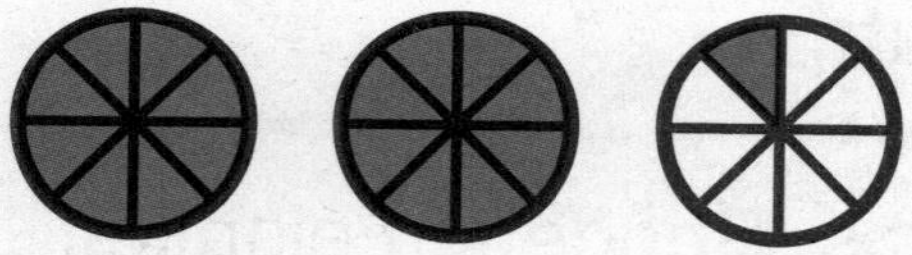

○ 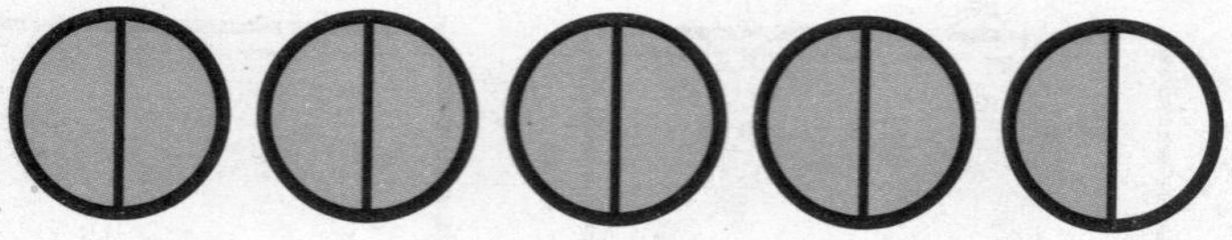

10. Which is the same as fourteen eighths?

○ one whole and two eighths

○ eight wholes and four eighths

○ two wholes and one eighth

○ one whole and six eighths

11. **Extend Your Thinking** Tina's class is having a pizza party.
The pizzas are cut into eighths.
There are 30 students in her class.
How many pizzas does Tina's class need so that each student will get one slice?

_____ pizzas

Name _____

Another Look You can make fractions with more than one whole.

These shapes are each one eighth of larger shapes.

Color to show the eighths.

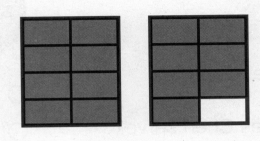

🏠 **HOME CONNECTION**
Your child used words to describe fractional parts greater than one whole and made models for those fractions.

HOME ACTIVITY Draw three squares. Ask your child to divide the squares into fourths and color nine fourths. Ask your child to tell you how many wholes and fourths he or she colored.

Fifteen eighths is equal to __one__ whole and __seven__ eighths.

Color to show halves or fourths.
Complete the sentence.

1. seven halves

Seven halves is equal to _____ wholes and _____ half.

2. ten fourths

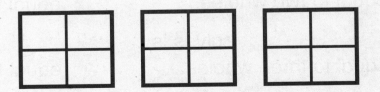

Ten fourths is equal to _____ wholes and _____ fourths.

3. Chen serves one fourth of each loaf to the six students at his lunch table.

How many fourths does Chen serve?

_____ fourths

How many whole loaves does Chen serve?

_____ whole

How many fourths does Chen have left over?

_____ fourths

4. What would this picture show if three of the parts in the second circle were **NOT** shaded?

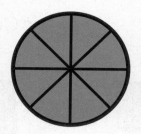 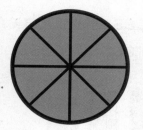

○ two wholes and one eighth

○ five wholes and one eighth

○ one whole and five eighths

○ one whole and seven eighths

Extend Your Thinking For each problem, complete the sentences. Look for a pattern.

5. _____ halves is equal to one whole.

_____ halves is equal to two wholes.

_____ halves is equal to three wholes.

_____ halves is equal to four wholes.

6. _____ fourths is equal to one whole.

_____ fourths is equal to two wholes.

_____ fourths is equal to three wholes.

_____ fourths is equal to four wholes.

7. _____ eighths is equal to one whole.

_____ eighths is equal to two wholes.

_____ eighths is equal to three wholes.

_____ eighths is equal to four wholes.

Name _____

Solve & Share

Here is a parking lot that will be used for the school carnival. Draw lines on the first shape to show how the lot could be divided into 4 equal parts to make game booths.
Show how the second shape could be divided into 8 equal parts.

⬟ **TEKS 2.1D** Communicate mathematical ideas, reasoning, and their implications using multiple representations ... . Also, 2.3A, 2.3D. **Mathematical Process Standards 2.1A, 2.1B, 2.1G.**

Digital Resources at SavvasTexas.com

  Solve Learn Glossary Check Tools Games

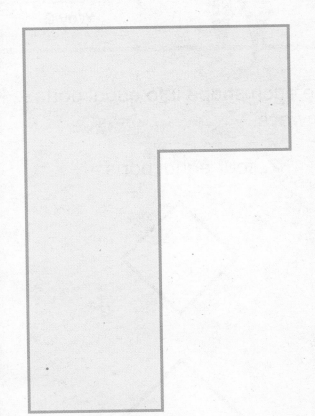

Analyze

Joanne and 3 friends are planting small gardens on this lot. How could they divide the lot into 4 equal parts?

Plan

Draw lines to show how the lot could be divided equally.

Solve, Justify, and Evaluate

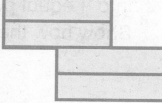

Each part is one fourth of the whole shape!

Here is one way:

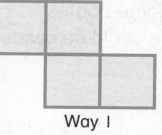

Way 1

Here is another way:

Way 2

Do You Understand?

Show Me! When you divide a shape into two equal parts, what are the parts called?
Four equal parts?
Eight equal parts?

☆ Guided Practice ☆

Draw lines to divide each shape into equal parts. Show two different ways.

1. two equal parts

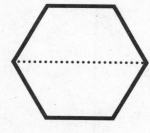

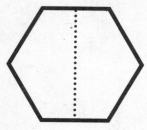

2. four equal parts

Name _____

Draw lines to divide each shape into equal parts. Show two different ways.

3. halves

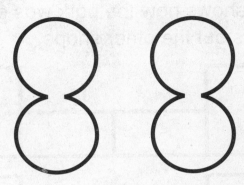

4. fourths

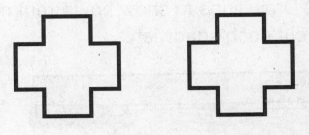

5. eighths

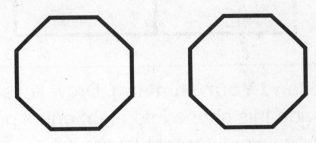

6. halves

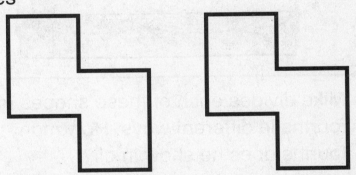

7. Extend Your Thinking Draw two ways to divide this shape into halves. Then draw two ways to divide this shape into fourths.

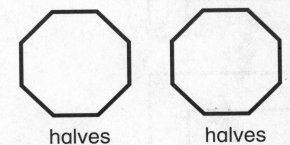

halves   halves

fourths   fourths

Problem Solving — Solve each problem.

8. Brent has these two sandwiches. He cuts one sandwich into four equal parts. He cuts the other sandwich into eight equal parts. Draw lines to show how Brent might have cut each sandwich.

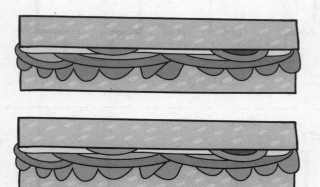

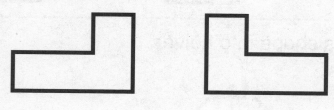

9. A town wants to divide the park into four equal sections. Circle the shape that shows how the park was divided. Cross out the other shape.

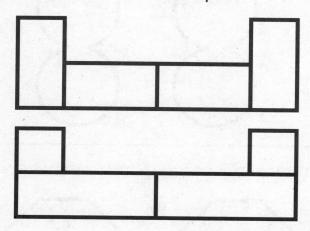

10. ⭐ Mike divides each of these shapes into fourths in different ways. How many fourths does he show in all?

○ 12
○ 8
○ 16
○ 4

11. Extend Your Thinking Draw lines to divide this shape into eight equal parts. Show two different ways.

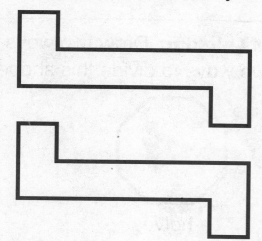

Topic 12 | Lesson 7

Name _____

Another Look You can draw lines to divide a shape into equal parts.

Divide this shape into fourths and then into eighths.

Look for a smaller shape inside the shape. Check that you have four equal parts.

You can divide the whole shape into even smaller shapes. Now you have eight equal parts.

 **HOME CONNECTION**
Your child drew pictures to divide shapes into two, four, or eight equal parts.

HOME ACTIVITY Draw a simple shape such as a circle or rectangle. Ask your child to divide it into four equal parts.

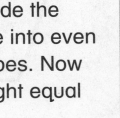

Draw lines to divide each shape into equal parts.

1. Divide into halves.
   Then divide into fourths.

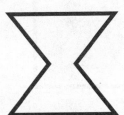

2. Divide into halves.
   Then divide into fourths.

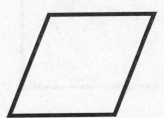
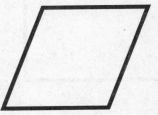

3. Amir divided a shape into halves and then into fourths. Which shows the shape Amir divided?

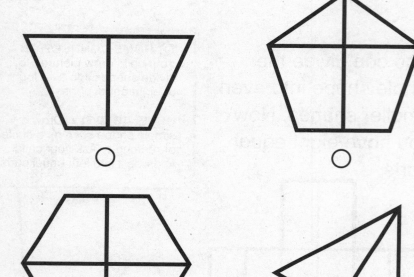

○

○

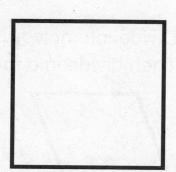

○

4. Extend Your Thinking Sue is making a flag for her team. It is in the shape of a triangle. Sue wants her flag to be made up of four small triangles that are the same shape and size. Draw lines to show what the flag will look like.

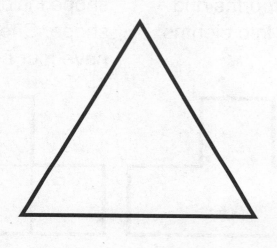

5. Draw lines to divide each square into fourths. Show four different ways.

Name _____

Draw a picture to **connect** your fraction sense to these problems!

1. You bake two pans of cornbread.
   Both pans are the same size and shape.
   Draw lines to show how to cut each pan
   of cornbread into eighths. Fold two pieces
   of paper into eighths to help.

   How many eighths are there in all?

   _____

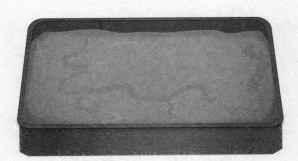

2. One whole pan of cornbread is eaten at dinner.
   Write a fraction for that amount of cornbread.

   _____

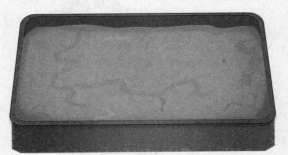

3. Suppose one whole pan and 4 pieces of
   the second pan of cornbread are eaten at
   dinner. How many eighths would be eaten
   in all?

   _____

4. You bake 4 pans of cornbread for a charity
   bake sale.
   Each pan sells for $5.
   How much did the cornbread sell for in all?

   $_____

Fraction Fill-In

1. Shade one part less than the whole.

Each type of food has a different size and shape. What is always the same?

_____

_____

What's Wrong?

2. Zack wants to draw lines to make halves or fourths. He says that fourths will have larger parts than halves. Do you agree? Explain.

_____

_____

_____

_____

Code Math

3. Use the code to solve the number sentences.

▼ = 2	☐ = 3
✱ = 5	⬠ = 8

☐ × ☐ = 24

⬠ ÷ ▼ = ☐

Set A

TOPIC 12

You can split a whole into parts.

equal parts 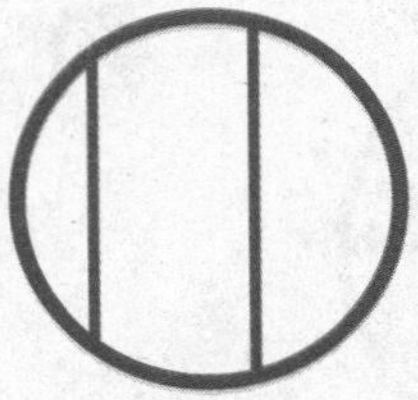   not equal parts

Does this shape
have equal parts?

(yes)   no

How many equal parts? 4

| 2 equal parts are **halves**. | 4 equal parts are **fourths**. | 8 equal parts are **eighths**. |

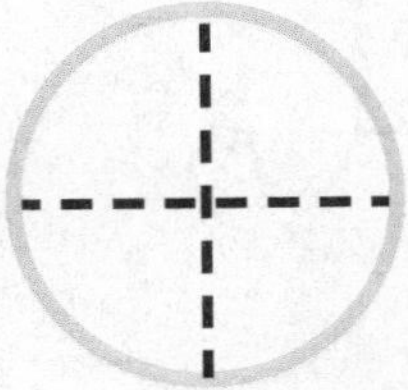

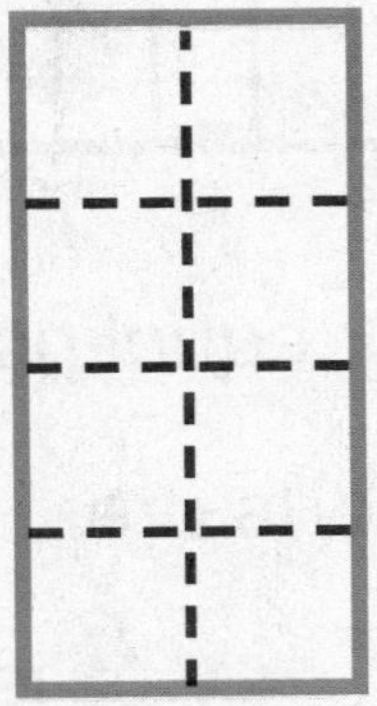

Reteaching

Circle shapes that show the
fraction word.
Draw an X on shapes that do
not show the fraction word.

1. halves

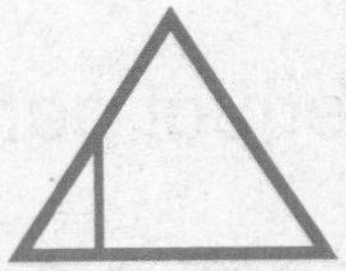

2. fourths

3. eighths

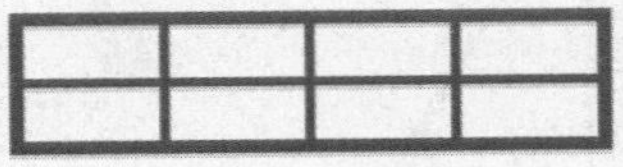

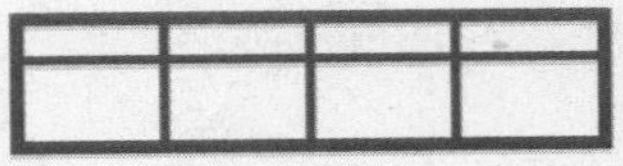

Tell if each shape shows
halves, fourths, or eighths.

4.   5.   6.

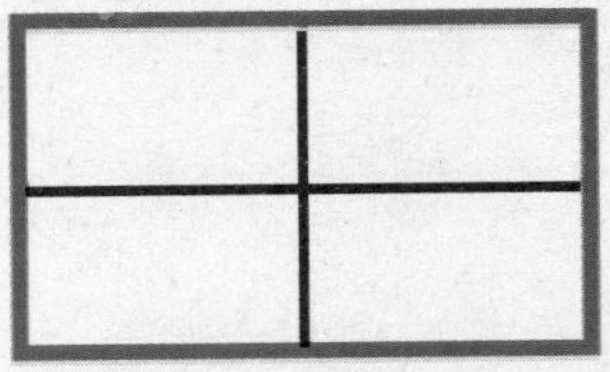

You can write a fraction to name equal parts of a whole.

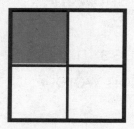

__4__ equal parts

The parts are __fourths__.

__One fourth__ is red.

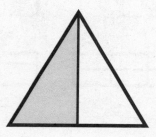

__2__ equal parts

The parts are __halves__.

__One half__ is yellow.

Name the parts.
Then write the fraction.

7.

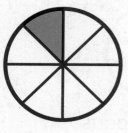

_____ equal parts

The parts are _____.

_____ is green.

8.

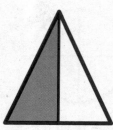

_____ equal parts

The parts are _____.

_____ is blue.

9.

_____ equal parts

The parts are _____.

_____ is pink.

10.

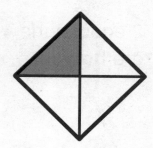

_____ equal parts

The parts are _____.

_____ is purple.

Set C _____

Fractions can name more than one part of a whole.

Name the parts.
Then write the fraction.

4 equal parts

The parts are __fourths__.

__Three fourths__ is orange.

8 equal parts

The parts are __eighths__.

__Four eighths__ is green.

11.

_____ equal parts

The parts are _____.

_____ is green.

12.

_____ equal parts

The parts are _____.

_____ is blue.

13.

_____ equal parts

The parts are _____.

_____ is yellow.

14.

_____ equal parts

The parts are _____.

_____ is red.

Fractions can name all of the parts of a whole.

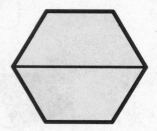

__2__ equal parts

The parts are __halves__.

__Two halves__ equal one whole.

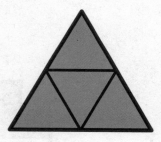

__4__ equal parts

The parts are __fourths__.

__Four fourths__ equal one whole.

Name the parts.
Then write the fraction.

15.

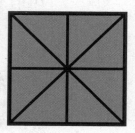

_____ equal parts

The parts are _____.

_____ equal one whole.

16.

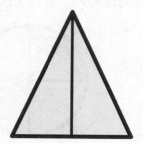

_____ equal parts

The parts are _____.

_____ equal one whole.

17.

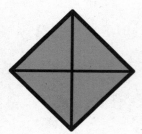

_____ equal parts

The parts are _____.

_____ equal one whole.

18.

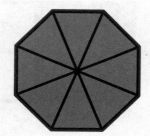

_____ equal parts

The parts are _____.

_____ equal one whole.

Name _____

1. Tracy cut a watermelon slice in half. How many equal parts did she make?

○ 1

○ 2

○ 3

○ 4

2. Megan ate one part of her sandwich.
What part of her sandwich did she eat?

○ one whole

○ one half

○ one fourth

○ one eighth

3. Jay has a green and yellow kite. What fraction of the kite is green?

○ one fourth

○ two fourths

○ one half

○ three fourths

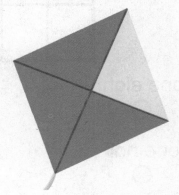

4. Maria has an umbrella. What fraction of the umbrella is blue?

○ one fourth

○ two fourths

○ one eighth

○ four eighths

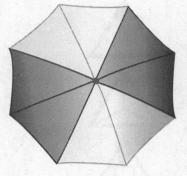

5. Ray cut a small pizza into fourths.
He ate the whole pizza.
What fraction of the whole pizza did
he eat?

○ four fourths

○ three fourths

○ two fourths

○ one fourth

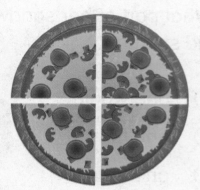

6. Leah cut two squares into fourths.
She colored some of the parts.
What parts did Leah color?

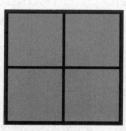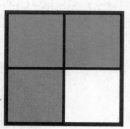

○ one whole and one fourth

○ one whole and two fourths

○ one whole and three fourths

○ three wholes and one fourth

7. Ms. Camire asked her class to show
a triangle cut in half.
Which picture shows halves?

○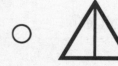

○

○

○

8. Drew colored one part of this rectangle.
What fraction of the rectangle did he color?

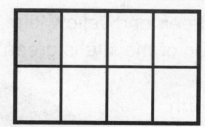

one eighth
○

one fourth
○

one half
○

one whole
○

Topic 12

9. Which shape shows one whole shaded?

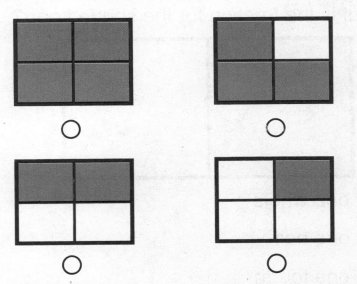

○   ○

○   ○

10. Arif divides a square into halves. Toni divides a square that is the same size into fourths. Which sentence correctly compares the squares?

○ Toni's square has larger parts.

○ Arif's square has more parts.

○ Arif's square has larger parts.

○ Toni's square has fewer parts.

11. Which shows two different ways to show fourths?

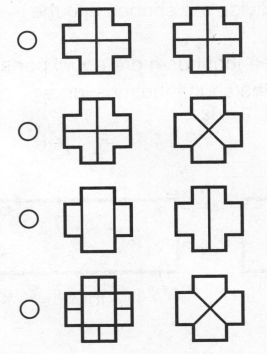

12. Tania colors parts of the circles. Which shows the parts Tania colors?

○ six halves

○ one whole and one sixth

○ one whole and one half

○ five halves

13. This cracker is divided into fourths.

How many equal parts does the cracker have?

○ 8

○ 4

○ 2

○ 1

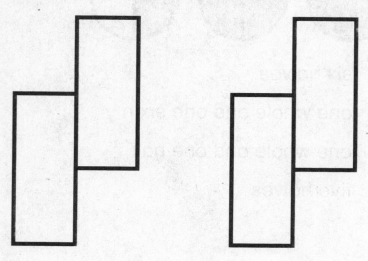

14. Mark shaded part of this rectangle. What is the fraction for the shaded part?

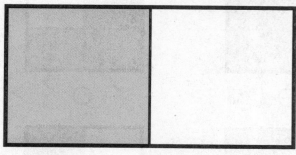

○ one whole

○ one half

○ one fourth

○ one eighth

15. Draw lines to show two different ways to divide these shapes into fourths.

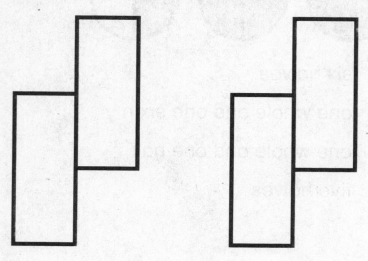

16. Draw lines to divide the shapes into the given fractions.

Circle the shape that has more equal parts. Draw an **X** on the shape that has larger equal parts.

halves

fourths

Geometry

Essential Question: How can shapes and solids be described, compared, and used to make other shapes?

A cookie could be a circle, square, rectangle—or any other shape!

The heat from the oven bakes the cookies.

Wow! Let's do this project and learn more.

Math and Science Project: Light and Heat

Find Out Look at recipes in the cookie section of a cookbook. Find out how cookies can be made in circles, squares, rectangles, and triangles. Then compare the recipes. What steps are always included?

Journal: Make a Book Draw and label pictures of cookies in different shapes. In your book, also:

• List the important steps for baking cookies.

• Describe how the cookies change after baking.

• Draw cookies in the shapes of pentagons, hexagons, or other polygons.

Name _____

Review What You Know

Vocabulary

1. Circle the shape that shows **equal parts**.

2. Circle the shape that shows **fourths**.

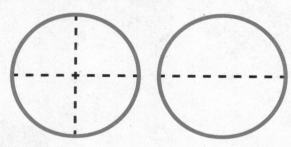

3. Circle the shape that shows **eighths**.

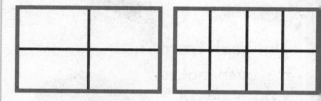

Fractions

4. Write the fraction shown.

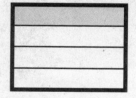

_____

5. Write the fraction shown.

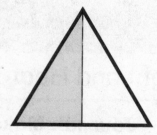

_____

Missing Numbers

6. Find the pattern in the table to finish filling in the output. Then write the rule.

Input	Output
2	4
4	6
6	8
8	
10	

rule: _____

My Word Cards

Study the words on the front of the card.
Complete the activity on the back.

A-Z

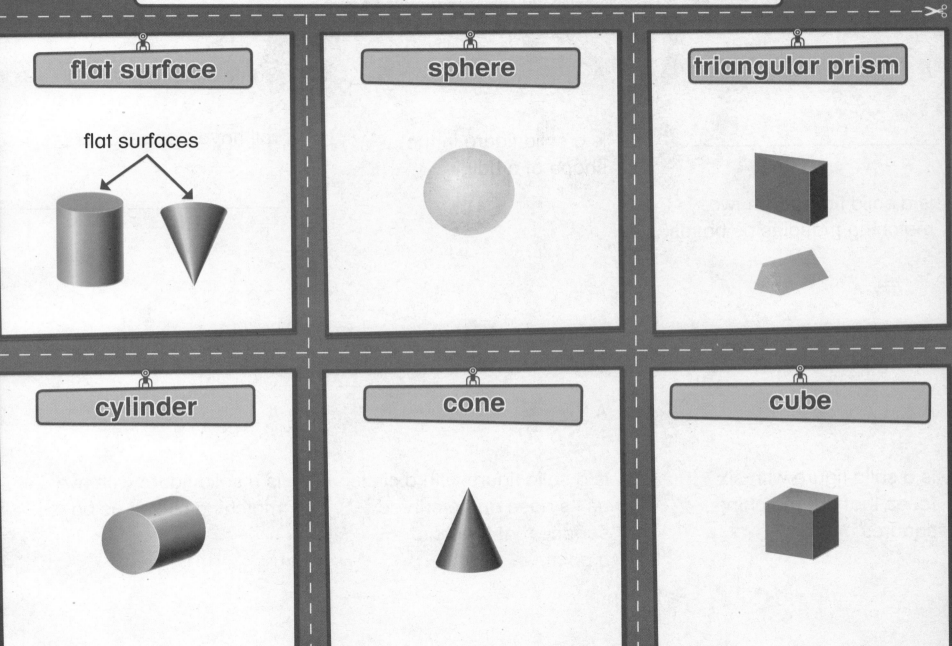

flat surface

flat surfaces

sphere

triangular prism

cylinder

cone

cube

My Word Cards

Use what you know to complete the sentences.
Extend learning by writing your own sentence using each word.

A _____

_____

is a solid figure with two
matching triangles as bases.

A _____

is a solid figure in the
shape of a ball.

Some solid figures that

roll have _____

_____.

A _____

is a solid figure with six
faces that are matching
squares.

A _____

is a solid figure with a circle
as its base and a curved
surface that meets at
a point.

A _____

is a solid figure with two
matching circles as bases.

My Word Cards

Study the words on the front of the card.
Complete the activity on the back.

A-Z

rectangular prism

face

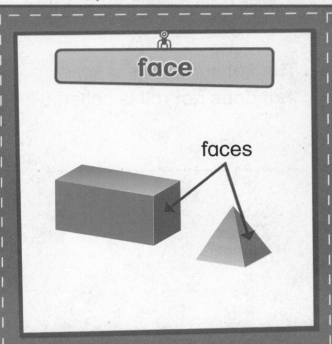

faces

edge

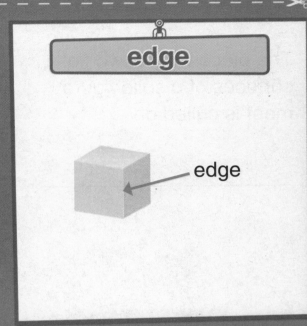

edge

vertex

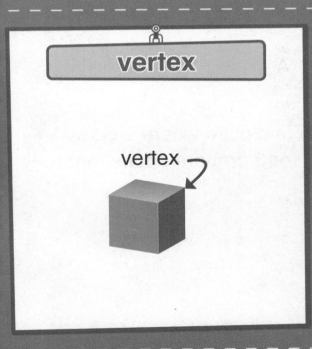

vertex

polygon

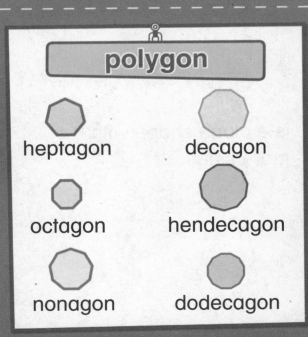

heptagon   decagon

octagon   hendecagon

nonagon   dodecagon

side

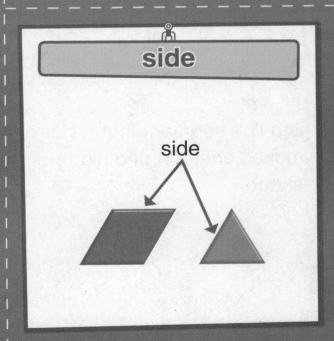

side

My Word Cards

Use what you know to complete the sentences.
Extend learning by writing your own sentence using each word.

The place where two flat surfaces of a solid figure meet is called an

_____.

The flat surface of a solid that does not roll is called a

_____.

A _____

_____

is a solid figure with bases that are rectangles.

A _____

is a line segment that makes one part of a plane shape.

A _____

is a plane shape with 3 or more sides.

A _____

is a point where 2 sides or 3 or more edges meet.

My Word Cards

Study the words on the front of the card.
Complete the activity on the back.

A-Z

quadrilateral

pentagon

hexagon

pyramid

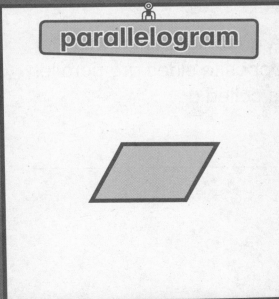

parallelogram

trapezoid

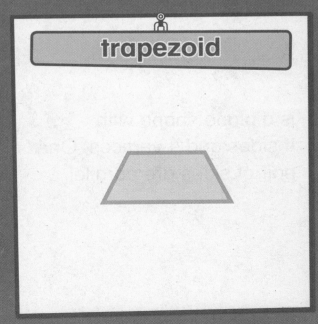

My Word Cards

Use what you know to complete the sentences.
Extend learning by writing your own sentence using each word.

A _____

is a polygon with 6 sides.

A _____

is a polygon with 5 sides.

A _____

is a polygon with 4 sides.

A _____

is a plane shape with
4 sides and 4 vertices. One
pair of sides are parallel.

A quadrilateral in which
opposite sides are parallel
is called a

_____.

A _____

is a solid figure with a base
that is a polygon and faces
that are triangles that meet
in a point.

Name _____

☆ **Independent** ☆
☆ **Practice**

Write how many flat surfaces or faces, edges, and vertices each solid figure has. Then circle the matching objects.

3. A rectangular prism has __6__ faces, __12__ edges, and __8__ vertices.

> The matching objects look like the solid figure!

4. A triangular prism has __5__ faces, __6__ edges, and __8__ vertices.

  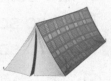 

5. A sphere has __0__ flat surfaces, __0__ edges, and __0__ vertices.

6. Extend Your Thinking Why are the flat surfaces on these solids called faces?

__be_____

_____

Problem Solving Use the clues to solve each problem.

7. Sandy's solid figure has 1 flat surface.
It has 0 edges and 1 vertex.
Which figure is it?

_____

8. I have 2 more vertices than faces.
I have 4 more edges than vertices.
My edges are all the same length.

What solid figure am I?

I am a _____.

9. Andrew has two solid figures.
One of the figures can roll and
has no vertices or flat surfaces.
The other figure has more vertices
than a cone. It has fewer vertices than a
rectangular prism.

Which of Andrew's figures is shown?

  ○   ○

  ○   ○

10. **Extend Your Thinking** Nadine is thinking
of two solids.
The two solids have 3 flat surfaces in all.
The two solids have 1 vertex in all.

What two solids could Nadine be
thinking of?

_____ and _____

Explain your thinking.

_____

_____

_____

Name _____

Another Look Some solid figures have flat surfaces and others have faces. Some have edges and vertices.

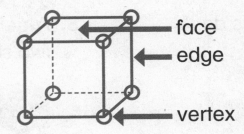

← face
← edge
← vertex

🏠 **HOME CONNECTION**
Your child learned to recognize solid figures and classify them by their attributes.

HOME ACTIVITY Take your child on a hunt for solid figures in your home or neighborhood. Ask your child to describe each solid figure he or she sees.

Put an X on the solid figures that have edges.
Underline the solid figures that have vertices.
Circle the solid figure that does not have a flat surface.

sphere   triangular prism   cylinder   cone   cube   rectangular prism

Write the number of flat surfaces or faces, edges, and vertices each solid figure has.

1.  flat surfaces _____
   edges _____
   vertices _____

2. 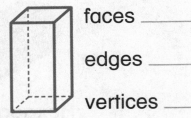 faces _____
   edges _____
   vertices _____

3. flat surfaces _____
   edges _____
   vertices _____

Write a number sentence to solve.

4. **Algebra** How many flat surfaces do these two shapes have in all?

_____ + _____ = _____

_____ flat surfaces

5. **Algebra** How many vertices do these two shapes have in all?

_____ + _____ = _____

_____ vertices

6. Jackie says that if a solid figure cannot roll, then it has faces.
Is Jackie correct? Explain.

_____

_____

_____

7. Ming's shape has fewer than 8 faces.
⭐ It has fewer than 10 edges.
Which could **NOT** be Ming's shape?

○   ○   ○   ○

8. **Extend Your Thinking** Use what you know about triangular prisms to describe the solids below.

Pentagonal Prism

faces _____

vertices _____

edges _____

Hexagonal Prism

faces _____

vertices _____

edges _____

Name ______________________________

Solve & Share

What are some ways these solid figures are alike? How are they different? Explain.

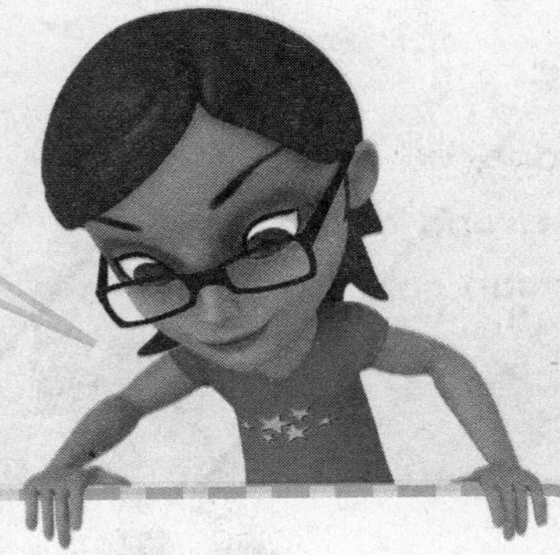

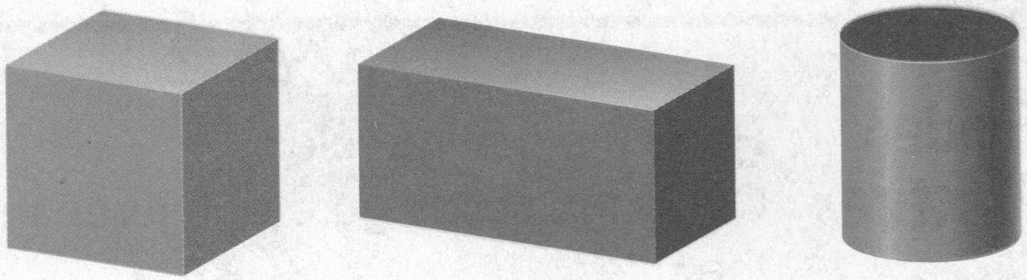

Lesson 13-2
Sorting Solid Figures

TEKS 2.8B Classify and sort three-dimensional solids . . . based on attributes using formal geometric language. Also, 2.8.
Mathematical Process Standards 2.1A, 2.1C, 2.1D, 2.1F.

Digital Resources at SavvasTexas.com

Solve | Learn | Glossary | Check | Tools | Games

Find the solid figure that rolls and has two flat surfaces.

A cone, a cylinder, and a sphere can roll.

A cone and a cylinder roll and have flat surfaces.

A cylinder rolls and has two flat surfaces.

Do You Understand?

Show Me! How are a cone and a cube alike and different?

Guided Practice Read the sorting rule.
Circle the solid figure or figures that follow the rule.

1. has faces, cannot roll

2. can roll, no flat surfaces

Topic 13 | Lesson 2

☆ **Independent**
☆ **Practice**

Read the sorting rule. Circle the solid figure or figures that follow the rule.

3. at least 1 vertex

4. no vertices, has flat surfaces

5. at least 10 edges

6. has 8 vertices

7. Extend Your Thinking Ricardo says that if a solid figure has a vertex, it cannot roll. Is Ricardo correct? Explain.

_____

_____

8. Joan collects things that have no vertices. She found a marble and a pencil box. Which will she put in her collection?

_____

9. Fumi has a sphere, a cylinder, and a cone. He chooses the solid figure that has no vertices and two flat surfaces. Which solid figure did he choose?

10. Sharla found one object that cannot roll. Then she found another object that cannot roll. Which two objects could Sharla have found?

11. **Extend Your Thinking** Write a sorting rule for these solid figures. Then circle the solid figure or figures that follow the rule.

_____

_____

_____

Name _____

Another Look You can sort solid figures in many different ways.

Some figures have faces and cannot roll.

Some figures have flat surfaces and can roll.

Some figures have vertices.

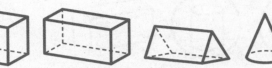

Some figures have no vertices.

🏠 **HOME CONNECTION**
Your child described how solid figures are alike and different and sorted them by a sorting rule, such as number of vertices.

HOME ACTIVITY Find two or three solid objects and ask your child to tell you how they are alike and different.

Circle any solid figures that follow the sorting rule.

1. It has flat surfaces and can roll.

 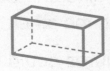

2. It has faces, edges, and vertices.

Draw a line to match one shape to one description.
No description should be used more than once.

3.

| I vertex | cannot roll | 0 vertices | 0 flat surfaces |

4.

| 12 edges | 5 faces | all faces the same | can roll |

Write a sorting rule for the circled solid figures.

5.

_____

_____

6. 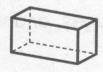

_____

_____

7. ⭐ Which rule describes both figures?

○ more edges than vertices

○ more faces than edges

○ fewer vertices than faces

○ fewer edges than vertices

8. **Extend Your Thinking** Mariah drew two solid figures. Both figures have some faces that are the same. Both figures have some faces that are different. One figure has one more face than the other.

What solid figures could Mariah have drawn?

_____

_____

Name _____

☆ ☆
Solve & Share

Find the solid figure that has the same shape as this present. If you traced one of the faces, what shape would it make? Show your work.

⊕ **TEKS 2.8B** Classify and sort three-dimensional solids ... based on attributes using formal geometric language. **Mathematical Process Standards** 2.1B, 2.1D, 2.1F.

Digital Resources at SavvasTexas.com

Solve   Learn   Glossary   Check   Tools   Games

solid traced _____

shape drawn _____

The flat surfaces of solid figures are plane shapes.

circle

square

triangle

rectangle

The faces of a cube are squares.

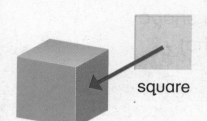

square

cube

The flat surfaces of a cylinder are circles.

circle

cylinder

The faces of a triangular prism are triangles and rectangles.

Plane shapes with 3 or more sides are called **polygons**.

So, a circle can't be a polygon!

Do You Understand?

Show Me! When you trace the flat surfaces of a cone and a cylinder, do you find the same plane shape? What is the shape?

Guided Practice

Circle the plane shape or shapes you can make by tracing the flat surfaces or faces of each solid figure shown. Use models if needed.

1.

2.

648 six hundred forty-eight

Topic 13 | Lesson 3

Name _____

Circle the solid figure or figures that have flat surfaces or faces you can trace to make the plane shape.

3.

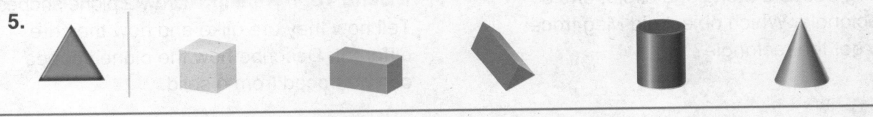

4.

5.

6.

7. **Extend Your Thinking** Jon says he traced the flat surfaces of a sphere and made a circle. Is he correct? Explain.

_____

_____

_____

8. T.J. traces a square using his block. Which block does T.J. have?

9. This cheese has the same shape as what solid figure? If you traced each face, what shapes would they make?

_____

10. Meg traced a triangle, a circle, and a rectangle. Which object did Meg trace to get the rectangle?

○

○

GUM ○

○

11. Extend Your Thinking Draw 2 plane shapes. Tell how they are alike and how they are different. Describe how the plane shapes can be traced from a solid.

_____

_____

_____

Name _____

Another Look If you trace the flat surfaces or faces of solid figures, you can make plane shapes.

The cylinder has two flat surfaces, but they are both circles!

square   rectangle

circle

🏠 **HOME CONNECTION**
Your child learned to identify the plane shapes that are the flat surfaces and faces of solid figures.

HOME ACTIVITY Have your child trace the flat surfaces of a solid shape such as a can or a box. Ask your child to name the plane shapes that he or she made.

Draw the plane shapes you could make if you traced the flat surfaces or faces of each of these solid figures. Write the name of the plane shapes.

1.

_____

2.

_____

3.

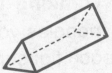

_____

4. Circle the solid figure or figures Vincent can trace to help draw the bug.

5. Circle the solid figure or figures Emma can trace to help draw the house.

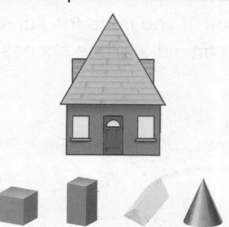

---

6. ⭐ Dion traces a square using a solid figure. Then he traces another square using a different solid figure. Which two solid figures could he have used?

◯   ◯   ◯   ◯

---

7. Extend Your Thinking Count how many circles, squares, and triangles you would draw if you traced each flat surface of each solid. Then complete the problems.

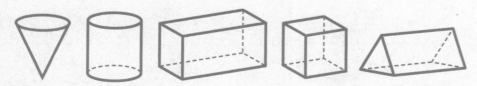

Which plane shape would you trace the greatest number of times? _____

Which plane shape would you trace the least number of times? _____

Topic 13 | Lesson 3

Name _____

☆ **Solve & Share**

Use your cubes to build a rectangular prism. Draw and write about the shape you made.

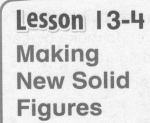

TEKS 2.8D Compose two-dimensional shapes and three-dimensional solids with given properties or attributes. **Mathematical Process Standards** 2.1A, 2.1B, 2.1C, 2.1F.

Digital Resources at SavvasTexas.com

 Solve Learn Glossary Check Tools Games

I used _____ cubes.

My shape has _____ faces.

My shape has _____ vertices.

You can combine solid figures to make bigger solid figures.

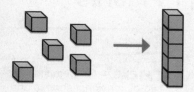

You can build a rectangular prism from cubes.

You can make a big cube from smaller cubes.

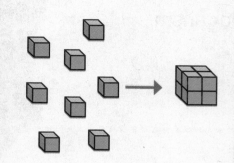

You can also use solid figures to make objects that you know.

A pyramid and a cube make a house!

A cube, a cylinder, and a cone make a rocket!

Do You Understand?

Show Me! How can you find the solid figures that make an object?

Guided Practice Circle the 2 solid figures that could be put together to make the object.

1.

2.

Name _____

Independent Practice

Circle the 2 or 3 solid figures that could be put together to make the object.

3.    (sphere)

4.    (pyramid) (cone)

5.

6. 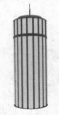    (rectangular prism) (triangular prism)

7. Extend Your Thinking Jon wants to combine cubes to make a new shape with 6 faces and 8 vertices. Use cubes to model. Then draw and name your new shapes.

8. Ralph made the skateboard ramp below with 2 solid figures.

What are the 2 solid figures?

_____

_____

9. Kirsten has 100 ice cubes. She wants to combine the ice cubes to make an ice sculpture.

What solid figures could Kirsten make with the ice cubes?

_____

10. Which object could be made with a cone and a cylinder?

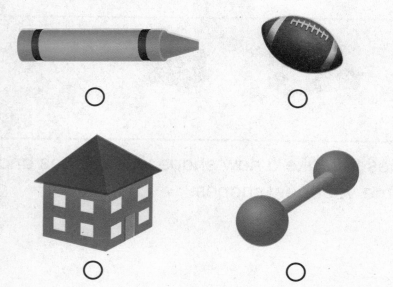

○   ○

○   ○

11. Extend Your Thinking Ellen used 2 of the same shape to build a bigger solid figure. Her new figure has 2 flat surfaces and 0 vertices.

What 2 shapes did Ellen use?

_____

What bigger solid figure did Ellen build?

_____

Name _____

Another Look You can combine 2 solid figures to make a new shape.

Count the faces, vertices, and edges for each solid figure.
Then count the faces, vertices, and edges for the new shape.

🏠 **HOME CONNECTION**
Your child learned to combine solid figures to make new solid figures.

HOME ACTIVITY Ask your child to show you how to make a new solid figure by using household objects such as shoe boxes, soup cans, and funnels.

 and  →

pyramid

faces _5_

vertices _5_

edges _8_

cube

faces _6_

vertices _8_

edges _12_

faces _9_

vertices _9_

edges _16_

The new shape has _9_ faces, _9_ vertices, and _16_ edges.

 Two shapes were combined to make a new shape.
Write the number of flat surfaces or faces, vertices, and edges for the new shape.

1.

flat surfaces _____

vertices _____

2.

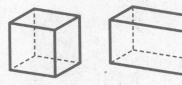

faces _____

vertices _____

edges _____

Write the number of flat surfaces or faces, vertices, and edges for each shape. Then write the number and type of solid figures that make the shape.

3.

faces _____

vertices _____

edges _____

The solid figures are _____

_____ .

4.

flat surfaces _____

vertices _____

edges _____

The solid figures are _____

_____ .

5.

faces _____

vertices _____

edges _____

The solid figures are _____

_____ .

6.

faces _____

vertices _____

edges _____

The solid figures are _____

_____ .

7. Which shape could **NOT** be used to make the milk carton?

○ rectangular prism

○ triangular prism

○ cylinder

○ cube

Milk

8. Extend Your Thinking Ramon combined a cone and a cylinder to make a new shape. How many flat surfaces and vertices does his new shape have?

_____

Name _____

Solve & Share

Model and draw some plane shapes that have 3 vertices.
Write the name for one of your shapes.
Is this name correct for all of the shapes you made?

⊕ **TEKS 2.8C** Classify and sort polygons with 12 or fewer sides according to attributes, including identifying the number of sides and number of vertices. Also, 2.8, 2.8A. **Mathematical Process Standards 2.1D, 2.1F.**

3 vertices

Digital Resources at SavvasTexas.com

Solve   Learn   Glossary   Check   Tools   Games

Triangles

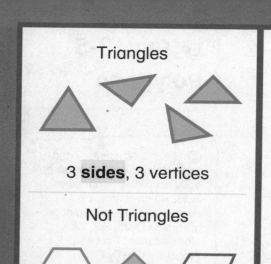

3 sides, 3 vertices

Not Triangles

Quadrilaterals

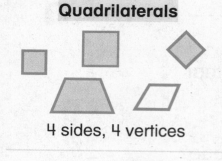

4 sides, 4 vertices

Not Quadrilaterals

Pentagons

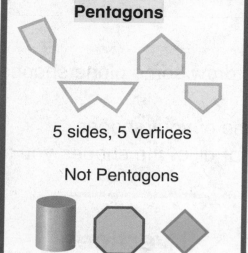

5 sides, 5 vertices

Not Pentagons

Hexagons

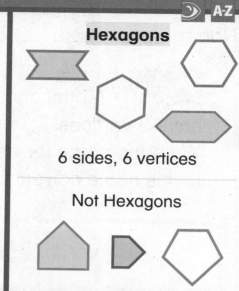

6 sides, 6 vertices

Not Hexagons

Do You Understand?

Show Me! How do sides and vertices help you name a polygon?

Guided Practice

Match each shape to its name.

1.

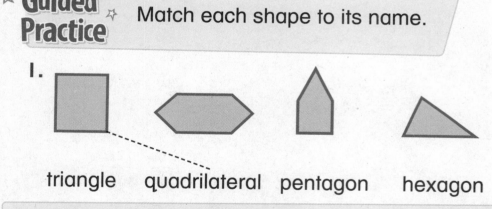

triangle   quadrilateral   pentagon   hexagon

Name each shape. Tell how many sides and vertices.

2.

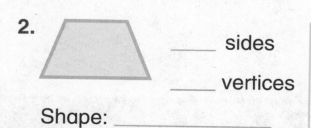

_____ sides

_____ vertices

Shape: _____

3.

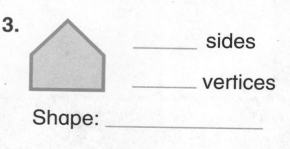

_____ sides

_____ vertices

Shape: _____

Topic 13 | Lesson 5

Name _____

☆ ☆
Independent
☆ **Practice**

Match each shape to its name.

4.

triangle   quadrilateral   pentagon   hexagon

5.

triangle   quadrilateral   pentagon   hexagon

Draw the shape. Tell how many sides and vertices.

6. Quadrilateral

_____ sides

_____ vertices

7. Hexagon

_____ sides

_____ vertices

8. Triangle

_____ sides

_____ vertices

9. Extend Your Thinking Bianca drew a triangle and a pentagon.
How many sides and vertices did she draw in all? Draw the shapes.

_____ sides   _____ vertices

10. Marcos has 4 toothpicks. He places them as shown. What shape can Marcos make if he adds one more toothpick?

_____

11. Connect all the dots to make two polygons. Name the shapes that you made.

_____   _____

12. Which polygon is **NOT** a hexagon?

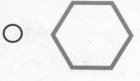

Think: What do I know about hexagons?

○

○

○

○

13. **Extend Your Thinking** Randall said that a square is a quadrilateral. Susan said that a square is a square, so it is not a quadrilateral. Who is correct? Explain.

_____

_____

_____

_____

_____

_____

Name _____

Another Look You can name shapes by their sides and their vertices.

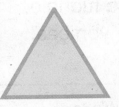 A triangle has
_3_ sides and
_3_ vertices.

 A quadrilateral has
_4_ sides and
_4_ vertices.

🏠 **HOME CONNECTION**
Your child identified various polygons and their attributes.

HOME ACTIVITY Look around your home for items that are shaped like triangles, quadrilaterals, pentagons, or hexagons. Ask your child to tell the number of sides and vertices for each shape.

 A pentagon has
_5_ sides and
_5_ vertices.

 A hexagon has
_6_ sides and
_6_ vertices.

 Name each shape.
Write the number of sides and vertices.

1.

Shape: _____

_____ sides

_____ vertices

2.

Shape: _____

_____ sides

_____ vertices

3.

Shape: _____

_____ sides

_____ vertices

Tell how many sides or vertices each student drew.

4. **Algebra** Leona drew
   2 pentagons.
   She drew _____ vertices.

5. **Algebra** Nestor drew
   3 quadrilaterals.
   He drew _____ sides.

6. **Algebra** Kip drew
   a hexagon and a triangle.
   He drew _____ vertices.

7. Draw 2 hexagons that look different from the one shown.

8. Draw 2 quadrilaterals that look different from the one shown.

9. ⭐ Jin drew two polygons.
   One of the polygons is shown below.
   If Jin drew 9 sides and 9 vertices in all,
   which other polygon could he have drawn?

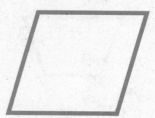

   ○ triangle   ○ rectangle
   ○ rhombus   ○ pentagon

10. **Extend Your Thinking** Tami traced
    the faces of this wooden block.
    What shapes did she draw?
    Name and draw the shapes.

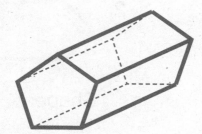

Name _____

Solve & Share

Draw a polygon with more than 5 sides.
Then draw another polygon with fewer than 4 sides.
Name the polygons you drew.

⭐ **TEKS 2.8C** Classify and sort polygons with 12 or fewer sides according to attributes, including identifying the number of sides and number of vertices. Also 2.8, 2.8A. **Mathematical Process Standards** 2.1B, 2.1D, 2.1F, 2.1G.

Digital Resources at SavvasTexas.com

 Solve   Learn   Glossary   Check   Tools   Games

_____

You have learned that polygons can be named by their number of sides and vertices. Here are some more polygons.

Heptagons	Octagons	Nonagons	Decagons	Hendecagons	Dodecagons
7 sides 7 vertices	8 sides 8 vertices	9 sides 9 vertices	10 sides 10 vertices	11 sides 11 vertices	12 sides 12 vertices

Circle the polygon with 8 sides and 8 vertices.

Do You Understand?

Show Me! What is the difference between a heptagon and a hendecagon?

1.

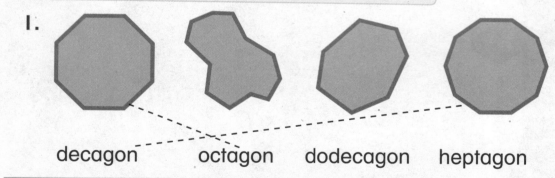

decagon   octagon   dodecagon   heptagon

2.

nonagon   hendecagon   heptagon   octagon

Topic 13 | Lesson 6

Name _____

☆ Independent ☆ Practice

Circle the polygon that has the given number of sides and vertices. Then write the name of the polygon.

3. 9 sides and 9 vertices _____

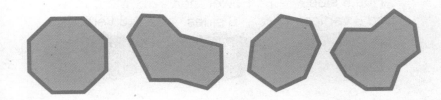

4. 12 sides and 12 vertices _____

5. 8 sides and 8 vertices _____

6. 11 sides and 11 vertices _____

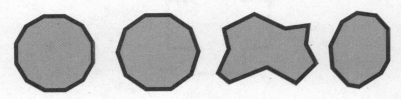

7. 7 sides and 7 vertices _____

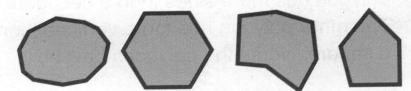

8. 10 sides and 10 vertices _____

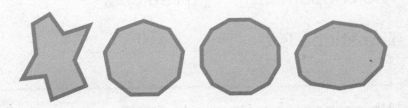

9. Extend Your Thinking Tyson drew a polygon that has 2 times as many sides as a quadrilateral. Draw the polygon.

What polygon did Tyson draw? _____

10. Winnie drew the shape of the plus sign for a math project.

The shape has _____ sides.

The shape has _____ vertices.

The shape is a _____.

11. Ty wants to put exactly one shape in each box. Name each shape. Then draw a line to the correct box.

| Has 8 sides and 8 vertices | Fewer than 8 sides | More than 8 vertices |

L   H   T

_____ _____ _____

12. Which polygon shown is **NOT** a decagon?

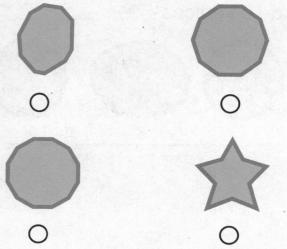

○   ○

○   ○

13. Extend Your Thinking Levi used 16 toothpicks to build two polygons. One polygon has more sides than a decagon. The other polygon has more vertices than a square. Name the polygons Levi built.

_____ and _____

Name _____

Another Look You can sort polygons by using the number of sides and the number of vertices.

Draw lines to sort the polygons.

Heptagon
7 sides
7 vertices

Octagon
8 sides
8 vertices

Each heptagon has 7 sides and 7 vertices. Each octagon has 8 sides and 8 vertices.

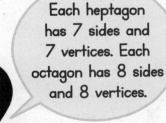

🏠 **HOME CONNECTION** Your child learned to name and sort polygons based on the number of sides and vertices of the polygons.

HOME ACTIVITY Have your child look at a stop sign on a street or a picture of a stop sign. Ask your child to name the polygon and tell you how many sides and vertices it has.

Draw lines to sort the polygons.

1.

Decagon
10 sides
10 vertices

Dodecagon
12 sides
12 vertices

2.

Nonagon
9 sides
9 vertices

Hendecagon
11 sides
11 vertices

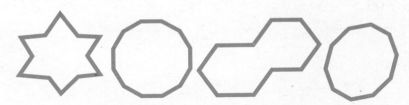

3. Draw a triangle and a dodecagon.

How many sides and vertices did you draw in all?

_____ sides and _____ vertices

4. Lois drew one shape with fewer than 5 vertices. She drew another shape with more than 7 sides.
Which two shapes could Lois have drawn?

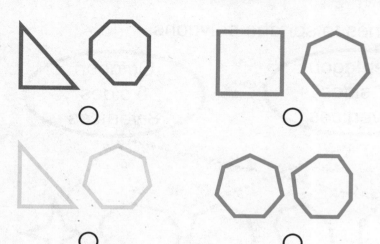

○   ○

○   ○

5. Extend Your Thinking Name each polygon. Then draw a line from the shape to the box that describes it.

| fewer than 5 sides | from 5 to 8 sides | more than 8 sides |

Name _____

Solve & Share

Model a polygon with 3 sides that are the same length. Then model a polygon with 3 sides that are different lengths. Draw your polygons in the spaces below.

TEKS 2.8A Create two-dimensional shapes based on given attributes, including number of sides and vertices. **Mathematical Process Standards** 2.1C, 2.1D, 2.1F, 2.1G.

Digital Resources at SavvasTexas.com

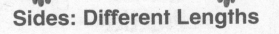

Solve   Learn   Glossary   Check   Tools   Games

Sides: Same Length

Sides: Different Lengths

Do You Understand?

Show Me! You are asked to draw a shape with 4 vertices and 4 sides of equal length. What are the names of some different shapes you could draw?

☆ Guided Practice ☆ Draw each shape. Complete the sentences.

1. Draw a polygon with 3 vertices.

The polygon has _____ sides.

The polygon is a

_____.

2. Draw a polygon with 6 sides that are the same length.

The polygon has _____ vertices.

The polygon is a

_____.

Topic 13 | Lesson 7

Name _____

Draw each shape. Complete the sentences.

3. Draw a polygon with 8 vertices.

The polygon has _____ sides.

The polygon is an _____.

4. Draw a quadrilateral with 2 pairs of sides that are the same length.

The polygon has _____ vertices.

The polygon is a _____.

5. Draw a polygon with 7 vertices.

The polygon has _____ sides.

The polygon is a _____.

6. Draw a polygon with 4 sides that are different lengths.

The polygon has _____ vertices.

The polygon is a _____.

7. Draw a polygon with 5 vertices and 3 sides that are the same length.

The polygon has _____ sides in all.

The polygon is a _____.

8. Extend Your Thinking Can you draw a polygon with 3 vertices and 4 sides? Explain.

9. Draw a rectangle with 4 equal sides.

What is another name for this shape?

_____

10. Create a pattern of 3 shapes. The number of vertices in each shape increases by two.

Name the shapes.

_____, _____, _____

11. Dmitri drew two different polygons. One of the polygons was a square. If Dmitri drew 9 sides and 9 vertices in all, what other polygon did Dmitri draw?

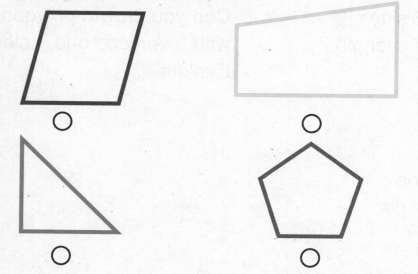

○   ○

○   ○

12. **Extend Your Thinking** The owner of Joe's Fish Market wants a new sign. He wants the sign to have 0 straight sides. Draw a sign for Joe's Fish Market.

The sign has _____ vertices.
Is the sign a polygon? Explain.

_____

_____

Name _____

Another Look The number of sides in a polygon is the same as the number of vertices.

Draw a polygon with 6 vertices.

The sides can be the same length.   The sides can be different lengths.

🏠 **HOME CONNECTION**
Your child created two-dimensional shapes based on attributes such as number of sides and vertices.

HOME ACTIVITY Ask your child to draw a polygon with 4 vertices. Then ask your child to tell you the name of the polygon and how many sides it has.

Each polygon has ___6___ vertices.

Each polygon has ___6___ sides.

Both polygons are _____hexagons_____.

 Draw two different polygons for each number of vertices.

1. 4 vertices

2. 5 vertices

Each polygon has _____ sides.

Both polygons are _____.

Each polygon has _____ sides.

Both polygons are _____.

Draw each polygon. Then complete the sentences.

3. It has 2 fewer sides than a heptagon.

The shape is a _____.

4. It has 3 more vertices than a triangle.

The shape is a _____.

5. It has 1 more vertex than an octagon and 2 fewer sides than a hendecagon.

The shape is a _____.

6. Kit drew a polygon that has 4 vertices. Which could **NOT** be Kit's polygon?

quadrilateral
○

rectangle
○

triangle
○

square
○

7. Reg drew a polygon with more sides than a square and fewer vertices than a heptagon. Which could Reg have drawn?

decagon
○

nonagon
○

octagon
○

pentagon
○

8. Extend Your Thinking Tanika had 7 toothpicks. She used them all to create two polygons. Draw two polygons that Tanika could have created.
Write the names of your shapes.

Name _____

Solve & Share

Use two or more shapes to make a shape with 4 sides and 4 vertices.
Use two or more shapes to make a shape with 6 sides and 6 vertices.
Trace your shapes below.

⊕ TEKS 2.8D Compose two-dimensional shapes and three-dimensional solids with given properties or attributes. Mathematical Process Standards 2.1B, 2.1C, 2.1D, 2.1F.

Digital Resources at SavvasTexas.com

Solve   Learn   Glossary   Check   Tools   Games

4 sides
4 vertices

6 sides
6 vertices

You can put shapes together to make another shape.

triangle

parallelogram

trapezoid

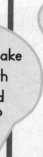 How can I make a shape with 6 sides and 6 vertices?

I can make a hexagon.

_6_ sides _6_ vertices

You can make many larger shapes with smaller shapes.

I made a triangle and a parallelogram using smaller shapes.

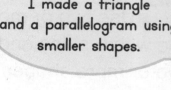

Do You Understand?

Show Me! You made a new shape using two smaller shapes. Can the new shape have the same number of sides and vertices as the two smaller shapes? Explain.

☆ **Guided Practice** ☆

Put your shapes together to make another shape with the given number of sides and vertices. Trace and color to show the shapes you use. Name the shape you make.

1. 4 sides
4 vertices

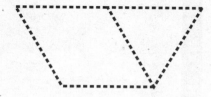

I made a ___trapezoid___.

2. 5 sides
5 vertices

I made a _____.

Independent Practice

Put your shapes together to make another shape with the given number of sides and vertices. Trace and color to show the shapes you use. Name the shape you make.

3. 3 sides
3 vertices

4. 6 sides
6 vertices

5. 8 sides
8 vertices

I made a _____.

I made a _____.

I made an _____.

6. Extend Your Thinking Rico has 4 shapes that are all the same. He puts the 4 shapes together to make another shape. The shape he makes is the same shape, only bigger. Draw and name a shape that Rico could have made.

Rico made _____.

7. Make this shape with 4 smaller shapes. Trace and color to show the shapes you use.

_____
name of shape

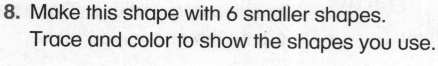

_____ sides

_____ vertices

8. Make this shape with 6 smaller shapes. Trace and color to show the shapes you use.

_____
name of shape

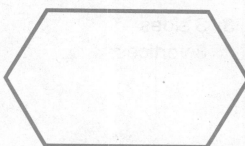

_____ sides

_____ vertices

9. Ethan puts 2 trapezoids together. Which new shape does he make?

○

○

○

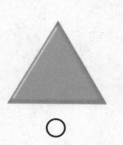
○

10. **Extend Your Thinking** Use 2 or more shapes to make a new shape. Draw the new shape. Write the number of sides and vertices.

_____ sides

_____ vertices

Name _____

Another Look You can use pattern blocks to make larger shapes from smaller shapes.

← vertex

← side

hexagon   parallelogram

🏠 **HOME CONNECTION**
Your child composed larger shapes from smaller shapes.

HOME ACTIVITY Cut out triangles, rectangles, and squares from paper or cardboard. Ask your child to combine these shapes to create new shapes.

Put 2 parallelograms and a hexagon together to make the larger shape.

_6_ sides   _6_ vertices

This shape is a ___hexagon___.

Use the shapes shown to make a larger shape with the given number of sides and vertices. Draw and name the larger shape.

1.

6 sides   6 vertices

2.

8 sides   8 vertices

Topic 13 | Lesson 8   Digital Resources at SavvasTexas.com   six hundred eighty-one **681**

Follow the directions to make each shape.
Then draw a picture to show how you made the shape.

3. Make a triangle with 5 smaller shapes.

4. Make an octagon with 3 smaller shapes.

5. Which two shapes **CANNOT** be put together to make a hexagon?

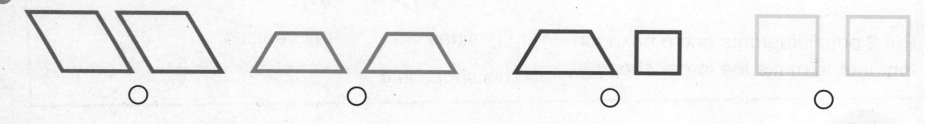

○   ○   ○   ○

6. **Extend Your Thinking** Make the same parallelogram in three different ways.
Draw lines to show the shapes you use.

Use 6 shapes.   Use 7 shapes.   Use 8 shapes.

Topic 13 | Lesson 8

Name _____

Solve & Share

What new shapes can you make from this shape if you cut it apart? Show how you cut your shape. Then draw and name the new shapes you made.

⭐ **TEKS 2.1D** Communicate mathematical ideas, reasoning, and their implications using multiple representations .... **TEKS 2.8E** Decompose two-dimensional shapes ... and identify the resulting geometric parts. **Mathematical Process Standards 2.1B, 2.1E, 2.1G.**

Digital Resources at SavvasTexas.com

Solve   Learn   Glossary   Check   Tools   Games

Analyze and Plan

How can you cut shapes apart to make new shapes?

I can draw lines to cut the shape into parts. The parts will make smaller shapes.

Solve, Justify, and Evaluate

The blue line cuts the square into 2 triangles.

The purple lines cut the square into 4 smaller squares.

The green lines cut the square into 4 triangles.

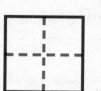

Do You Understand?

Show Me! How many lines do you need to draw to cut a triangle into three smaller shapes? Explain your reasoning.

☆ Guided Practice ☆

Draw lines to make new shapes.

1. Draw 1 line to make 2 triangles.

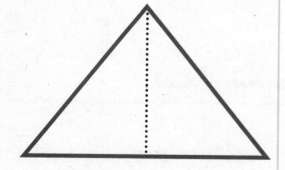

2. Draw 2 lines to make 3 rectangles.

Name _____

Draw lines to make new shapes.

3. Draw 2 lines to make 4 rectangles.

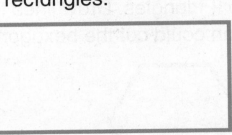

4. Draw 3 lines to make 6 triangles.

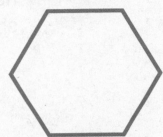

5. Draw 1 line to make 2 triangles.

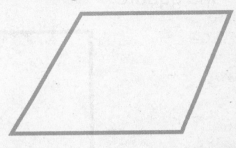

6. Draw 2 lines to make 1 square and 2 triangles.

7. Draw 2 lines to make 2 parallelograms and 2 triangles.

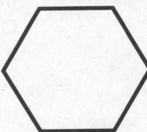

8. Draw 2 lines to make 1 hexagon and 2 triangles.

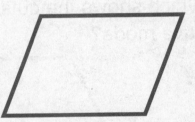

9. Extend Your Thinking List new shapes you could make by cutting apart a hexagon. Draw the cuts you would make.

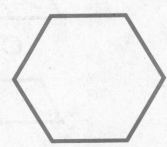

_____

_____

Problem Solving Solve the problems below.

10. Jenny is making a quilt. She wants to cut this square piece of fabric into 8 triangles. Draw lines to show how Jenny could cut the square.

11. Dan is drawing a picture to plan a garden. The garden will be in the shape of a hexagon. Dan draws 3 lines to cut the hexagon into 4 triangles. Draw lines to show how Dan could cut the hexagon.

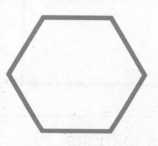

12. Mr. Weber cut this trapezoid into triangles. Which shows the cuts he could **NOT** have made?

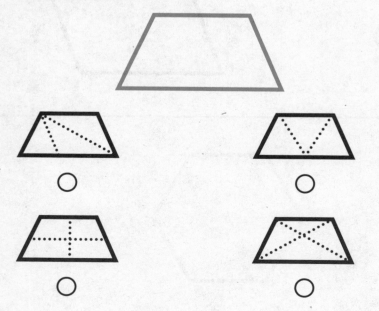

13. **Extend Your Thinking** A rectangular treasure map has been cut into 3 shapes. One of the shapes is shown. The other 2 shapes are missing. Draw lines to show how the map may have been cut.

What could the two missing shapes be?

_____

Name _____

Another Look You can draw lines to cut a large shape into smaller shapes.

Draw 1 line to make more triangles.

Now there are 2 triangles and 4 squares!

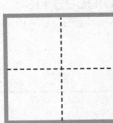

⌂ **HOME CONNECTION**
Your child learned to cut apart large shapes into smaller shapes to solve problems.

HOME ACTIVITY Cut out large shapes such as rectangles, triangles, and hexagons from a piece of paper. Have your child cut apart these shapes to make new shapes. Identify the new shapes together.

Draw 2 lines to make more squares.

 Draw lines to make new shapes.

1. Draw 2 lines to cut the square into 4 triangles.

2. Draw 1 line to cut the hexagon into 2 trapezoids.

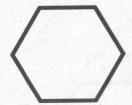

3. Draw 2 lines to cut the pentagon into 3 triangles.

Solve the problems below.

4. Ana has a poster board in the shape of a rectangle. She draws 1 line to cut the poster board into two new shapes. The two new shapes have 7 sides and 7 vertices in all.

Draw a line to show how the poster board may have been cut.
What could the two new shapes be?

5. Trey made pasta in the shape of a square. He draws 2 lines to cut the pasta into smaller pieces. The smaller pieces have 12 sides and 12 vertices in all.

Draw lines to show how the pasta may have been cut.
What shapes could the smaller pieces be?

6. Cassie draws 1 line to cut a square into two smaller shapes.
Which could **NOT** be the two smaller shapes?

2 triangles   2 squares   2 rectangles   1 triangle, 1 pentagon
   ○   ○   ○   ○

7. Extend Your Thinking Draw 2 lines to cut each triangle into the given shapes.

1 rectangle and 2 triangles   1 pentagon and 2 triangles   1 triangle and 2 trapezoids

Name _____

Explain the math you know to connect ideas about shapes.

1. Choose one of the solids above. Describe it.

   My solid is called a _____.

   It has _____ flat surfaces, _____ vertices,

   and _____ edges.

2. Think about the plane shapes your solid has. Circle one or more of them below.

3. Draw lines to divide your plane shapes into fourths. How many fourths do you have?

   _____ fourths

4. What smaller polygons could you use to make this shape?
   Draw lines. Name each polygon you use.

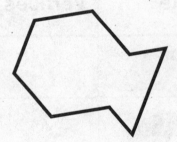

5. Write a sorting rule about sides and vertices for the shapes in Exercise 2.
   Explain which shapes fit your rule.
   Sorting rule: _____.

   _____

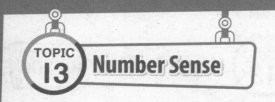

Complete It!

1. Build a "snake" with a tan head and a blue body.
Count its sides and vertices.
Write the numbers in the table.

Add 1 more blue rhombus at a time to make the "snake" grow. Fill in the table.

Snake	Vertices	Sides
Head + 1		
Head + 2		
Head + 3		
Head + 4		

What happens as the "snake" grows?

_____

What's Wrong?

2. Pete has saved $112. He says if he saves $20 more he will have $312. Fix Pete's mistake. Explain.

Number Word Puzzle

3. Write each answer as a number word in the boxes.

- 57 − 42 = ?
- 42 + ? = 61
- ? + 11 = 22

The letters in the blue boxes spell _____.

Name _____

Set A

Identify a solid figure by finding the number of faces, edges, and vertices.

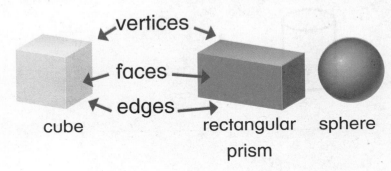

vertices

faces

edges

cube   rectangular   sphere
              prism

A cube has __6__ faces,
__12__ edges, and __8__ vertices.

Write how many faces, vertices, and edges.

1. rectangular prism _____ faces

_____ edges

_____ vertices

2. sphere _____ faces

_____ edges

_____ vertices

Set B

You can use a sorting rule to sort solid figures.
Sorting rule: has faces

Sorting rule: does not have any vertices

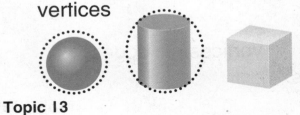

Circle the solid figure or figures that follow the sorting rule.

3. can roll and has flat surfaces

4. has 6 faces

You can trace plane shapes from the faces of solid figures.

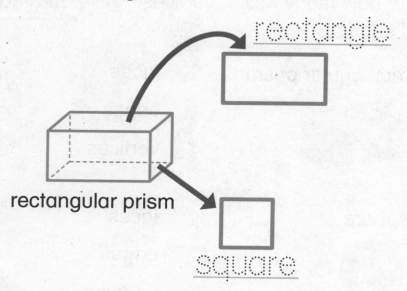

rectangle

rectangular prism

square

Draw the shape or shapes you can trace from the solid figure.
Name the shape or shapes.

5.

_____

6.

_____

You can combine solid figures to make bigger solid figures.
Combine 2 cubes.

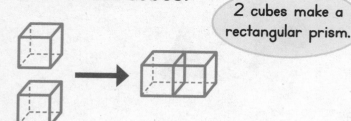

2 cubes make a rectangular prism.

6   8   12
faces vertices edges

Two shapes were combined to make a new shape. Write the number of flat surfaces, vertices, and edges for the new shape.

7.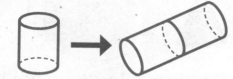

_____   _____   _____
flat   vertices   edges
surfaces

692 six hundred ninety-two

Name _____

Set E _____

You can name shapes by sides and vertices.

name <u>triangles</u>

sides <u>3</u>

vertices <u>3</u>

name <u>quadrilaterals</u>

sides <u>4</u>

vertices <u>4</u>

Name the shape. Write the number of sides and vertices.

8.

name _____

sides _____

vertices _____

9.

name _____

sides _____

vertices _____

Set F _____

You can draw a polygon with a given number of sides or vertices.

Draw a polygon with 4 sides.

Draw a polygon with 5 vertices.

I can draw a quadrilateral.

I can draw a pentagon.

Draw a polygon with the number of sides or vertices shown.

10. 6 sides

11. 3 vertices

Set G

You can use shapes to make new shapes.

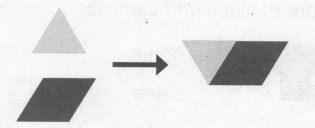

The new shape is a ⟨trapezoid⟩.

It has 4 sides.

It has 4 vertices.

Make a larger shape.
Draw and name the shape.
Write the number of sides and vertices.

12.

name _____

sides _____ vertices _____

13.

name _____

sides _____ vertices _____

Set H

You can make new shapes by cutting shapes apart.

The square is cut into 3 rectangles.

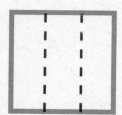

The triangle is cut into 3 smaller triangles.

Draw lines to make new shapes.

14. Draw 2 lines to make 4 squares.

15. Draw 3 lines to make 6 triangles.

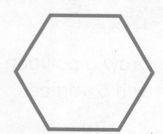

694 six hundred ninety-four

Topic 13

Name _____

1. In what way are these 3 solid figures alike?

○ They roll.

○ They do not roll.

○ They have vertices.

○ They do not have vertices.

2. Katie puts three triangles together to make a bigger shape. Which shape did she make?

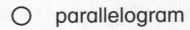

○ trapezoid

○ parallelogram

○ hexagon

○ square

3. Which object could be made with a triangular prism and a rectangular prism?

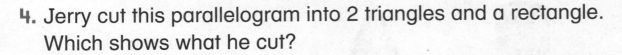

○   ○   ○   ○

4. Jerry cut this parallelogram into 2 triangles and a rectangle. Which shows what he cut?

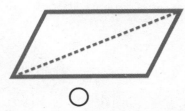 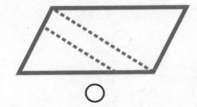 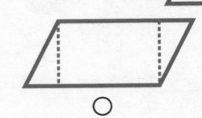 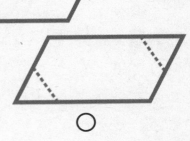

○   ○   ○   ○

5. Rita drew a polygon. It has fewer sides than an octagon and more vertices than a pentagon.
Which shape could be Rita's polygon?

○ triangle

○ rectangle

○ hexagon

○ decagon

6. I have 0 flat surfaces.
I have 0 vertices. I roll.
Which shape am I?

○ cone

○ sphere

○ cube

○ cylinder

---

7. Which plane shape can be traced from the solid figure?

circle   rectangle   parallelogram   square

○   ○   ○   ○

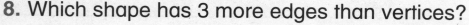

---

8. Which shape has 3 more edges than vertices?

○   ○   ○   ○

9. Which group of solid figures can roll?

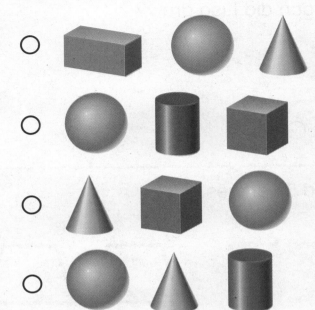

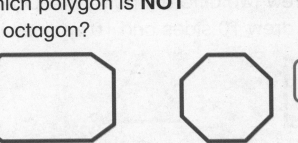

10. Which polygon is **NOT** an octagon?

○

○

○

○

11. Mandy draws a shape with 5 vertices.
Which shape did Mandy draw?

○ triangle

○ quadrilateral

○ pentagon

○ hexagon

12. Jason wants to trace a solid figure to make a triangle.
Which solid figure could Jason trace?

○ cube

○ cylinder

○ pyramid

○ rectangular prism

13. Lisa drew two different polygons. One of the polygons was a hexagon.
If Lisa drew 10 sides and 10 vertices in all, which other polygon did Lisa draw?

○   ○   ○   ○

14. Paul uses two shapes to make a new shape with 5 sides and 5 vertices.
Which two shapes did he use?

○   ○   ○   ○

15. Draw 4 lines to make new shapes.
Write the names of the shapes you made.

_____

16. Two shapes were combined to make a new shape.
Write the number of faces, vertices, and edges for the new shape.

_____ faces, _____ vertices, _____ edges

Measurement

Essential Question: What are ways to measure length, area, and time?

These sunflowers all face the same direction. That's because they always face the sun!

Plants and animals change over time.

Wow! Let's do this project and learn more.

Math and Science Project: Natural Clocks

Find Out Find a log or tree branch that has been cut so you can see the rings, or find a photo of a cut-open log. Count the rings that you see. Each ring shows one year of the tree's life.

Journal: Make a Book Draw a picture of tree rings. In your book, also:

• Count the tree rings and write the age of the tree.

• Draw pictures of plants, animals, or people. Use each picture to show an example of measurement.

Name _____

Review What You Know

Vocabulary

1. Draw a line to show the **length** of the bat.

2. Circle to show which is the **hour hand**.

long red hand

short blue hand

3. Circle to show which is the **minute hand**.

long red hand

short blue hand

Estimating and Measuring Length

4. Estimate the length. Then measure using cubes.

Estimate

about ___ cubes

Measure

about ___ cubes

5. Estimate the length. Then measure using cubes.

Estimate

about ___ cubes

Measure

about ___ cubes

Skip Counting

6. Skip count by 5s. Write the missing numbers.

5, 10, ___, 20, ___, ___,

35, ___, ___, ___, ___

My Word Cards Study the words on the front of the card. Complete the activity on the back.

A-Z

a.m.

p.m.

quarter past

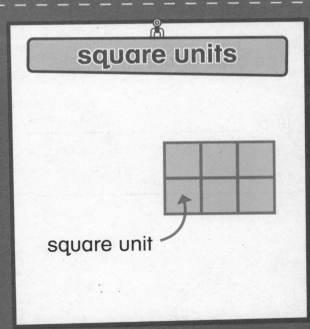

It is quarter past 4.

half past

It is half past 9.

quarter to

It is quarter to 4.

square units

square unit

Use what you know to complete the sentences.
Extend learning by writing your own sentence using each word.

A _____

_____

is 15 minutes after the hour.

The half of the day from midday to midnight can be described as

_____

The half of the day from midnight to midday can be described as

_____

The area of the rectangle

is 6 _____

_____.

A _____

_____

is 15 minutes before the hour.

30 minutes past the hour is

_____

_____.

My Word Cards

Study the words on the front of the card. Complete the activity on the back.

A-Z

area

 = 6 square units

length

The length is about 1 yard.

inch

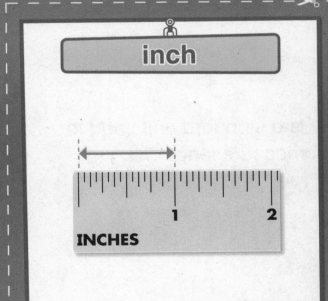

INCHES

foot

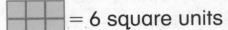

A foot is 12 inches.

yard

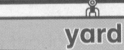

estimate

I think the book is about 1 foot long.

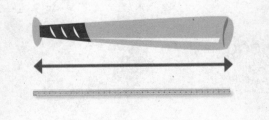

My Word Cards

Use what you know to complete the sentences.
Extend learning by writing your own sentence using each word.

An ____________________

is a standard unit used to measure length.

The ____________________

is the distance from one end to the other end of an object.

The ____________________

is the number of square units needed to cover a plane shape.

When you ________________,

you make a good guess.

A baseball bat is about a

____

long.

One ____________________

is 12 inches.

Study the words on the front of the card. Complete the activity on the back.

A-Z

nearest inch

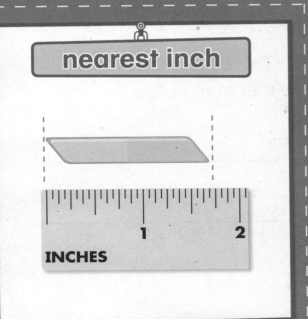

INCHES

unit

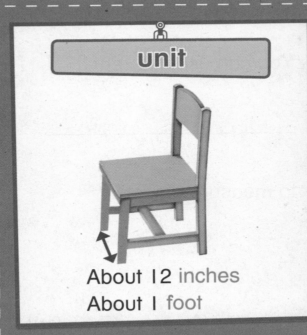

About 12 inches
About 1 foot

height

centimeter

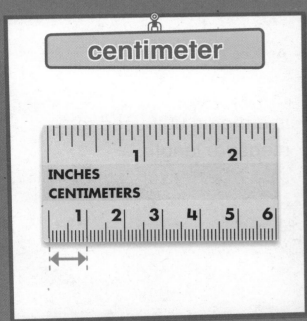

INCHES
CENTIMETERS

meter

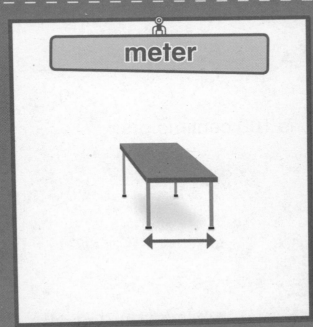

nearest centimeter

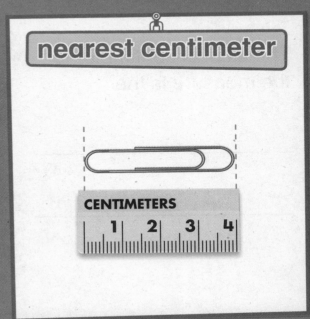

CENTIMETERS

My Word Cards

Use what you know to complete the sentences.
Extend learning by writing your own sentence using each word.

____

is how tall something is.

You can use different

____

to measure objects.

The closest inch to the measure is the

____

______________________.

The closest centimeter to the measure is the

____

______________________.

A ______________________

is 100 centimeters.

A ______________________

is a metric unit used to measure length.

Name _____

☆ **Solve & Share**

An airplane is due to arrive at 3:37.
How can you show this time on the clock below? Explain.

TEKS 2.9G Read and write time to the nearest one-minute increment using analog and digital clocks and distinguish between a.m. and p.m. Also, 2.9. **Mathematical Process Standards** 2.1A, 2.1C, 2.1D, 2.1F.

Digital Resources at SavvasTexas.com

Solve Learn Glossary Check Tools Games

You can use clocks to tell time. Both clocks show 8:05.

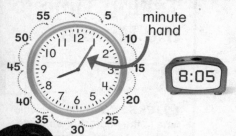

minute hand

8:05

The minute hand moves from number to number in 5 minutes.

Both clocks show 8:27.

8:27

The minute hand moves from mark to mark in 1 minute.

There are 60 minutes in 1 hour.

8:00

hour hand

9:00

The hour hand moves from number to number in 60 minutes.

You can also use the terms **a.m.** and **p.m.** to tell about time.

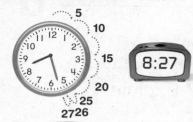

Use a.m. for morning times. I woke up at 8 a.m.

Use p.m. for afternoon or evening times. I went to bed at 8 p.m.

Do You Understand?

Show Me! What might you be doing at 6:15 a.m.? At 6:15 p.m.?

☆ **Guided Practice** ☆   Complete the clocks so both clocks show the same time.

1.

6:45

2.

3:23

3.

7:57

4.

5:38

Topic 14 | Lesson 1

Name _____

Another Look You can use two kinds of clocks to tell time.

The minute hand moves from mark to mark in 1 minute.
There are 5 marks between each number. So, the minute hand moves from number to number in 5 minutes.

There are 30 minutes in a half hour and 60 minutes in an hour.
The hour hand moves from number to number every 60 minutes.

🏠 **HOME CONNECTION**
Your child learned how to tell time to the minute.

HOME ACTIVITY Draw three clock faces showing 3:22, 10:49, and 7:05. Have your child tell you the time each clock shows.

Count by 5s and 1s. Write the time.

1.

2.

3. The clock shows the time that Sharon left her house to walk to the library. It takes her 12 minutes to walk there. At what time will Sharon arrive at the library?

- ○ 5:22
- ○ 5:12
- ○ 5:10
- ○ 5:48

4. The time is 6:05 p.m. What number is the minute hand pointing to on a clock?

The minute hand will be on the _____.

Extend Your Thinking Each riddle is about a different clock. Solve the riddle and write the time.

5. My hour hand is between the 3 and the 4. My minute hand is pointing to the 7.

What time do I show? _____

6. My hour hand is between the 5 and the 6. My minute hand is pointing to the 4.

What time do I show? _____

---

7. My hour hand is between the 11 and the 12. My minute hand is pointing to the first mark after the 12.

What time do I show? _____

8. My hour hand is between the 1 and the 2. My minute hand is pointing to the mark that comes just before the 1.

What time do I show? _____

Name _____

Solve & Share

Both of these clocks show the same time. How many different ways can you say this time? Write each way.

⭐ **TEKS 2.9G** Read and write time to the nearest one-minute increment using analog and digital clocks and distinguish between a.m. and p.m. Also, 2.9. **Mathematical Process Standards** 2.1B, 2.1D, 2.1E, 2.1G.

Digital Resources at SavvasTexas.com

Solve   Learn   Glossary   Check   Tools   Games

Look at the times.
How many minutes after the hour is each time?

1:15   **1:30**   **1:53**

| 15 minutes after 1, **quarter past** 1 | 30 minutes after 1, **half past** 1 | 53 minutes after 1 |

Times after the half hour are often read as times before the next hour.

3:30   **3:45**   **3:48**

| 30 minutes before 4 | 15 minutes before 4, **quarter to** 4 | 12 minutes before 4 |

Do You Understand?

Show Me! Write two ways to say 5:27.

 **Guided Practice**

Complete the clocks so both clocks show the same time. Then circle another way to say the time.

1.

2:30

half past 2

30 minutes before 2

2.

6:45

quarter to 7

quarter past 6

714 seven hundred fourteen

Topic 14 | Lesson 2

☆ Independent ☆
☆ Practice

Complete the clocks so both clocks show the same time.
Then write the time before or after the hour.

3.

_____ minutes before 5

4.

quarter past _____

5.

23 minutes after _____

Extend Your Thinking Look at the clock to solve each problem.

6. What time will it be in 30 minutes?
Write this time in two different ways.

_____

_____

7. What time will it be in 47 minutes?
Write this time in two different ways.

_____

_____

8. James arrives home at 6:00.
15 minutes later, he starts his homework.
At what time does James start his
homework?

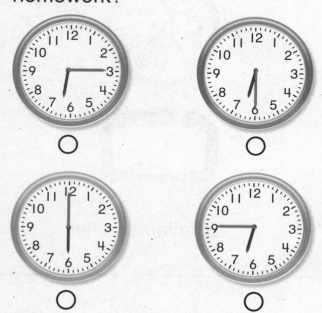

9. A train left the station at 6:54.
What are two other ways to say this time?

_____

_____

10. Miguel is meeting a friend at half past 4.
Draw the clock hands to show this time.

11. Extend Your Thinking Draw a clock
with hands that show 11:45.
Then write two ways to say the time.

_____

_____

Name _____

Another Look There are different ways to say time before and after the hour.

6:15

15 minutes after 6 or quarter past 6

6:30

30 minutes after 6 or half past 6

6:45

45 minutes after 6 or quarter to 7

2:39

21 minutes before 3 or 39 minutes after 2

🏠 **HOME CONNECTION** Your child learned to tell time before and after the hour.

HOME ACTIVITY Draw several clock faces. Have your child draw the time for 7:15, 2:30, and 5:45. Then have your child say the time using the terms *quarter past, half past,* and *quarter to.*

 Count by 5s and 1s to tell the time. Write the time on the line below the clock.

1.

30 minutes after _____ or half past _____

_____

2.

_____ minutes after _____ or
_____ minutes before _____

_____

3. Joyce woke up at 10 minutes after 7. It took her 40 minutes to get ready and walk to school. What time did Joyce get to school?

○   ○

○   ○

4. The time is 6:09. Is the hour hand closer to 6 or 7? Explain.

_____

_____

_____

_____

_____

Extend Your Thinking Write the time. Then answer each question.

5. Nancy arrives at 10 minutes before 8.

School starts at

Is Nancy early or late for school?

_____   _____

6. Sean arrives at quarter to 7.

Dinner starts at

Is Sean early or late for dinner?

_____   _____

Name ______________________

Solve & Share

How many squares do you need to cover this shape? Explain how you know.

Lesson 14-3
Measuring Area

TEKS 2.9F ... find the area of a rectangle by covering it ..., counting to find the total number of square units, and describing the measurement .... Also, 2.9. **Mathematical Process Standards** 2.1C, 2.1D, 2.1F.

Digital Resources at SavvasTexas.com

Solve | Learn | Glossary | Check | Tools | Games

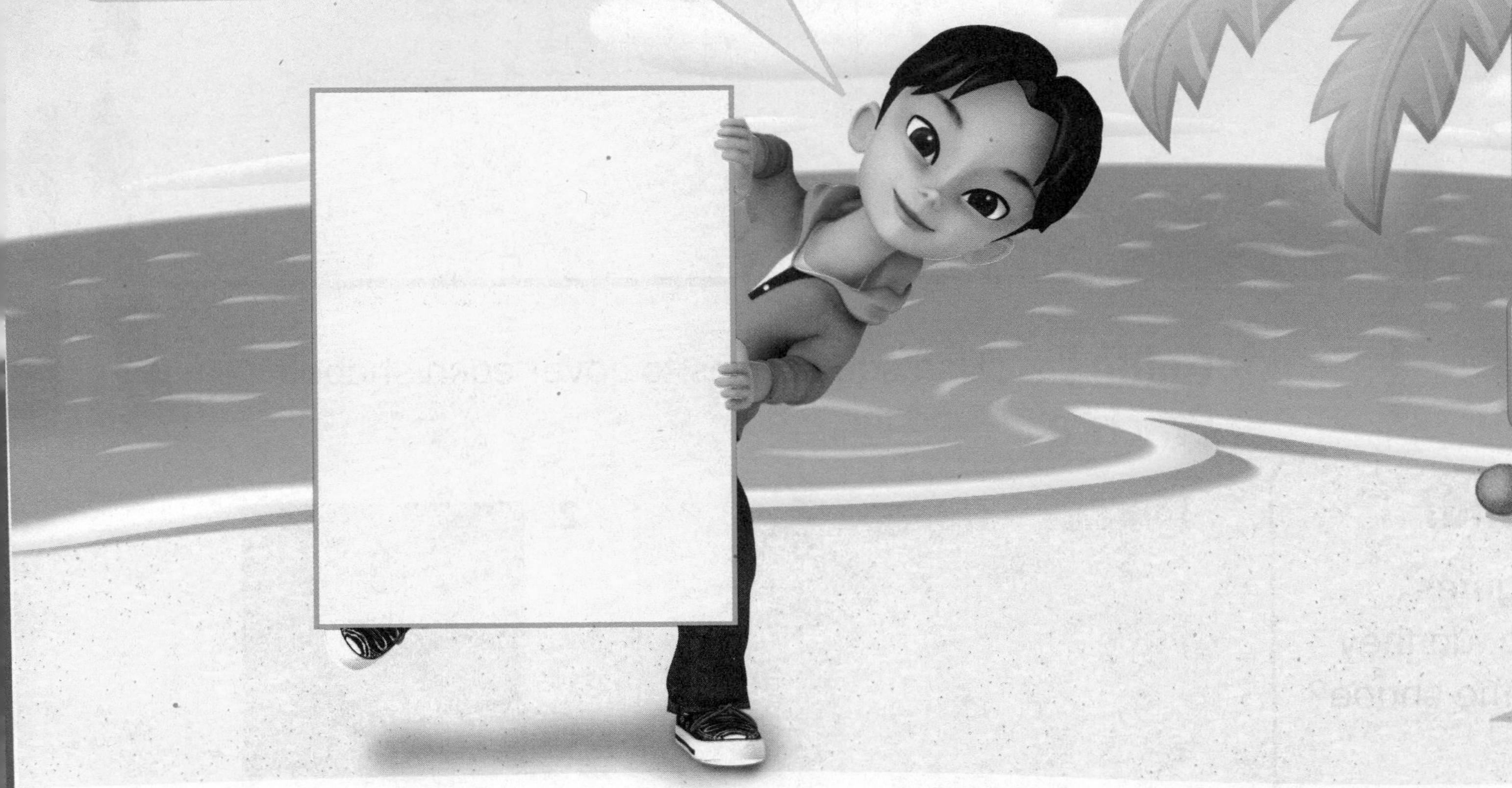

_______ squares

What is the **area** of this shape?

Area is how many square units it would take to cover the shape.

You can use square units to measure area.

Count the square units inside the shape.

There are 15 square units inside the shape. The area is 15 square units.

Do You Understand?

Show Me! If two figures have the same area, do they always have the same shape? Explain.

☆ **Guided Practice** ☆ Use square tiles to cover each shape. Find the area.

1.

3 square units

2.

_____ square units

Name _____

Independent ☆ Practice

Use square tiles to cover each shape. Find the area.

3.

_____ square units

4.

_____ square units

5.

_____ square units

6. Extend Your Thinking Draw two different shapes
that each have an area of 4 square units.
Show the units in your drawing.

Use square tiles to help.

Problem Solving

Solve each problem.

7. Ken is making a puzzle. The area of the blue square is 1 square unit. What are the areas of some other pieces of the puzzle?

Purple: _____ square units

Green: _____ square units

8. ⭐ What is the area of the yellow piece of Ken's puzzle?

7 square units ○   5 square units ○

3 square units ○   1 square unit ○

9. ⭐ Which figure has an area of exactly 4 square units?

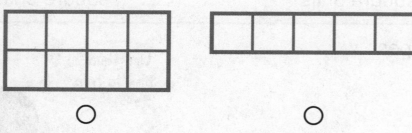

○   ○

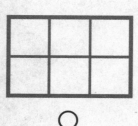   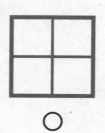

○   ○

10. **Extend Your Thinking** Draw two rectangles that have different areas. Find their areas. Explain how you found their areas.

_____ square units   _____ square units

Topic 14 | Lesson 3

Name _____

Another Look

Look at this shape.

To find the area, count how many squares fit inside the shape.

Remember: Area is how many units it would take to cover the shape.

To help you keep track, make an x in each square as you count it.

⌂ **HOME CONNECTION**
Your child used square tiles to find the area of figures.

HOME ACTIVITY Have your child choose a flat surface and then measure the area with square self-stick notes or other square items that can be used as units to measure the area. Have your child tell you how many units cover the surface.

The area of the shape is __8__ square units.

Find the area of each shape. Mark each square as you count.

1.

Area: _____ square units

2.

Area: _____ square units

3.

Area: _____ square units

4. What is the area of the striped part of this flag?

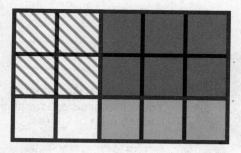

_____ square units

5. What is the area of all the parts of the flag that are not striped?

○ 9 square units

○ 11 square units

○ 15 square units

○ 16 square units

6. Suppose you had a garden that had an area of 10 square units.
Draw what your garden would look like.
Show the square units.

7. Extend Your Thinking Draw a figure that has the same area as the figure below but a different shape.
Find the area of each shape.

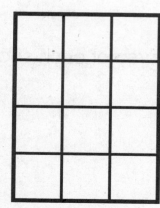

_____ square units   _____ square units

Topic 14 | Lesson 3

Name _____

Solve & Share

Use six squares to make one shape. Copy your shape and your partner's shape below. What is the area of each shape? What is the distance around each shape?

⊗ **TEKS 2.1C** Select tools ... and techniques ... to solve problems. Also, 2.9, 2.9F. **Mathematical Process Standards** 2.1B, 2.1C, 2.1F.

Digital Resources at SavvasTexas.com

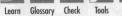

Solve   Learn   Glossary   Check   Tools   Games

My shape

area: _____ square units

distance
around: _____ units

My partner's shape

area: _____ square units

distance
around: _____ units

Analyze

Make two different shapes that have an area of 8 square units. Count the distance around the shapes.

Plan

I can use 8 square tiles to make the shapes.

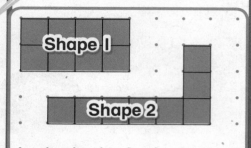

Shape 1

Shape 2

Solve, Justify, and Evaluate

Count to find the distance around the shapes.

The areas are the same. The distance around is different.

Distance around
Shape 1 = __12__ units

Distance around
Shape 2 = __18__ units

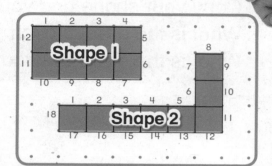

Shape 1

Shape 2

Do You Understand?

Show Me! If the areas of two shapes are the same, does the distance around have to be the same? Explain.

726 seven hundred twenty-six

Guided Practice

Use square tiles to make two shapes with the same area. Then draw your shapes on the grid. Find the distance around each shape.

1. The area is 5 square units.

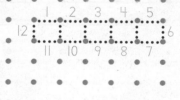

Distance around
Shape 1 = __12__ units

Distance around
Shape 2 = _____ units

2. The area is 4 square units.

Distance around
Shape 1 = _____ units

Distance around
Shape 2 = _____ units

Topic 14 | Lesson 4

Use square tiles to make two shapes with the same area.
Then draw your shapes on the grid. Find the distance around each.

3. The area is 7 square units.

Distance around
Shape 1 = _____ units

Distance around
Shape 2 = _____ units

4. The area is 6 square units.

Distance around
Shape 1 = _____ units

Distance around
Shape 2 = _____ units

5. The area is 9 square units.

Distance around
Shape 1 = _____ units

Distance around
Shape 2 = _____ units

Extend Your Thinking Draw two different shapes that follow each rule.

6. The distance around is 8 units.

7. The distance around is 10 units.

8. Sandy used square tiles to make a rectangle. The distance around the rectangle is 14 units.
Which of the following shows how many tiles she could have used?

○ 7   ○ 8   ○ 9   ○ 10

9. Dan used small square tiles to make a big square.
The distance around the big square is 16 units. Which of the following shows how many small square tiles he could have used?

○ 16   ○ 9   ○ 8   ○ 4

10. Ms. Robb wants to build a square fence around her garden to keep out rabbits. The area of the inside of the garden is 9 square units.
How many units of fence does Ms. Robb need for the garden?

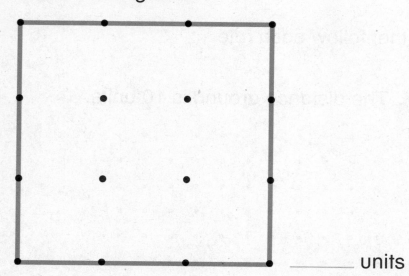

_____ units

11. **Extend Your Thinking** Draw two rectangles that have the same area but have a distance around that is different. Describe the rectangles.

Name _____

Another Look

Find the area.

Count the square units inside the shape.

The area is _6_ square units.

Now, find the distance
around the shape.

The distance around is _10_ units.

Area is space
inside a shape.

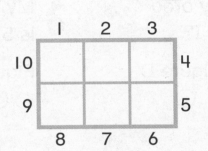

🏠 **HOME CONNECTION**
Your child used objects to
make shapes and to find
the area of and the distance
around the shapes.

HOME ACTIVITY Have your
child draw a shape with an
area of 3 square units. Ask
your child to show you how
to find the distance around
the shape.

Find the area and the distance around each shape.

1.

The area is _____ square units.

The distance around is _____ units.

2.

The area is _____ square units.

The distance around is _____ units.

Use the figures below to solve the riddles.

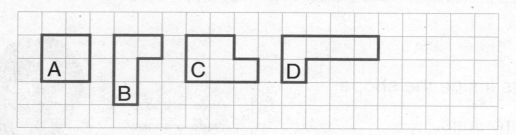

3. My distance around is 10 units. My area is 4 square units. Which figure am I?

    Figure A   Figure B   Figure C   Figure D

      ○   ○   ○   ○

4. My distance around is 12 units. My area is 5 square units. Which figure am I?

    Figure D   Figure C   Figure B   Figure A

      ○   ○   ○   ○

Extend Your Thinking Find the distance around and the area of each shape.

5.

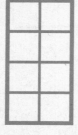

Distance around: _____ units
Area: _____ square units

6.

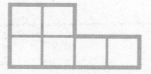

Distance around: _____ units
Area: _____ square units

7.

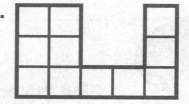

Distance around: _____ uni
Area: _____ square units

8. Color the shape with the longest distance around red.

9. Color the shape with the smallest area blue.

Topic 14 | Lesson 4

Name _____

Solve & Share

Find three objects in the classroom that are each about 1 paper clip long.
Draw these objects below.

⭐ **TEKS 2.9A** Find the length of objects using concrete models for standard units of length. **Mathematical Process Standards** 2.1A, 2.1C, 2.1D.

Digital Resources at SavvasTexas.com

Solve   Learn   Glossary   Check   Tools   Games

about 1 paper clip

You can use different **units** to measure **length**. This is 1 **inch**.

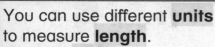

INCHES

There are 12 inches in 1 foot. There are 3 feet in 1 yard.

These are objects that are about 1 inch, 1 foot, and 1 yard tall.

about 1 inch

about 1 foot

about 1 yard

You can use these objects to measure.

 is about 2 , which is about 2 inches.

 is about 2 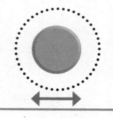, which is about 2 feet.

Estimate first. Measure to check your estimate.

is about 2 , which is about 2 yards.

Do You Understand?

Show Me! Is your height closer to 4 feet or 4 yards? How do you know?

✰ **Guided Practice** ✰ Circle the object that is about each length.

1. about 1 inch

2. about 1 foot

3. about 1 yard

☆ Independent ☆ Practice

Estimate. Then measure the lengths of the objects shown.
Use a paper clip, a book, and an object that is about 1 yard to measure.

	Estimate	Measure	Standard Units
4. 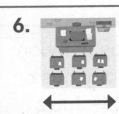	about _____ paper clips	about _____ paper clips	about _____ inches
5.	about _____ books	about _____ books	about _____ feet
6.	about _____ objects	about _____ objects	about _____ yards

7. Extend Your Thinking What is the best unit to measure the length of a baseball card? How do you know?

_____

_____

8. Extend Your Thinking What is the best unit to measure the height of a building? How do you know?

_____

_____

Problem Solving — Solve each problem.

9. Calvin measures the length of a car. He says it is about 3 units long. Circle the unit Calvin used.

paper clip
inch
yard
foot

10. Which real object is about 1 inch long?

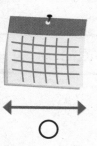 ○

 ○

 ○

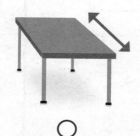 ○

11. Estimate the length from your fingertips to your elbow. Then measure.

Estimate	Measure	Standard Units
about _____ paper clips	about _____ paper clips	about _____ inches

12. Extend Your Thinking Joe has a ribbon that is about 12 inches long. Marty has a ribbon that is about 1 foot long. Is Joe's ribbon longer than Marty's ribbon? Explain.

_____

_____

_____

Name _____

Another Look

A paper clip is about 1 inch long.

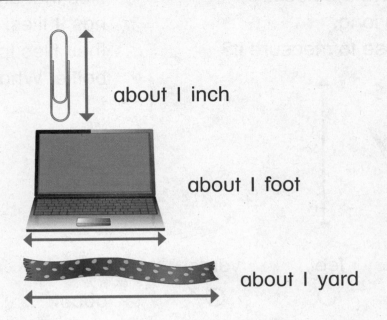

about 1 inch

A laptop computer is about
1 foot wide.
There are 12 inches in 1 foot.

about 1 foot

A scarf is about 1 yard long.
There are 3 feet in 1 yard.

about 1 yard

🏠 **HOME CONNECTION**
Your child learned about inches, feet, and yards.

HOME ACTIVITY Have your child identify three objects at home that are about 1 inch, 1 foot, and 1 yard in length or height.

About how long is each object?
Circle the answer.

1.

about 1 inch

about 1 foot

about 1 yard

2.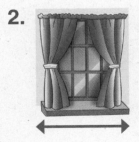

about 1 inch

about 1 foot

about 1 yard

3.

about 1 inch

about 1 foot

about 1 yard

4. Chris measures the height of a hockey stick. She says the hockey stick is about 4 units long. Which unit did she use to measure it?

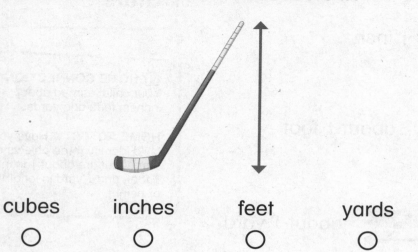

cubes	inches	feet	yards
○	○	○	○

5. Extend Your Thinking Mia and Jake have tiles that are each about 1 inch long. Mia has 4 tiles. Jake has 5 tiles. They use all of their tiles to measure the height of this water bottle. What is the height of the water bottle?

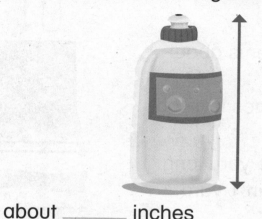

about _____ inches

Find three objects and measure their length or height.
Draw a picture or write the name of each object.
Then measure one object using inches, one using feet, and one using yards.

6.

about _____ inches

7.

about _____ feet

8.

about _____ yards

Solve & Share

How can you measure to find objects that are about 1 inch, about 6 inches, and about 12 inches long? Show these objects below.

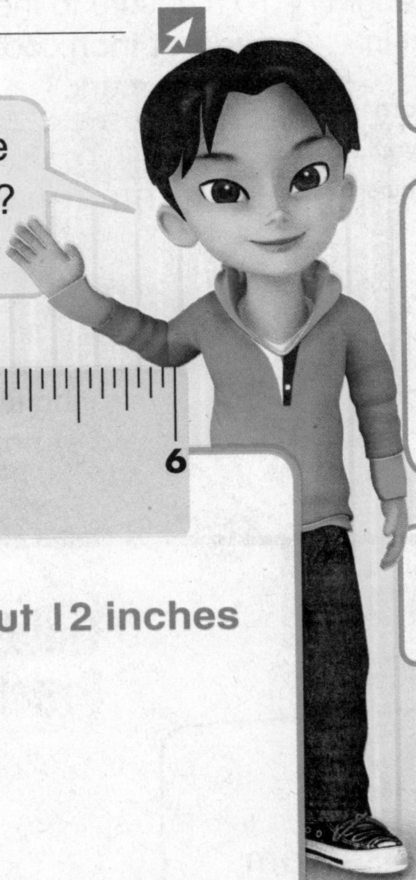

⭐ TEKS 2.9D Determine the length of an object to the nearest marked unit using rulers, yardsticks, meter sticks, or measuring tapes. Also, 2.9E. **Mathematical Process Standards** 2.1B, 2.1C, 2.1F, 2.1G.

0   1   2   3   4   5   6

INCHES

Digital Resources at SavvasTexas.com

Solve Learn Glossary Check Tools Games

about 1 inch	about 6 inches	about 12 inches

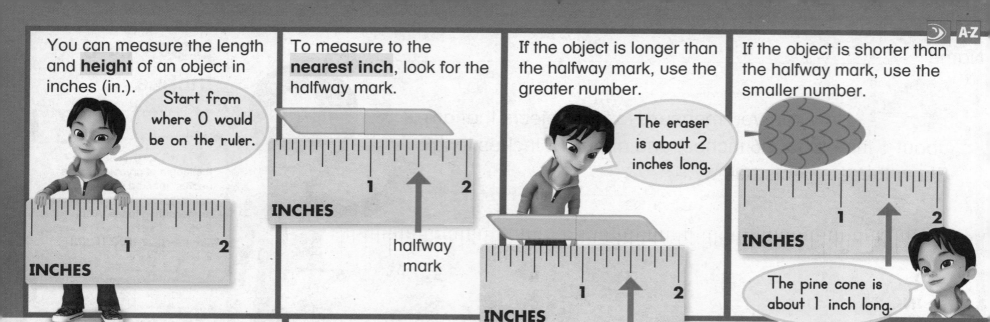

You can measure the length and **height** of an object in inches (in.).

Start from where 0 would be on the ruler.

INCHES

To measure to the **nearest inch**, look for the halfway mark.

INCHES

halfway mark

If the object is longer than the halfway mark, use the greater number.

The eraser is about 2 inches long.

INCHES

If the object is shorter than the halfway mark, use the smaller number.

INCHES

The pine cone is about 1 inch long.

Do You Understand?

Show Me! What classroom objects are about 12 inches long?

✰ **Guided Practice** ✰ Estimate the height or length of each object. Then use a ruler to measure.

1.

height of a juice box

2.

length of a pencil case

Estimate	Measure
about _6_ inches	about _4_ inches
about ___ inches	about ___ inches

Name _____

Estimate the height or length of each object. Then use a ruler to measure.

3.

length of a
book bag

Estimate	Measure
about _____ inches	about _____ inches
about _____ inches	about _____ inches

4.

length of a
paintbrush

5.

height of
a cup

Estimate	Measure
about _____ inches	about _____ inches
about _____ inches	about _____ inches

6.

length of a
crayon box

Extend Your Thinking Think about how to use a ruler to solve each problem.

7. Jason measures an object. The object is just shorter than the halfway mark between 8 and 9 on his inch ruler. How long is the object?

about _____ inches

8. Gina measures an object. The object is just longer than the halfway mark between 9 and 10 on her inch ruler. How long is the object?

about _____ inches

Problem Solving Solve each problem.

9. Pam and José eat cherries. Pam says that each cherry is about 1 inch wide. José says each cherry is about 6 inches wide. Who is correct?

_____

10. Yona bought two stamps. She measured one of them. Yona put the two stamps next to each other. About how many inches wide are the two stamps together?

4 inches ○   3 inches ○

2 inches ○   1 inch ○

11. Find an object in the classroom that measures about 6 inches. Draw the object. Write two sentences to describe it.

_____

_____

_____

12. **Extend Your Thinking** Explain how to use an inch ruler to measure the length of an object.

_____

_____

_____

740 seven hundred forty

Topic 14 | Lesson 6

Name _____

Another Look You can use a ruler to measure inches.

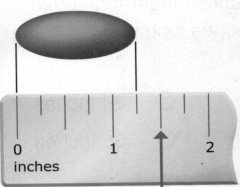

This bead is about
<u>1</u> inch long.

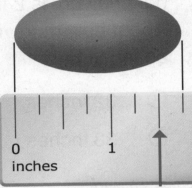

This bead is about
<u>2</u> inches long.

To measure to the nearest inch, look at the halfway mark between inches. If the object is longer, use the greater number. If the object is shorter, use the lesser number.

🏠 **HOME CONNECTION**
Your child measured the length of classroom objects to the nearest inch.

HOME ACTIVITY Ask your child to find items at home that are about 1 inch, about 6 inches, and about 12 inches long.

Estimate the height or length. Then use a ruler to measure.

1. height of a book

My Favorite Book

2. length of a pencil

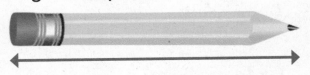

Estimate	Measure
about ____ inches	about ____ inches
about ____ inches	about ____ inches

3. Measure the length of this straw in inches. About how long is the straw?

about _____ inches

Use a ruler to measure!

4. Jeremy measured his baseball bat to be about 34 inches. Luke's baseball bat is 3 inches shorter than Jeremy's. Pat's baseball bat is 2 inches longer than Luke's. About how many inches long is Pat's baseball bat?

○ 32 inches   ○ 34 inches

○ 33 inches   ○ 35 inches

5. **Extend Your Thinking** Estimate how long the path is to get out of this maze.

about _____ inches

6. Draw a path from the start to the exit. Use a ruler to measure each part of your path. Add the lengths together. About how long is the path?

about _____ inches

7. How close to the answer was your estimate?

_____ inches

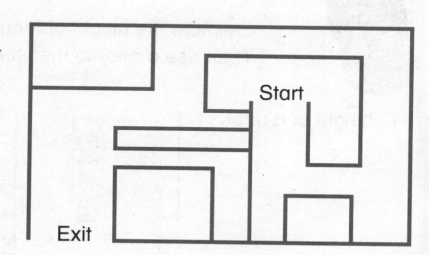

Name _____

Solve & Share

How can you measure to find objects that are about 1 inch, about 1 foot, and about 1 yard long? Show these objects below.

⊕ **TEKS 2.9D** Determine the length of an object to the nearest marked unit using rulers, yardsticks, meter sticks, or measuring tapes. Also, 2.9, 2.9E. **Mathematical Process Standards** 2.1A, 2.1C, 2.1F.

Digital Resources at SavvasTexas.com

Solve   Learn   Glossary   Check   Tools   Games

about 1 inch

about 1 foot

about 1 yard

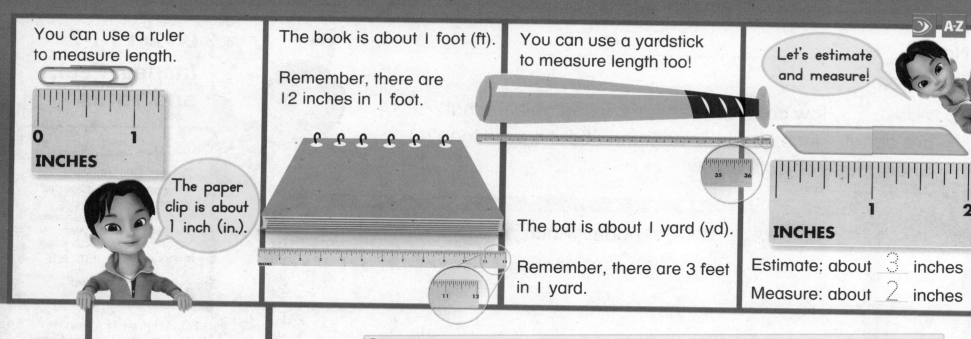

You can use a ruler to measure length.

INCHES

The paper clip is about 1 inch (in.).

The book is about 1 foot (ft).

Remember, there are 12 inches in 1 foot.

You can use a yardstick to measure length too!

The bat is about 1 yard (yd).

Remember, there are 3 feet in 1 yard.

Let's estimate and measure!

INCHES

Estimate: about ___3___ inches

Measure: about ___2___ inches

Do You Understand?

Show Me! Would it be easier to use inches or yards to measure the length of a school building? Why?

Guided Practice

Match each object with a reasonable estimate of its length.

1.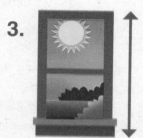

   about 1 yard

2.

   about 1 inch

3.

   about 1 foot

Independent ☆ Practice Estimate the length of each object shown. Use a ruler or a yardstick to measure.

	Estimate	Measure
4. 	about _____ inches	about _____ inches
5. 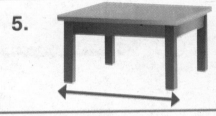	about _____ feet	about _____ feet
6.	about _____ yards	about _____ yards

Extend Your Thinking Tell what each length equals.

7. 1 foot = _____ inches

2 feet = _____ inches

3 feet = _____ inches

8. 1 yard = _____ feet

2 yards = _____ feet

3 yards = _____ feet

9. 1 yard = _____ inches

2 yards = _____ inches

3 yards = _____ inches

10. Circle the real object that is about 6 feet in length.

11. Jon lays two of the same real object together. Together, they have a length of about 12 inches. Which is the object Jon uses?

○    ○

○    ○

12. Find an object in the classroom that measures about 2 feet. Draw the object. Write two sentences to describe it.

13. Extend Your Thinking Explain how to use a yardstick to measure the length of an object.

_____

_____

_____

Name _____

Another Look You can use a yardstick to measure objects to the nearest foot.

Remember, 12 inches = 1 foot,
24 inches = 2 feet, and
36 inches = 3 feet.

Think: Is the string closer to 2 feet or closer to 3 feet?

🏠 **HOME CONNECTION**
Your child learned about inches, feet, and yards.

HOME ACTIVITY Have your child identify three objects at home that are about 1 inch, 1 foot, and 1 yard in length.

This string is about
_2_ feet long.

This string is about
_3_ feet long.

Estimate the height or length of each object. Then measure.

1. the height of the doorway

Estimate: about ____ feet

Measure: about ____ feet

2. the height of a chair

Estimate: about ____ feet

Measure: about ____ feet

3. the width of a window

Estimate: about ____ feet

Measure: about ____ feet

4. Draw a picture of or name an object that measures:

more than 6 inches

less than 2 feet

more than 3 yards

5. About how long is the crayon?

○ about 1 inch

○ about 2 inches

○ about 4 inches

○ about 6 inches

6. Which could be the height of a real shovel?

○ 2 inches

○ 2 cubes

○ 2 feet

○ 2 yards

7. **Extend Your Thinking** Do you need more feet or more yards to measure the height of a tree? Explain.

_____

_____

_____

_____

Topic 14 | Lesson 7

Name _____

Solve & Share

Choose an object to measure with cubes and paper clips.

Do you need more cubes or more paper clips to measure your object? Why?

⊕ TEKS 2.9B Describe the inverse relationship between the size of the unit and the number of units needed to equal the length of an object. Also, 2.9D. **Mathematical Process Standards** 2.1C, 2.1D, 2.1E, 2.1F.

Digital Resources at SavvasTexas.com

Solve   Learn   Glossary   Check   Tools   Games

about _____ cubes long

about _____ paper clips long

more cubes   more paper clips

You can use different units to measure objects.
Which would you use more of to measure the length of the bookcase, feet or yards?

Measure the bookcase with feet.

It is about 3 feet long.

1 2 3

Measure the bookcase with yards.

It is about 1 yard long.

1

I used more feet than yards because a foot is the smaller unit.

Do You Understand?

Show Me! Would it be easier to measure the height of a door in inches or feet? Why?

★ **Guided Practice** ★ Measure each object using different units. Circle the unit you need more of to measure each object.

1.

about _____ feet   about _____ yards

more feet

more yards

2.

about _____ inches   about _____ feet

more inches

more feet

Topic 14 | Lesson 8

Independent Practice Measure each object using different units.
Circle the unit you need fewer of to measure each object.

3.

about _____ inches   about _____ feet

fewer inches

fewer feet

5.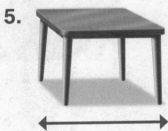

about _____ feet

about _____ yards

fewer feet

fewer yards

4.

about _____ feet   about _____ yards

fewer feet

fewer yards

Extend Your Thinking Estimate the length of each object.

6. About how long is a key?

about 2 yards

about 2 inches

about 2 feet

7. About how long is a suitcase?

about 2 yards

about 2 inches

about 2 feet

8. Which unit would you need fewest of to measure the length of the table?

inches ◯

feet ◯

yards ◯

all the same ◯

9. Which is the best estimate for the length of a vegetable garden?

about 1 inch ◯

about 3 yards ◯

about 1 foot ◯

about 20 inches ◯

10. Measure an object in your classroom using two different units.

Object: _____ about _____

about _____

Which unit did you use more of? _____

11. Extend Your Thinking Andrew wants to measure the length of a football field in feet or yards. Which unit is easier to measure with? Explain.

_____

_____

_____

_____

Name _____ 🔍 ⭙

Another Look You can measure using different units.

Derrick measured the gift box in inches and in feet.

The gift box is about

⫶ inches long.

The gift box is about

⌶ foot long.

🏠 **HOME CONNECTION**
Your child used inches, feet, and yards to measure objects.

HOME ACTIVITY Have your child use a foot ruler to measure objects. Then ask your child if he or she measured each object with more inches or more feet.

It takes more inches than feet to measure the gift box because an inch is a smaller unit.

If you use smaller units, you need to use more units.

Measure each object using different units.
Circle the unit you need more of to measure each object.

1.

about _____ feet   about _____ yards

more feet

more yards

2.

about _____ inches   about _____ feet

more inches

more feet

3. What is the best estimate for the length of an umbrella?

- ○ about 3 inches
- ○ about 1 foot
- ○ about 1 yard
- ○ about 3 yards

4. What is the best estimate for the length of a pen?

- ○ about 10 inches
- ○ about 6 inches
- ○ about 5 feet
- ○ about 10 yards

5. Extend Your Thinking Trina says that her dollhouse is about 8 yards tall. Do you think this is a good estimate? Explain.

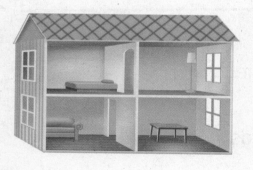

6. Extend Your Thinking Sarah wants to measure the length of her math book. Should she use inches, feet, or yards? Explain.

MATH

Name _____

☆ **Solve & Share**

What objects in the classroom are about 3 cubes long?
Use the cubes to measure and show what you found on the workmat.

⊘ **TEKS 2.9A** Find the length of objects using concrete models for standard units of length. **Mathematical Process Standards** 2.1C, 2.1D, 2.1F.

about 3 cubes

Digital Resources at SavvasTexas.com

  A-Z
Solve   Learn   Glossary   Check   Tools   Games

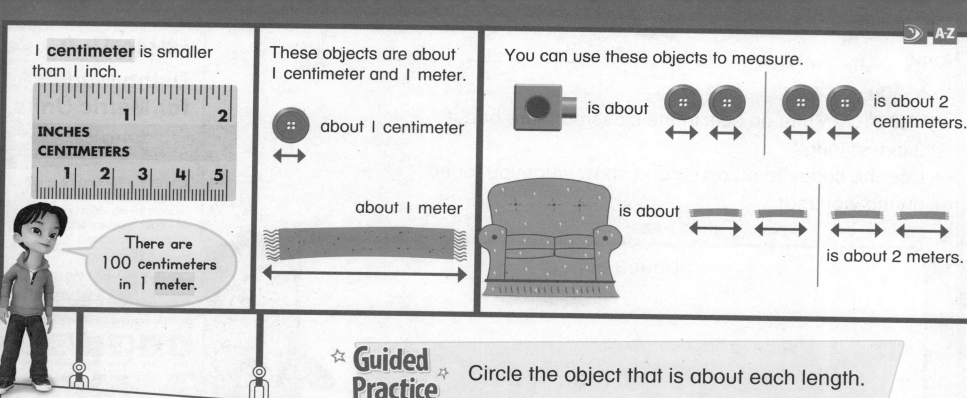

I centimeter is smaller than I inch.

INCHES
CENTIMETERS

There are 100 centimeters in I meter.

These objects are about I centimeter and I meter.

about I centimeter

about I meter

You can use these objects to measure.

is about

is about 2 centimeters.

is about

is about 2 meters.

Do You Understand?

Show Me! Would you use a button that is about I centimeter long to measure the length of a table? Explain why or why not.

Guided Practice

Circle the object that is about each length.

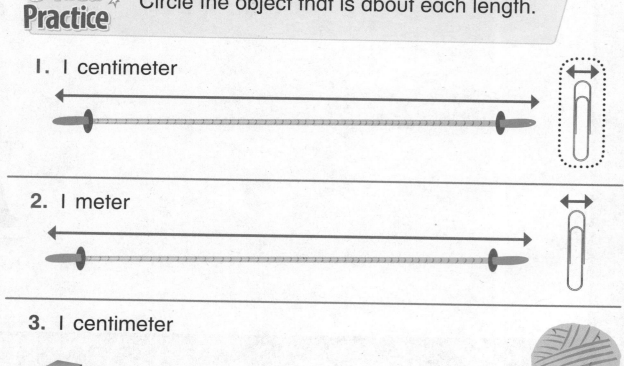

I. I centimeter

2. I meter

3. I centimeter

☆ **Independent** ☆
☆ **Practice**

Estimate. Then measure the lengths of the objects shown.
Use paper clips, ones cubes, string, or other objects to measure.

4.

	Estimate	Measure	Standard Units
4.	about _____ paper clip tops	about _____ paper clip tops	about _____ centimeters
5.	about _____ strings	about _____ strings	about _____ meters
6.	about _____ ones cubes	about _____ ones cubes	about _____ centimeters
7.	about _____ strings	about _____ strings	about _____ meters

8. Extend Your Thinking Juan says that his
toy truck is about 6 meters long.
Do you think this is a good estimate? Why
or why not?

_____

_____

_____

Solve each problem.

9. There are two of the same animal sitting on a bench. They take up about 2 centimeters of space. Which animal could they be?

○   ○

○   ○

10. Three of the same object next to each other equals 3 meters in length. Which object could it be?

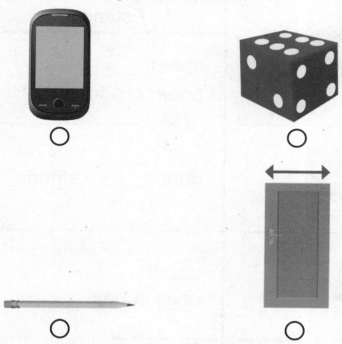

○   ○

○   ○

11. Use an object that is about 1 centimeter to estimate and measure the length of your shoe.

Estimate   Measure   Standard Units

about _____   about _____   about _____
objects   objects   centimeters

12. **Extend Your Thinking** Mr. Gavin has a ladder that is 200 centimeters tall. Mr. Cornell has a ladder that is 8 meters tall. Whose ladder is taller? Explain.

_____

_____

 Topic 14 | Lesson 9

Name _____

Another Look

This bead is about 1 centimeter long.

> You would need 100 of these beads to make 1 meter!

There are 100 centimeters in 1 meter.

...

About how long is each object? Circle the better estimate.

1.    about 1 centimeter

   about 1 meter

2. 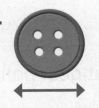   about 1 centimeter

   about 1 meter

3. 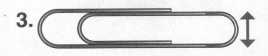   about 1 centimeter

   about 1 meter

4.    about 3 centimeters

   about 3 meters

5. Two of which object would be about 2 centimeters long?

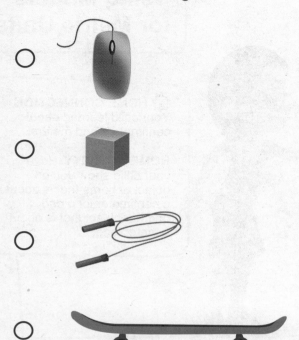

○ (mouse)

○ (cube)

○ (jump rope)

○ (skateboard)

6. Name an animal that is about 1 meter long.

_____

If your animal is about 1 meter, about how many centimeters long is it? Explain.

_____

_____

_____

_____

7. Extend Your Thinking Draw a line from each mouse to the cheese below it.
Use an object that is about 1 centimeter to measure each path.
Record the lengths.
Circle the mouse with the longest path.

Mouse A: _____ centimeters

Mouse B: _____ centimeters

Mouse C: _____ centimeters

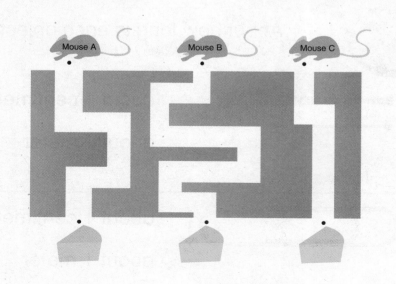

Name _____

Solve & Share

What objects in the classroom are about 1 centimeter, about 10 centimeters, and about 100 centimeters long? Show these objects below.

TEKS 2.9D Determine the length of an object to the nearest marked unit using rulers, yardsticks, meter sticks, or measuring tapes. Also, 2.9E. **Mathematical Process Standards** 2.1C, 2.1D, 2.1E.

Digital Resources at SavvasTexas.com

| Solve | Learn | Glossary | Check | Tools | Games |

```
|1  |2  |3  |4  |5  |6  |7  |8  |9  |10 |11 |12 |13 |14 |15
```

CENTIMETERS

about 1 centimeter	about 10 centimeters	about 100 centimeters

You can measure the length of an object in centimeters (cm).

CENTIMETERS

To measure to the **nearest centimeter,** look for the halfway mark.

CENTIMETERS
halfway mark

If the object is longer than the halfway mark, use the greater number.

The cube is about 2 centimeters long.

CENTIMETERS

If the object is shorter than the halfway mark, use the smaller number.

CENTIMETERS

This paper clip is about 3 centimeters long.

Do You Understand?

Show Me! Explain how you know the length of a paper clip is about 3 centimeters long.

Guided Practice

Estimate the height or length of each object.
Then use a ruler to measure.

1.
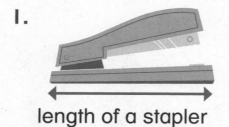
length of a stapler

2.

height of a book

Estimate	Measure
about 15 centimeters	about 18 centimeters
about ___ centimeters	about ___ centimeters

Topic 14 | Lesson 10

Name _____

Estimate the width, height, or length of each object. Then use a ruler to measure.

3.

width of
a shoelace

Estimate	Measure
about _____ centimeters	about _____ centimeters
about _____ centimeters	about _____ centimeters

5.

length of
a pencil

Estimate	Measure
about _____ centimeters	about _____ centimeters
about _____ centimeters	about _____ centimeters

4.

width of
a chair

6.

height of
scissors

Extend Your Thinking Explain whether each estimate is reasonable or not.

7. Josh estimated that the length of his reading book is about 6 centimeters.

_____

_____

8. Shae estimated that the height of her desk is about 10 centimeters.

_____

_____

Problem Solving Solve each problem.

9. Mary wants to know how long her eraser is to the nearest centimeter. Which shows about how many centimeters long Mary's eraser is?

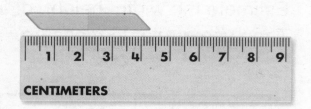

2 centimeters ○   3 centimeters ○   4 centimeters ○   5 centimeters ○

10. Nick wants to put another pen end to end with this one. About how long would the two pens be together?

_____ centimeters

11. Draw an object that is about 10 centimeters long. Write two sentences to describe your object.

12. **Extend Your Thinking** Paul says that a toothbrush is about 19 centimeters long. Sarah says it is about 150 centimeters long. Who is correct? Explain.

Name _____

Another Look You can use a ruler to measure centimeters.

To measure to the nearest centimeter, look at the halfway mark between centimeters. If the object is longer, use the greater number. If the object is shorter, use the smaller number.

🏠 **HOME CONNECTION**
Your child used a ruler to measure objects to the nearest centimeter.

HOME ACTIVITY Ask your child to find items at home that measure about 1 centimeter, about 10 centimeters, and about 100 centimeters. If possible, use a ruler to measure each object.

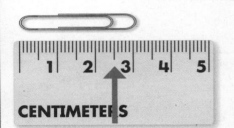

The paper clip is about

_3_ centimeters long.

This pencil is about

_9_ centimeters long.

Estimate the height or length.
Then use a ruler to measure.

I. length of a tape dispenser

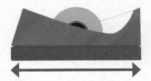

2. height of a book

	Estimate	Measure
	about _____ centimeters	about _____ centimeters
	about _____ centimeters	about _____ centimeters

3. Measure the length of this spoon in centimeters. About how long is the spoon?

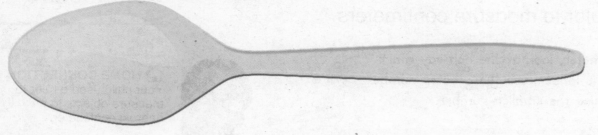

About _____ centimeters

4. Measure this paper clip. If you added 3 centimeters to it, about how many centimeters long would the paper clip be?

4 centimeters   3 centimeters   8 centimeters   6 centimeters

○   ○   ○   ○

5. Extend Your Thinking Mia has a string that is about 15 centimeters long. Circle the shapes that Mia can make with her string.

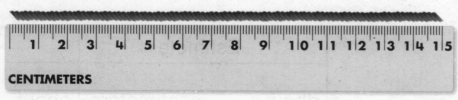
CENTIMETERS

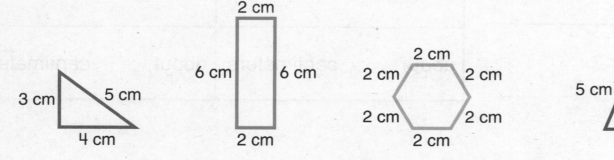

Name _____

Solve & Share

What objects in the classroom are about 3 centimeters long?

What objects are about 1 meter long?

Show these objects below.

⊙ **TEKS 2.9D** Determine the length of an object to the nearest marked unit using rulers, yardsticks, meter sticks, or measuring tapes. Also, 2.9, 2.9E. **Mathematical Process Standards** 2.1A, 2.1C, 2.1D.

Digital Resources at SavvasTexas.com

 Solve Learn A-Z Glossary Check Tools Games

about 3 centimeters

about 1 meter

You can use a ruler or a meter stick to measure length.

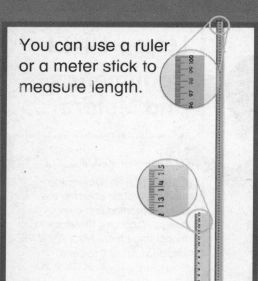

The button is about 1 centimeter (cm) long.

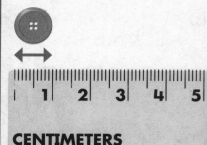

CENTIMETERS

This table is about 1 meter (m) long.

There are 100 centimeters in 1 meter!

Estimate and measure.

CENTIMETERS

Estimate: about ___3___ cm

Measure: about ___2___ cm

Do You Understand?

Show Me! Would it be easier to use centimeters or meters to measure the length of a house? Why?

Guided Practice

Match each object with a reasonable estimate of its length.

1.

I centimeter

2.

10 centimeters

3.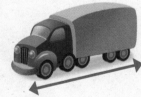

I meter

4.

10 meters

Topic 14 | Lesson 11

Name _____

Estimate the length of each object shown.
Use a ruler or a meter stick to measure.

	Estimate	Measure
5.	about ____ centimeters	about ____ centimeters
6.	about ____ meters	about ____ meters
7.	about ____ centimeters	about ____ centimeters
8.	about ____ meters	about ____ meters

9. Write the missing numbers.

I meter = ____ centimeters

2 meters = ____ centimeters

3 meters = ____ centimeters

10. **Extend Your Thinking** Debbie says that her doll is about 30 meters long. Do you think this is a good estimate? Why or why not?

_____

_____

11. Find an object in the classroom that measures about 10 centimeters.
Draw the object.
Write two sentences to describe it.

_____

_____

12. Circle the real object that would be about 2 meters long.

13. Measure each line. If you added another line of the same length, which would be about 12 centimeters long?

○ ────────────

○ ──────────

○ ───

○ -

14. Extend Your Thinking Explain how you use a centimeter ruler to measure the length of an object.

_____

_____

_____

_____

770 seven hundred seventy

Topic 14 | Lesson 11

Name _____

Another Look You can use a meter stick to measure length in meters.

Line up a meter stick with one end of an object. Mark the spot where the other end of the meter stick sits on the object. Then move the meter stick so the 0 end starts where you marked.

🏠 **HOME CONNECTION**
Your child learned about centimeters and meters.

HOME ACTIVITY Have your child show you an object at home that is about a centimeter long and another object that is about a meter long.

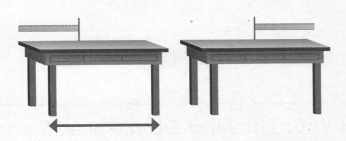

You can measure to the nearest unit.

The table is about
2 meters long.

Estimate the height or length of each object. Then use a meter stick to measure.

1. the length of a table

Estimate:
about _____ meters

Measure:
about _____ meters

2. the height of a chair

Estimate:
about _____ meters

Measure:
about _____ meters

3. the length of your room

Estimate:
about _____ meters

Measure:
about _____ meters

4. Name or draw a picture of two objects with these measurements:

more than 3 meters

less than 3 centimeters

5. What would be a reasonable measurement for the length of a calculator?

about _____ centimeters

---

6. ⭐ Which is the best estimate for the length of a bedroom?

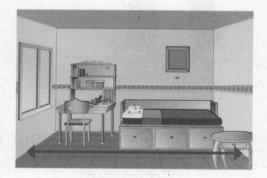

5 centimeters ○   2 meters ⦿

5 meters ○   50 meters ○

7. Extend Your Thinking Do you need fewer centimeters or fewer meters to measure the height of a doorway? Explain.

_____

_____

_____

_____

Name ____________________

Solve & Share

Measure this pencil in inches. Then measure it again in centimeters. Which measurement is the greater number?

Lesson 14-12
Measuring Length Using Metric Units

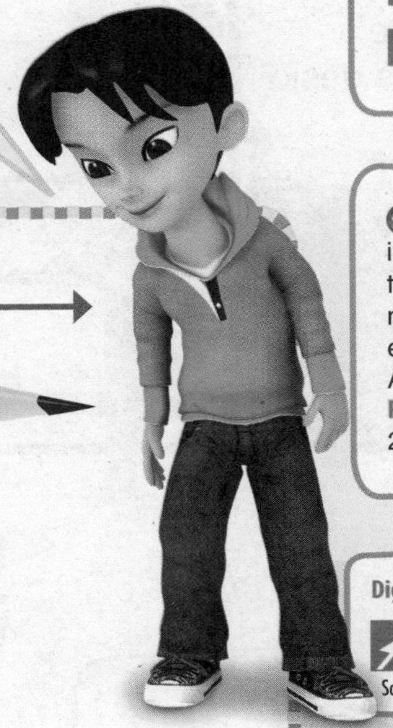

TEKS 2.9B Describe the inverse relationship between the size of the unit and the number of units needed to equal the length of an object. Also, 2.9D. **Mathematical Process Standards** 2.1A, 2.1C, 2.1D, 2.1G.

Digital Resources at SavvasTexas.com

Solve Learn Glossary Check Tools Games

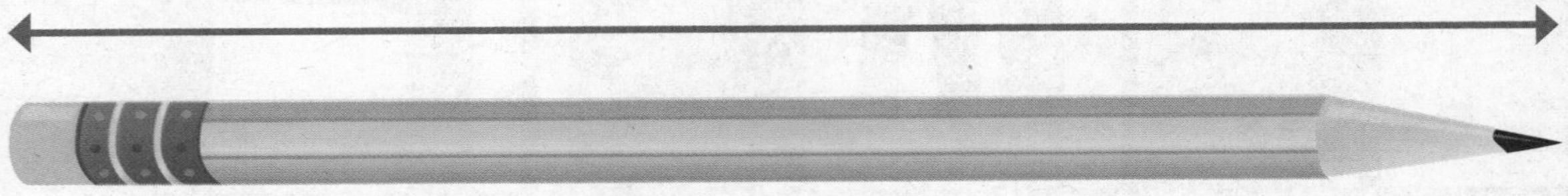

_____ inches _____ centimeters

Which number is greater? _____

You can use different units to measure the lengths of objects. Would you use more centimeters or more meters to measure the length of the teacher's desk?

Measure the desk using centimeters.

It is about 91 centimeters long!

89 90 91 92 93

Measure the desk using meters.

It is about 1 meter long!

I used more centimeters than meters because a centimeter is a much smaller unit than a meter.

Do You Understand?

Show Me! Would it be easier to measure the height of a wall in centimeters or in meters? Why?

Guided Practice

Measure each object using different units. Circle the unit you need more of to measure each object.

1.
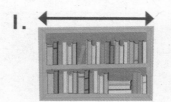
about _____ centimeters   more centimeters

about _____ meters   more meters

2.
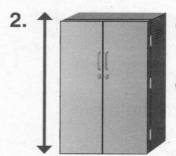
about _____ centimeters   more centimeters

about _____ meters   more meters

774   seven hundred seventy-four

Topic 14 | Lesson 12

Name _____

☆ **Independent** ☆
☆ **Practice** ☆

Measure each object using different units.
Circle the unit you need fewer of to measure each object.

3.

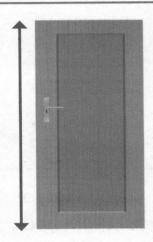

about _____ meters

about _____ centimeters

fewer centimeters

fewer meters

4.

about _____ meters

about _____ centimeters

fewer centimeters

fewer meters

---

5. Extend Your Thinking Jax measured the
height of his bedroom in both centimeters
and meters. Did he use fewer centimeters
or fewer meters? Explain.

_____

_____

_____

_____

6. Which unit would you need the fewest of to measure the jump rope?

  ○ centimeters

  ○ inches

  ○ meters

  ○ all the same

7. Estimate the length of a baseball bat in centimeters and meters.

_____ centimeters

_____ meters

Which number must be greater? Explain.

_____

_____

_____

_____

8. Extend Your Thinking If you had to measure the length of the hallway outside of your classroom, would you use centimeters or meters? Explain.

_____

_____

9. Extend Your Thinking If you had to measure the length of your math book using centimeters or meters, which would you use? Explain.

_____

_____

Name _____

Another Look You can measure using different units.

Andy measures the length of the television using both centimeters and meters.

The television is about

⌊ meter long.

The television is about

88 centimeters long.

🏠 **HOME CONNECTION**
Your child used centimeters and meters to measure objects.

HOME ACTIVITY Select two objects in your home, such as a table or a window. Ask your child if he or she would use more centimeters or meters to measure each object.

It takes fewer meters than centimeters to measure the television.
If you use larger units, you will use fewer of them.

Measure each object using centimeters and meters.
Circle the unit you need fewer of to measure each object.

1.

about ____ centimeters   fewer centimeters

about ____ meters   fewer meters

2.

about ____ centimeters   fewer centimeters

about ____ meters   fewer meters

3. Which would you use if you were to measure the length of the couch?

○ more centimeters than meters

○ fewer centimeters than meters

○ more meters than centimeters

○ both the same number of centimeters and meters

4. Circle the objects that are easier to measure using centimeters. Cross out the objects that are easier to measure using meters.

5. Extend Your Thinking Shane and Karen want to measure the length of a soccer field in centimeters or meters.
Which unit is easier to measure with? Explain.

Name _____

Solve & Share

Circle two paths. Estimate which one is longer.
How can you check if your estimate is correct?

⊕ **TEKS 2.1G** Display, explain, and justify mathematical ideas… in written or oral communication. **TEKS 2.9E** Determine a solution … involving length, including estimating lengths. **Mathematical Process Standards** 2.1B, 2.1C, 2.1E, 2.1F.

Digital Resources at SavvasTexas.com

| Solve | Learn | Glossary | Check | Tools | Games |

Estimate: The _____ path is longer.

Measure: The _____ path is longer.

Analyze and Plan

Which path is longer? How much longer?

Think about both parts of the path when you estimate and measure.

Estimate: _5_ cm

Estimate: _6_ cm

Solve and Justify

One part of the blue path is about 2 cm. The other part is about 2 cm. Add 2 + 2 to find the length.

2 + 2 = 4
The blue path is about 4 cm long.

CENTIMETERS

One part of the red path is about 1 cm. The other part is about 4 cm. 1 + 4 = 5
The red path is about 5 cm long.

CENTIMETERS

Evaluate

5 – 4 = 1
The red path is about 1 cm longer than the blue path.

Subtract to compare lengths. The blue path is about 4 cm long. The red path is about 1 cm longer.

Do You Understand?

Show Me! How can you find the length of a path that is not straight?

Guided Practice Estimate the length of each path. Then use a centimeter ruler to measure each path. Answer the questions.

1. **Path A**

Estimate: about __9__ centimeters

Measure: about __10__ centimeters

2. **Path B**

Estimate: about _____ centimeters

Measure: about _____ centimeters

3. Which path is longer?

_____

4. How much longer? about _____ centimeters longer

Topic 14 | Lesson 13

Name _____

Estimate the length of each path.
Then use a centimeter ruler to measure each path.

5.

Path C

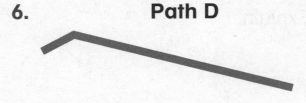

Estimate: about _____ centimeters

Measure: about _____ centimeters

6.

Path D

Estimate: about _____ centimeters

Measure: about _____ centimeters

---

7. Which path is longer?

_____

8. How much longer?

_____ centimeters longer

Extend Your Thinking Think about the length of each object. Circle the best estimate.
Then use your estimates to complete the sentence.

9. a key

about 1 cm   about 6 cm   about 20 cm

Think about objects you know that are about 1 cm long to help.

10. a pen

about 2 cm   about 4 cm   about 15 cm

Estimate: A _____ is about _____ cm

longer than a _____.

Problem Solving Solve each problem.

11. A path has two parts.
The total length of the path is 12 cm.
If one part is 8 cm, how long is the
other part? Explain.

_____ cm

12. Peter measures a path that has a total
⭐ length of 12 cm.
Janna measures a path that has two parts.
Each part measures 7 cm.

How much longer is Janna's path than
Peter's path?

2 cm   5 cm   7 cm   14 cm
○   ○   ○   ○

13. **Extend Your Thinking** Draw a path
with two parts. Measure the length
to the nearest centimeter. Write a
number sentence to show the length
of your path.

about _____ centimeters

14. **Extend Your Thinking** Beth drew a
model of a bike path near her home.
Use a ruler. Measure the
length of the path. Write the   **Beth's Path**
total length.
Show your work.

_____ centimeters

Ken drew a bike path
that is 6 cm long.
Whose drawing is longer? _____

How much longer? _____ centimeters

Name _____

Another Look You can write a number sentence
to help you find the total length of a path.

What is the total length of the path?

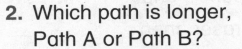

Measure each part of a path to find the total length.

🏠 **HOME CONNECTION**
Your child measured to compare the lengths of two paths.

HOME ACTIVITY Draw a path that is made up of two parts. Have your child use a centimeter ruler to measure each part.

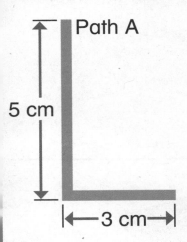

Path A

5 cm

←3 cm→

3 + 5 = 8

The path is __8__ centimeters long.

Use a centimeter ruler to measure the path.

1. Path B

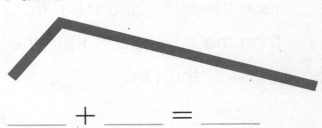

____ + ____ = ____

_____ centimeters long

2. Which path is longer, Path A or Path B?

Path A   Path B

3. How much longer is the longer path?

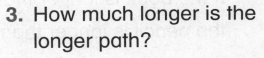

_____ centimeter longer

4. What is the total length of the path?

- ○ 2 centimeters
- ○ 4 centimeters
- ○ 6 centimeters
- ○ 8 centimeters

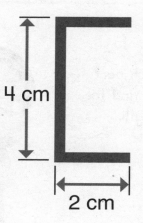

4 cm

2 cm

5. Nadine drew a path that is 7 cm longer than Nancy's path. Nadine's path is 15 cm long. How long is Nancy's path?

_____ − _____ = _____ centimeters

Use the pictures on the right to solve each problem.

6. Kristin cleans out her desk. Write the items she finds in order from longest to shortest. Then fill in the blanks for each sentence below.

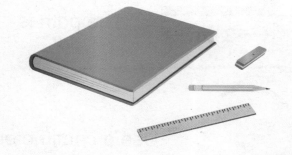

_____   _____   _____   _____

longest   shortest

7. If the book is longer than the pencil, and the pencil is longer than the eraser, then the _____ is longer than the eraser .

8. Extend Your Thinking If the pencil is _____ than the ruler, and the ruler is _____ than the _____, then the pencil is _____ than the _____.

Name _____

Have a classroom *Measure Hunt!* **Estimate** and **use tools** to explore lengths.

1. Pick one long object and one short object in your classroom.
   Estimate the length of the long object.
   Estimate the length of the short object.
   Then measure.
   Choose the units you will use.

Item	Estimate	Measure
long object	about _____ _____ long	about _____ _____ long
short object	about _____ _____ long	about _____ _____ long

2. Complete these sentences.

   I need _____ inches than feet to measure an object.

   I need _____ yards than inches to measure an object.

3. Ms. Jacobs made two posters for a charity event. She printed 247 copies of the first poster. She printed 136 copies of the second poster. How many posters did she print in all?

   _____ posters

What Number?

1. Pick a number between 500 and 800.
Follow the directions.
Write your new number each time.

My number	_____
Add 56	_____
Add 113	_____
Subtract 169	_____

What do you notice about the numbers in the top and bottom rows? Explain.

_____

_____

_____

What's Wrong?

2. Greta made an
Input/Output table.
It has 2 mistakes.
Fix the table.
Tell the pattern rule.

Input	Output
25	22
20	17
15	12
12	7
9	2

A-MAZE-ing!

3. Measure in centimeters to solve.

Path A   **Path B**

Path C is about 24 cm long. Demi
joins Path A, Path B, and Path C
together to make a new path. About
how long is the new path?

about _____ centimeters

Set A

It takes 5 minutes for the minute hand to move from one number to the next. So, you can skip count by 5s.

Start counting at 12.

5
10
15
20
21

What time does the clock show?

8:21

Write the time.

1.

:

2.

:

Set B

You can say the number of minutes before the hour or after the hour.

10 minutes before 5

(10 minutes after 5)

(10 minutes before 5)

10 minutes after 5

Circle the time the clocks show.

3.

2:55

5 minutes before 3   5 minutes after 3

4.

10:15

15 minutes before 10   15 minutes after 10

Set C

There are 12 inches in 1 foot.
There are 3 feet in 1 yard.
You can measure using objects that
are close to 1 inch, 1 foot, or 1 yard.

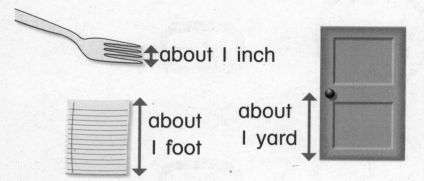

about 1 inch

about
1 foot

about
1 yard

Use a piece of paper to measure two
classroom objects in feet. Name each object
and tell about how many feet it measured.

5. Object: _____

about _____ feet

6. Object: _____

about _____ feet

Set D

You can measure the length of an
object to the nearest inch.

halfway
mark

The string is longer than halfway between
1 and 2.
So, use the greater number.
The string is about __2__ inches.

Find an object that is like the one shown.
Use a ruler to measure its length.

7.

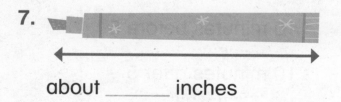

about _____ inches

8.

about _____ inches

Name _____

Set E

There are 100 centimeters in 1 meter.

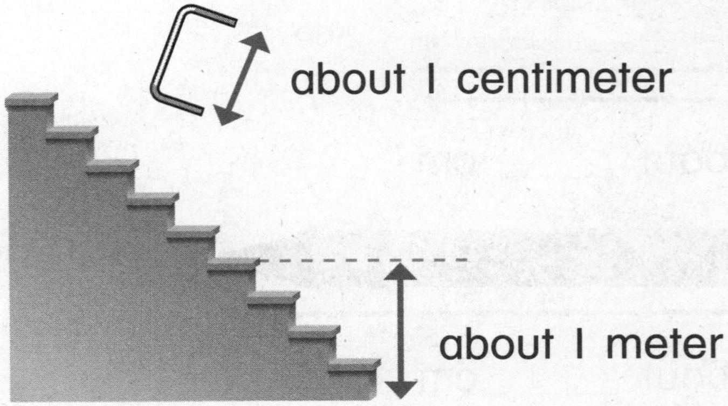

about 1 centimeter

about 1 meter

Circle the picture of the object that is about each length.

9. about 1 centimeter

10. about 1 meter

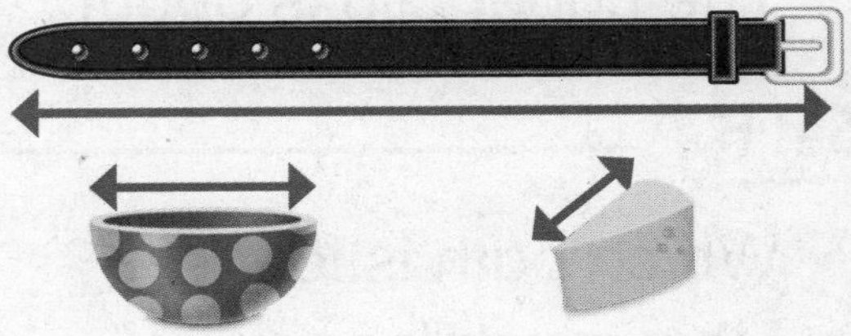

Set F

You can use square units to measure area. Count the square units inside the rectangle to find the area.

_6_ square units

Find the area. Use tiles to help.

11.

_____ square units

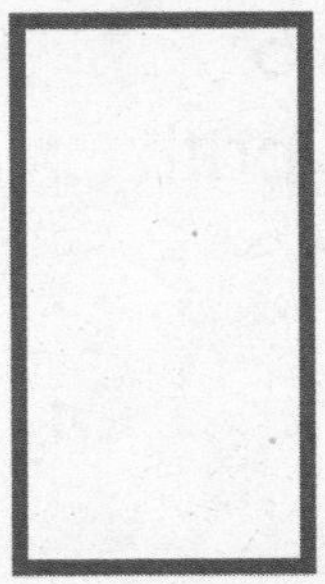

_____ square units   _____ square unit

You can measure the length of an
object to the nearest centimeter.

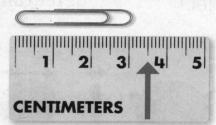

The paper clip is less than halfway
between 3 and 4.
So, use the lesser number.
The paper clip is about ⟍3 cm.

Find an object that is like the one shown.
Use a ruler to measure its length.

12.

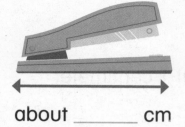

about _____ cm

13.

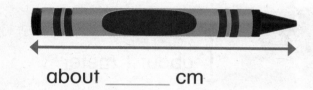

about _____ cm

Set H

Which path is longer?
How much longer?

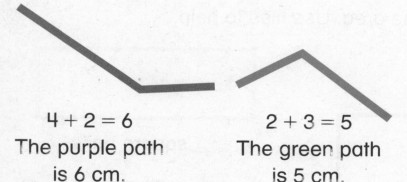

4 + 2 = 6
The purple path
is 6 cm.

2 + 3 = 5
The green path
is 5 cm.

Subtract the lengths to compare.

⟍6 – ⟍5 = ⟍1

The purple path is ⟍1 centimeter longer.

Use a centimeter ruler. Measure
each path.

14. Red path: _____ centimeters

15. Blue path: _____ centimeters

16. Which path is longer? _____

17. How much longer is it?
_____ centimeters longer

790 seven hundred ninety

Name _____

1. A baseball bat is about 1 yard long. Kim uses 3 bats to measure the length of the classroom chalkboard. About how long could the chalkboard be?

3 yards ○   3 inches ○

1 yard ○   1 foot ○

2. Sandy wakes up in the morning at the time shown on the clock. What time does Sandy wake up?

5:12 a.m. ○   6:12 a.m. ○   5:12 p.m. ○   6:12 p.m. ○

3. What is the area of this shape?

3 square units ○   6 square units ○

8 square units ○   9 square units ○

4. The playground at Ben's school has an area of 12 square units. Which shape has the same area?

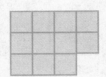 ○   ○

 ○   ○

5. About how long is the flower?

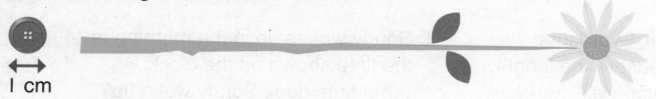

I cm

○ about 1 centimeter   ○ about 15 centimeters   ○ about 5 centimeters   ○ about 1 meter

---

6. Sarah's baseball game starts at the time shown on the clock.
What time does her game start?

4:45

half past 4   quarter past 5
○   ○

quarter past 4   quarter to 5
○   ○

7. About how many centimeters long is the marker?

I cm

16 centimeters   12 centimeters
○   ○

18 centimeters   4 centimeters
○   ○

8. A path has two parts. The total length of the path is 15 cm.
If one part of the path is 9 cm, how long is the other part?

24 cm   15 cm   9 cm   6 cm
○   ○   ○   ○

9. Which unit would you need the fewest of to measure the height of a fence?

Test
Continued

inches   feet
○   ○

yards   all the same
○   ○

10. Which is the best estimate for the width of a window?

I yard   I foot
○   ○

I inch   I cube
○   ○

11. Which line is about 1 centimeter long?

○ ───────────

○ ─────────────

○ ──

○ ▪

12. About how many inches long is this pencil?

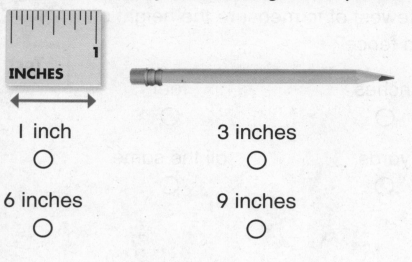

1 inch ○

3 inches ○

6 inches ○

9 inches ○

13. What is the area of this shape?

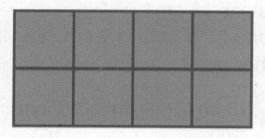

10 square units ○

8 square units ○

6 square units ○

4 square units ○

14. Circle the unit you need fewer of to measure the length of a kitchen.

fewer centimeters   fewer meters

Circle the unit you would need fewer of to measure the length of a table.

fewer feet   fewer yards

15. Draw lines to match each length to the correct object.

1 centimeter   1 meter   20 centimeters

ant   shoe   table

Topic 14

Data

Essential Question: How can bar graphs and pictographs be used to show data and answer questions?

Sometimes, the weather changes quickly.

Scientists can predict the weather.

Wow! Let's do this project and learn more.

Math and Science Project: Five Days of Weather

Find Out Have students select a newspaper or the Internet to find the temperature forecast for the next five days. Then, each day at noon, record whether the actual temperature is lower than the forecast, the same as the forecast, or higher than the forecast.

Journal: Make a Book Draw a picture to show the actual temperatures that you recorded. In your book, also:

• Make a bar graph or pictograph of the temperatures.

• Compare the temperatures that you recorded to the forecasts.

Review What You Know

Vocabulary

1. Circle the number that is 10 **more** than 50.

40   51   60

2. Circle the **tally marks**.

Favorite Toy	
Car	⊥⊥⊥ II
Building Blocks	IIII
Doll	⊥⊥⊥ I

3. Circle the **difference**.

$22 - 9 = 13$

Comparing Numbers

4. A zoo has 45 snakes.
It has 35 spiders.
Compare the snakes
and spiders.
Write > or <.

45 ◯ 35

5.

Picnic Tickets Sold	
Jean	16
Paulo	18
Fatima	12

Who sold the most picnic tickets?

_____

Addition and Subtraction

6. Byron scored 24 points in a game.
Ava scored 16 points in the game.
How many more points than Ava did Byron score?

_____ points

My Word Cards

Study the words on the front of the card.
Complete the activity on the back.

A-Z

bar graph

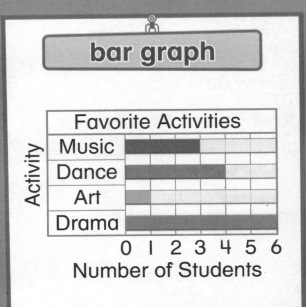

Favorite Activities

Activity: Music, Dance, Art, Drama

Number of Students

data

Favorite Fruit	
Apple	7
Peach	4
Orange	5

pictograph

Favorite Ball Games	
Baseball	⚲⚲
Soccer	⚲⚲⚲⚲⚲⚲⚲⚲
Tennis	⚲⚲⚲⚲

Each ⚲ = 1 student

symbol

The symbol will be ⚲.
Each ⚲ represents
1 student.

predict

There is a pattern in this cube train.
You can predict that the next two cubes will be green and yellow.

My Word Cards

Use what you know to complete the sentences.
Extend learning by writing your own sentence using each word.

A ______________________

uses pictures to show data.

____

are information you collect.

A graph that uses bars to show data is called a

____

______________________.

When you

______________________,

you say what you think will happen.

A character or picture used to represent something is called a

______________________.

Name _____

☆ Solve & Share

This graph shows the number of birthdays in each season for a class.
How can you use this graph to write the number of birthdays in the table? Tell how you know.

TEKS 2.10A Explain that the length of a bar in a bar graph … represents the number of data points for a given category. Also, 2.10, 2.10B, 2.10D. **Mathematical Process Standards** 2.1B, 2.1C, 2.1E, 2.1F.

Digital Resources at SavvasTexas.com

Solve   Learn   Glossary   Check   Tools   Games

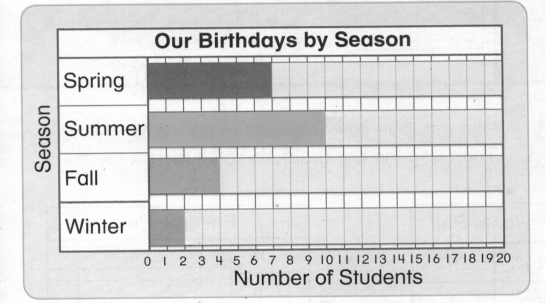

Our Birthdays by Season

Season	
Spring	
Summer	
Fall	
Winter	

Number of Students
0 1 2 3 4 5 6 7 8 9 10 11 12 13 14 15 16 17 18 19 20

Our Birthdays by Season	
Spring	
Summer	
Fall	
Winter	

Use the table to make a **bar graph**.
First, write a title and label the graph.

Favorite Activities

Music	3
Dance	4
Art	1
Drama	6

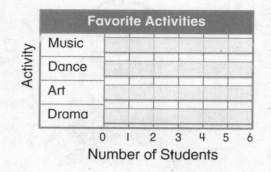

Favorite Activities

Activity: Music, Dance, Art, Drama

Number of Students: 0 1 2 3 4 5 6

Color boxes for each activity to match the **data**.

The bars tell you how many students like each activity.

Favorite Activities

Music	3
Dance	4
Art	1
Drama	6

Favorite Activities

Activity: Music, Dance, Art, Drama

Number of Students: 0 1 2 3 4 5 6

Do You Understand?

Show Me! Which activity did most of the students choose? Explain how you know.

☆ **Guided Practice** ☆ Use the table to complete the bar graph. Then use the bar graph to solve the problems.

Favorite Pet

Cat	4
Dog	6
Bird	2
Turtle	3

Favorite Pet

Pet: Cat, Dog, Bird, Turtle

Number of Students: 0 1 2 3 4 5 6

1. How many students chose cats?

4

2. Which pet did the most students choose?

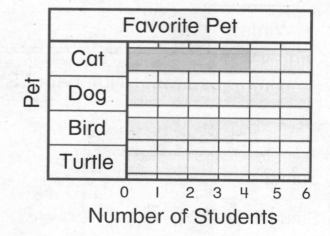

Independent Practice

Use the bar graph to solve the problems.

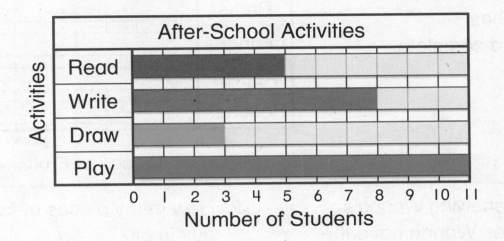

After-School Activities

Activities: Read, Write, Draw, Play

Number of Students

---

3. How many students write after school?

_____

4. Which activity do exactly 5 students do after school? _____

---

5. Which activity do the fewest students do after school? _____

6. How many students do the activity in Exercise 5? _____

---

7. Which activity do the most students do after school? _____

8. How many students do the activity in Exercise 7? _____

---

9. Extend Your Thinking How would the graph be different if 2 students changed their after-school activity from Play to Read?

_____

_____

_____

10. Wanda went to the farm.
She bought 8 pears, 5 oranges,
2 apples, and 9 peaches.
Use this information to complete
the bar graph.

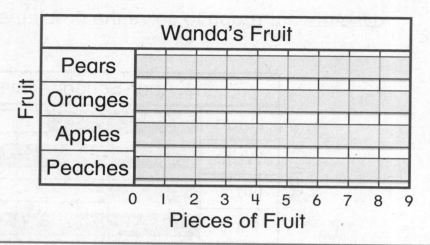

11. Look at the bar graph showing Wanda's fruit. Of which fruit does Wanda have the fewest pieces?

_____

12. How many pieces of fruit did Wanda ⭐ buy in all?

9 ○   15 ○

17 ○   24 ○

13. **Extend Your Thinking** Look at the graph for Exercise 10.
How would the graph change if Wanda bought 3 more pears?

_____

_____

Name _____

Another Look The table shows how students voted to name the class goldfish.

Use the data from the table to make a bar graph.

🏠 **HOME CONNECTION**
Your child used a table and a bar graph to represent data.

HOME ACTIVITY Gather three small groups of objects, such as 3 pens, 4 rubber bands, and 6 buttons. Make a table and a bar graph with your child to show how many of each object you have.

Goldfish Names	
Flash	5
Goldie	3
Rocky	6
Bubbles	8

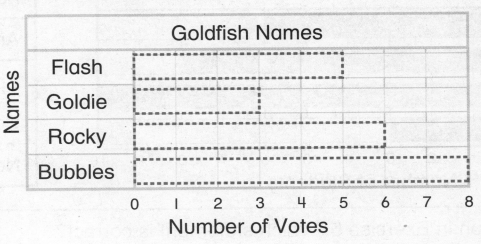

Goldfish Names

Names — Flash, Goldie, Rocky, Bubbles

Number of Votes 0 1 2 3 4 5 6 7 8

Use the bar graph above to solve the problems.

1. How many students voted for the name

   Goldie? _____

2. How many students voted for the name

   Flash? _____

3. Which name did the most students

   vote for? _____

4. Which name did the fewest students

   vote for? _____

Topic 15 | Lesson 1
Digital Resources at SavvasTexas.com
eight hundred three **803**

Use the bar graph to solve the problems.

5. The graph shows one class's favorite kinds of TV shows.
Write the number of students that chose each kind of show in the table.

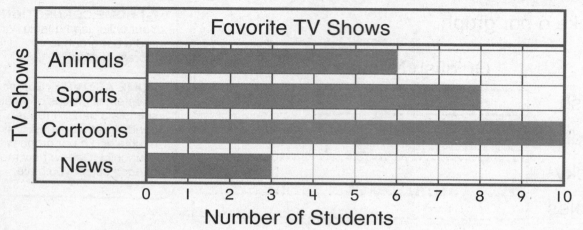

Favorite TV Shows	
Animals	
Sports	
Cartoons	
News	

6. Look at the bar graph in Exercise 5. Which statement is correct?

○ Fewer students chose sports than animals.

○ Fewer students chose sports than news.

○ More students chose news than animals.

○ More students chose cartoons than animals.

7. **Extend Your Thinking** Together, Marla, Derek, and Juan picked a total of 19 apples.
Write the missing numbers in the table and complete the bar graph.

Apple Picking	
Marla	3
Derek	
Juan	

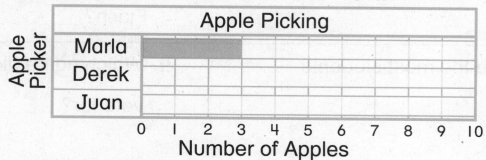

Topic 15 | Lesson 1

Name _____

☆
Solve & Share

This graph shows the favorite subjects for a class. How can you use this graph to write the data in the table? Tell how you know.

⭐ **TEKS 2.10A** Explain that ... the number of pictures in a pictograph represents the number of data points for a given category. Also, 2.10, 2.10B, 2.10D. **Mathematical Process Standards** 2.1B, 2.1D, 2.1E, 2.1F, 2.1G.

Digital Resources at SavvasTexas.com

Solve Learn Glossary Check Tools Games

Each = 1 student

Favorite School Subject	
Reading	
Math	
Science	
Social Studies	

Favorite School Subject	
Reading	
Math	
Science	
Social Studies	

Topic 15 | Lesson 2
Digital Resources at SavvasTexas.com
eight hundred five **805**

The tally chart shows the favorite ball games of Ms. Green's class.

Favorite Ball Games	
Baseball	II
Soccer	卌 III
Tennis	IIII

You can show the same data in another way.

Choose a **symbol** to represent the data.

The symbol will be 🕴. Each 🕴 represents 1 student.

A **pictograph** uses pictures to show data.
You can draw the symbols to show the data.

8 students chose soccer!

Favorite Ball Games	
Baseball	🕴🕴
Soccer	🕴🕴🕴🕴🕴🕴🕴🕴
Tennis	🕴🕴🕴🕴

Each 🕴 = 1 student

Do You Understand?

Show Me! How are the tally chart and pictograph for the favorite ball games of Ms. Green's class alike?

Guided Practice Use the tally chart to complete the pictograph. Then use the pictograph to solve the problems.

Favorite Colors	
Blue	卌
Red	卌 I
Purple	III

Favorite Colors	
Blue	╲ ╲ ╲ ╲ ╲
Red	
Purple	

Each = 1 vote

1. How many students like blue best?

    5

2. Which color is the favorite of most students?

    _____

Name _____

☆
Independent
☆ **Practice**   Use the pictograph to solve the problems.

Favorite Season	
Spring	𝕏 𝕏 𝕏 𝕏
Summer	𝕏 𝕏 𝕏 𝕏 𝕏 𝕏 𝕏 𝕏 𝕏
Fall	𝕏 𝕏 𝕏 𝕏 𝕏 𝕏
Winter	𝕏 𝕏

Each 𝕏 = I vote

3. How many students like fall best? _____

4. Which season do exactly 4 students like best? _____

5. Which season do the fewest students like?
_____

6. How many students like the season with the fewest votes? _____

7. Which season do the most students like?
_____

8. How many students like the season in Exercise 7? _____

9. Extend Your Thinking Look at the pictograph above. How would the graph change if 2 students changed their votes from Summer to Fall?

_____

_____

_____

Problem Solving

Use the tally chart to complete the pictograph. Use the pictograph to solve the problems.

10. Bob made a tally chart to show the trees in a park.

Trees in the Park	
Birch	III
Oak	THL I
Maple	THL
Pine	II

Trees in the Park	
Birch	
Oak	
Maple	
Pine	

Each 🌳 = I tree

How many oak trees are in the park? _____

11. Which type of tree is there the least of in the park?

_____

12. How many birch and maple trees are there in all?

   8   9   II   16
   ○   ○   ○   ○

13. Extend Your Thinking Draw a pictograph to show the data in the table.

Favorite Drink	
Milk	III
Juice	IIII
Water	I

Each 🥤 = I vote

808 eight hundred eight

Name _____

Another Look A pictograph uses pictures or symbols to show information.

Write how many students chose each snack.

There are 9 symbols
for popcorn.
So 9 students chose
popcorn.

🏠 HOME CONNECTION
Your child made pictographs
to represent data.

HOME ACTIVITY Tell
your child which snack
shown in the pictograph
is your favorite. Ask him
or her to explain how the
Favorite Snack pictograph
would change if your
response was added to the
pictograph.

Favorite Snacks	
Popcorn	☺☺☺☺☺☺☺☺☺
Fruit Cups	☺☺☺☺
Yogurt	☺☺☺☺☺☺☺
Cheese and Crackers	☺☺☺☺☺☺☺☺☺☺

9
_____

_____

_____

Each ☺ = I student

Use the pictograph above to solve the problems.

I. How many students like cheese and crackers best?

_____ students

2. How many students like yogurt best?

_____ students

3. Which snack is the least favorite?

_____

4. Which snack is most students' favorite?

_____

Use the pictograph to solve the problems.

5. Denise, Steve, Tom, and Lisa have tickets for rides at the amusement park.
The pictograph shows how many tickets each student has.
Use the pictograph to complete the tally chart.

Tickets We Have	
Denise	TICKET TICKET TICKET TICKET
Steve	TICKET TICKET
Tom	TICKET TICKET TICKET TICKET TICKET TICKET TICKET TICKET TICKET TICKET
Lisa	TICKET TICKET TICKET TICKET TICKET TICKET

Each TICKET = I ticket

Tickets We Have	
Denise	
Steve	
Tom	
Lisa	

6. How many tickets do Lisa and Steve have in all?

6 ○   9 ○

8 ○   21 ○

7. The roller coaster costs 5 tickets.
Who can ride on the roller coaster?

Denise and Steve ○   Steve and Tom ○

Tom and Lisa ○   Lisa and Denise ○

8. **Extend Your Thinking** Write your own story problem about the pictograph and the tally chart for the amusement park tickets.
Give it to a classmate to solve.

_____

_____

_____

810 eight hundred ten

Name _____

Solve & Share

How can you use the data in the table to make a bar graph? Explain to a partner. Complete the bar graph.

TEKS 2.10B Organize a collection of data with up to four categories using pictographs and bar graphs with intervals of one or more. Also, 2.10, 2.10D. **Mathematical Process Standards** 2.1B, 2.1C, 2.1E, 2.1F, 2.1G.

Favorite Meal	
Breakfast	10
Lunch	16
Dinner	14

Digital Resources at SavvasTexas.com

Solve   Learn   Glossary   Check   Tools   Games

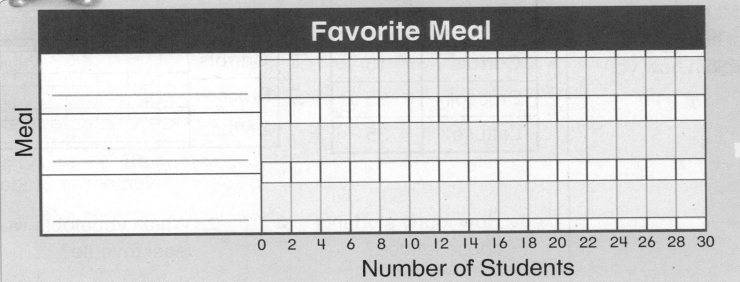

Favorite Meal

Meal

Number of Students

0 2 4 6 8 10 12 14 16 18 20 22 24 26 28 30

This table shows the number of cups of lemonade sold by each student.

What is another way to show this information?

Lemonade Sold	
Gwen	20
Mike	30
Elena	50
Lee	20

You can make a bar graph.

Lemonade Sold

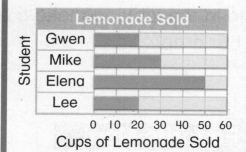

Student

Gwen
Mike
Elena
Lee

0 10 20 30 40 50 60
Cups of Lemonade Sold

You can also make a pictograph.

Lemonade Sold

Gwen	
Mike	
Elena	
Lee	

Each 🥤 = 10 cups sold

You can use either of these graphs to organize the data. Both graphs show the number of cups of lemonade sold.

Do You Understand?

Show Me! Which student sold the fewest cups of lemonade? Explain how you know.

☆ **Guided Practice** ☆ Use the table to make a bar graph. Then use the bar graph to solve the problems.

Favorite Vegetable	
Corn	30
Carrots	15
Broccoli	25
Lettuce	35

Favorite Vegetable

Vegetable

Corn	
Carrots	
Broccoli	
Lettuce	

0 5 10 15 20 25 30 35 40
Number of Students

1. How many students chose lettuce?

35

2. Which vegetable was the least favorite?

_____

Topic 15 | Lesson 3

Name ______________________

Independent Practice

Use the table to make a pictograph.
Then use the pictograph to solve the problems.

Ways to Get to School	
Walk	20
Car	50
Bus	90
Bike	30

Ways to Get to School	
Walk	
Car	
Bus	
Bike	

Each  = 10 students

3. How many students use a bike to get to school? ______

4. Which way do the most students use? ______

5. How many students use the way in Exercise 4? ______

6. Which way do 50 students use? ______

7. Which way do the fewest students use? ______

8. How many students use the way in Exercise 7? ______

9. **Extend Your Thinking** Look at the pictograph for the ways to get to school. If 10 students rode a skateboard to school, how would the pictograph change?

____

____

____

Problem Solving

Use the information about Shawna's collections to complete the bar graph. Then use the bar graph to solve the problems.

10. Shawna collected 18 shells, 8 marbles, 14 cards, and 16 stamps.

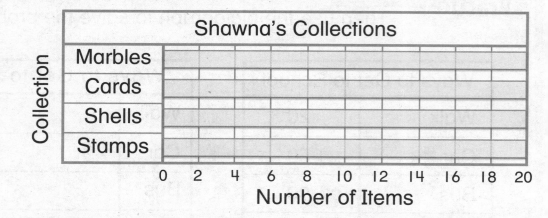

Shawna's Collections

Collection	
Marbles	
Cards	
Shells	
Stamps	

0 2 4 6 8 10 12 14 16 18 20
Number of Items

11. What is the total number of items in all four of Shawna's collections?

____ + ____ + ____ + ____ = ____

12. How many more items are in the largest collection than in the smallest collection?

- ○ 20
- ○ 18
- ○ 10
- ○ 8

13. Extend Your Thinking

Look at the bar graph showing Shawna's collections. Complete the tally chart and the pictograph to show the same data as the bar graph.

Shawna's Collections	
Marbles	
Cards	
Shells	
Stamps	

Shawna's Collections	
Marbles	
Cards	
Shells	
Stamps	

Each ▭ = 2 items

Topic 15 | Lesson 3

Name _____

Another Look Use data in the table to make a bar graph.

Students at Grand School sold tickets to their school play.

Complete the bar graph to show the number of tickets each grade sold.

Tickets Sold to School Play	
Grade 1	80
Grade 2	150
Grade 3	120

🏠 **HOME CONNECTION**
Your child learned how to organize data in different ways, such as making a bar graph or a pictograph.

HOME ACTIVITY Ask your child to explain how he or she used the data about ticket sales to make a bar graph. Then ask your child how he or she could make a pictograph to organize the same data.

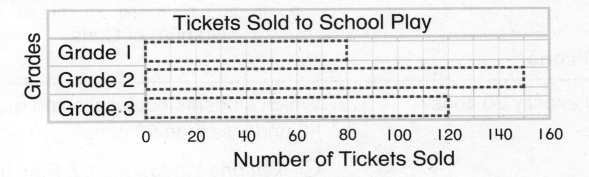

Use the bar graph to solve the problems.

1. How many tickets did Grade 3 sell?

_____

2. How many tickets did Grade 1 sell?

_____

3. Which grade sold the fewest tickets?

_____

4. Which grade sold the most tickets?

_____

Use the pictograph to solve the problems.

5. The pictograph shows how many cans each student collected for recycling. Make a bar graph that shows the same data.

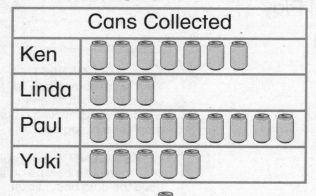

Each 🥫 = 10 cans

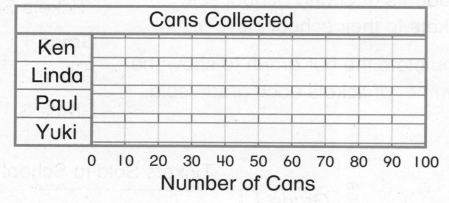

6. Which student collected exactly 30 cans?

_____

7. Which students each collected more than 40 and less than 90 cans?

○ Ken and Linda   ○ Paul and Ken

○ Yuki and Paul   ○ Ken and Yuki

8. **Extend Your Thinking** Write the missing number in the key. Then draw the symbols in the pictograph.

Favorite Home Activity	
Reading Books	12
Coloring Pictures	10
Playing Games	16

Favorite Home Activity	
Reading Books	
Coloring Pictures	☺ ☺ ☺ ☺ ☺
Playing Games	

Each ☺ = ____ students

Name _____

Solve & Share

14 students voted for Turtle as their favorite pond animal.
20 students voted for Frog. 8 students voted for Fish.
Make a pictograph to show the data.
Write two things you notice about the data.

★ TEKS 2.10D Draw conclusions and make predictions from information in a graph. **Mathematical Process Standards** 2.1D, 2.1E, 2.1F, 2.1G.

Digital Resources at SavvasTexas.com

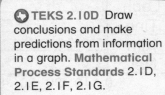
Solve   Learn   Glossary   Check   Tools   Games

Favorite Pond Animals

Turtle	
Frog	
Fish	

Each ★ = 2 votes

1. _____

2. _____

Look at the bar graph about the carnival ticket sales. What does it show?

The length of each bar shows how many tickets were sold.

Carnival Tickets Sold

Name	
Leah	
Tino	
Kim	
Neil	

0 10 20 30 40 50 60
Tickets Sold

Leah sold _20_ tickets.
Tino sold _10_ tickets.
Kim sold _50_ tickets.
Neil sold _40_ tickets.

You can also compare information.

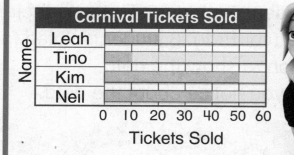

Kim sold the most tickets.

Leah sold more tickets than Tino.

Neil sold fewer tickets than Kim.

Carnival Tickets Sold

Name	
Leah	
Tino	
Kim	
Neil	

0 10 20 30 40 50 60
Tickets Sold

Do You Understand?

Show Me! Look at the graph above. How many more tickets did Kim sell than Neil? How do you know?

☆ **Guided Practice** ☆ Use the bar graph to solve the problems.

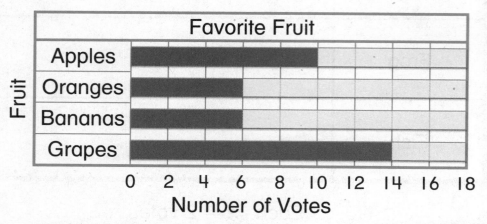

Favorite Fruit

Fruit: Apples, Oranges, Bananas, Grapes

0 2 4 6 8 10 12 14 16 18
Number of Votes

1. How many students voted for Apples? _10_

2. Did more students vote for Apples or Bananas?
_____

3. Which fruit got the most votes? _____

Name _____

Use the bar graph to solve the problems.

4. What do you notice about the number of students who went to the play on Tuesday?

_____

_____

_____

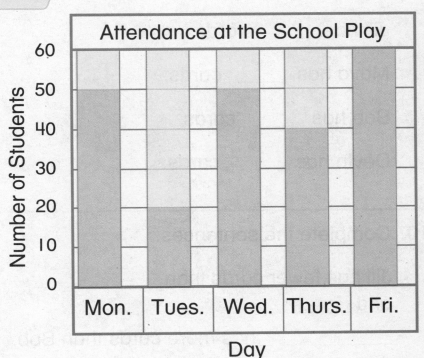

Attendance at the School Play

Number of Students

60
50
40
30
20
10
0

Mon. | Tues. | Wed. | Thurs. | Fri.

Day

5. Did fewer students attend the play on Monday or Friday? How many fewer?

_____

6. On which two days did the same number of students attend the play?

_____

7. Did more students attend the play on Wednesday or Thursday? How many more?

_____

8. Extend Your Thinking Write two different sentences that compare the number of students who attended the play on Friday to the number of students who attended the play on another day.

Sentence 1: _____

Sentence 2: _____

9. Write the number of cards in each student's collection.

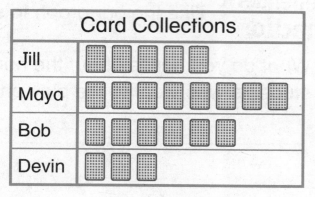

Card Collections	
Jill	
Maya	
Bob	
Devin	

Each ▦ = 10 cards

Jill has _____ cards.

Maya has _____ cards.

Bob has _____ cards.

Devin has _____ cards.

10. Complete the sentences.

Jill has fewer cards than _____
and _____.

_____ has more cards than Bob.

_____ has the fewest cards.

_____ has _____ more cards
than _____.

11. Who has fewer cards than Bob?

- ○ Maya
- ○ Devin and Maya
- ○ Devin and Jill
- ○ Maya and Jill

12. Extend Your Thinking Becky has more cards than Jill but fewer cards than Maya.
Is it possible for Becky to also have fewer cards than Bob? Explain.

_____

_____

_____

Name _____

Another Look You can draw conclusions from data in a graph.

This pictograph shows students' favorite types of fiction.

Write how many students chose each type of fiction.

The key shows how many votes each book stands for. Each book is 5 votes. Use the key to count the number of votes for each type of fiction.

35
25
20
45

Favorite Fiction

Fantasy	📘 📘 📘 📘 📘 📘 📘
Adventure	📘 📘 📘 📘 📘
Science Fiction	📘 📘 📘 📘
Mystery	📘 📘 📘 📘 📘 📘 📘 📘 📘

Each 📘 = 5 votes

Use the pictograph above to answer the questions.

1. Which was the least favorite type of fiction?

_____

2. Which type of fiction did most students vote for? _____

3. Did more students vote for fantasy or adventure? _____

4. If each student voted one time only, how many students voted in all? _____

Use the bar graph to answer the questions.

5. This bar graph shows the number of photos in 4 of Pierre's photo albums.

Which album has the most photos? _____

Does the Sports or People album have fewer photos? _____

How many fewer? _____

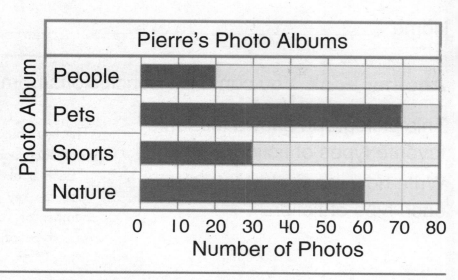

6. Explain something else you notice about the data.

_____

_____

7. ✪ Which album or albums have more photos than the Sports album?

- ○ Pets and Nature
- ○ People and Pets
- ○ Nature and People
- ○ People

8. Extend Your Thinking Look at the pictograph. Write four sentences to compare the number of rainy days in different months.

Rainy Days	
March	☂ ☂ ☂ ☂
April	☂ ☂ ☂ ☂ ☂
May	☂ ☂ ☂ ☂ ☂ ☂
June	☂ ☂ ☂

Each ☂ = 2 days

_____

_____

_____

_____

Solve & Share

This graph shows the total number of baseball cards in Addison's collection for the first four months of the year.

How many more cards do you think he will get in May?

Then how many total cards will he have? Explain.

⭐ **TEKS 2.10D** Draw conclusions and make predictions from information in a graph. **Mathematical Process Standards** 2.1A, 2.1D, 2.1E, 2.1F, 2.1G.

Digital Resources at SavvasTexas.com

Solve Learn Glossary Check Tools Games

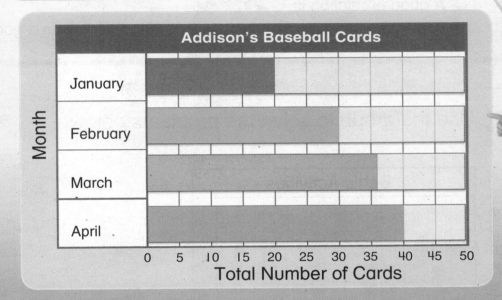

Addison's Baseball Cards

Month: January, February, March, April

Total Number of Cards: 0 5 10 15 20 25 30 35 40 45 50

Number of cards in May: _____

Total cards in collection: _____

_____

_____

Ms. Juarez's class is collecting bottle tops for 4 weeks. After 3 weeks, Adam, Bettina, and Carl made a bar graph to show how many bottle tops they had collected.

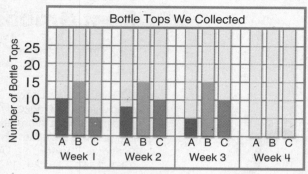

Bottle Tops We Collected

A is Adam B is Bettina C is Carl

How many bottle tops do you **predict** Bettina will collect in Week 4?

Bettina collected 15 bottle tops in Week 1, 15 in Week 2, and 15 in Week 3.

A good prediction is that she will collect 15 bottle tops in Week 4.

How many total bottle tops do you predict the students will collect in 4 weeks?

Week 1: 30 bottle tops
Week 2: about 32 bottle tops
Week 3: 30 bottle tops
Week 4: predict about 30 bott
tops. 30 + 32 + 30 + 30
is about 120.

120 bottle tops is a good prediction.

Do You Understand?

Show Me! Do you predict that Adam will collect more bottle tops or fewer bottle tops in Week 4 than in Week 3? Explain.

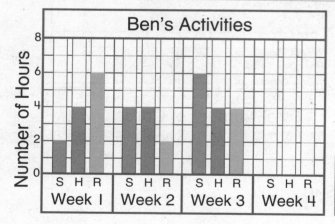

Ben's Activities

S is Sports
H is Homework
R is Reading

1. Which activity do you predict Ben will do most in Week 4?  Sports

2. How many hours in all do you predict Ben will spend on homework in 4 weeks?
_____ hours

Name _____

Use the graph to solve the problems.

3. How many blue T-shirts do you predict the store will sell in Week 4? _____

4. How many more gray T-shirts do you predict will be sold in Week 4 than in Week 3? _____

5. How many gray T-shirts in all do you predict the store will sell in all 4 weeks? _____

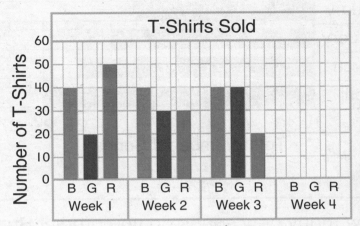

T-Shirts Sold

B is Blue
G is Gray
R is Red

6. Do you predict that the store will sell more blue T-shirts than gray T-shirts in Week 4? Explain.

_____

_____

_____

7. Which color T-shirt do you predict will have the fewest sales in Week 4? Explain.

_____

_____

_____

8. **Extend Your Thinking** If your predictions in Exercises 3–7 are correct, will the store sell more than 500 T-shirts in 4 weeks? Explain.

_____

_____

Problem Solving
Use the graph to solve the problems below.

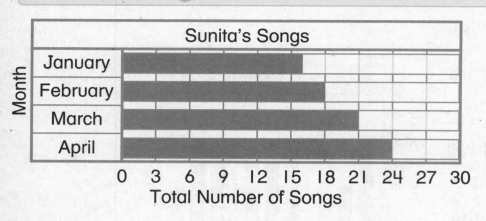

Sunita's Songs

Month	Total Number of Songs
January	
February	
March	
April	

0 3 6 9 12 15 18 21 24 27 30
Total Number of Songs

9. Sunita gets new songs for her music player every month. This graph shows the total number of songs on Sunita's music player for four months.

Sunita gets _____ new songs in February.

Sunita gets _____ new songs in March.

Sunita gets _____ new songs in April.

10. How many new songs do you predict Sunita will get in May? Explain.

_____ songs

_____

_____

11. ⭐ Which is the best prediction for the total number of songs Sunita will have on her music player in June?

20 ○   25 ○

24 ○   30 ○

12. **Extend Your Thinking** If your predictions in Exercises 10 and 11 are correct, what is a good prediction for the total number of songs on Sunita's music player in September? Explain.

_____ songs

_____

_____

Name _____

Another Look You can make predictions from a graph.

Andre did 5 sit-ups on Day 1, 10 on Day 2, and 15 on Day 3. A good prediction is that he will do ⟨20⟩ sit-ups on Day 4.

Blanca did 20 sit-ups on Day 1, 15 on Day 2, and 10 on Day 3. A good prediction is that she will do ⟨5⟩ sit-ups on Day 4.

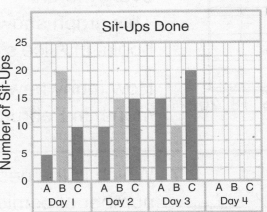

Sit-Ups Done

Number of Sit-Ups

A B C / A B C / A B C / A B C
Day 1 / Day 2 / Day 3 / Day 4

A is Andre
B is Blanca
C is Cam

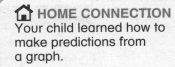
Andre does 5 more sit-ups each day.

Blanca does 5 fewer sit-ups each day.

HOME CONNECTION
Your child learned how to make predictions from a graph.

HOME ACTIVITY With your child, record the number of minutes he or she does homework each day for 3 days. Make a bar graph to show the data. Ask your child to use the graph to predict the number of minutes he or she will do homework on Day 4.

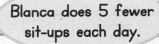
Use the graph above to make predictions and solve the problems.

1. How many more sit-ups does Cam do each day?

_____

2. How many sit-ups do you predict Cam will do on Day 4?

_____

3. How many sit-ups do you predict Andre will do in all 4 days?

_____

4. Who do you predict will do the most sit-ups in all in 4 days?

_____

Use the graph to solve the problems below.

5. Alice buys new comic books for her collection every month.

This graph shows the total number of comic books in Alice's collection for four months.

How many new comic books did Alice buy each month in February, March, and April? _____

6. How many comic books do you predict Alice will buy in May?

_____ comic books

7. Which is the best prediction for the total number of comic books that Alice will have in her collection in June?

12
○

18
○

14
○

20
○

8. Extend Your Thinking If your predictions for Exercises 6 and 7 are correct, in what month will Alice have 20 comic books in her collection? Explain.

Alice will have 20 comic books in _____.

_____

_____

Name _____

Solve & Share

Make a pictograph to show how many connecting cubes, counters, and ones cubes you have. Then write and solve a problem about your data.

⭐ TEKS 2.1E Create and use representations to … communicate mathematical ideas.
TEKS 2.10C Write and solve one-step word problems … using data represented within pictographs and bar graphs with intervals of one. **Mathematical Process Standards 2.1, 2.1B, 2.1D, 2.1F.**

Digital Resources at SavvasTexas.com

Solve   Learn   Glossary   Check   Tools   Games

Math Tools	
Connecting Cubes	
Counters	
Ones Cubes	

Each _____ = I math tool

_____

_____

Analyze

You can use the data to write and solve problems.

How many more stamps does Lara have than Gail?

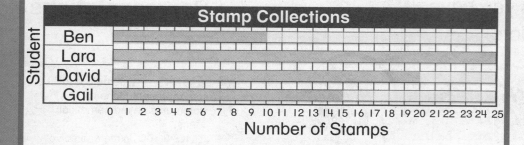

Stamp Collections

Student: Ben, Lara, David, Gail

Number of Stamps: 0 1 2 3 4 5 6 7 8 9 10 11 12 13 14 15 16 17 18 19 20 21 22 23 24 25

Plan and Solve

Lara has 25 stamps. Gail has 15 stamps. $25 - 15 = 10$

Lara has 10 more stamps than Gail.

Justify and Evaluate

I checked my answer by reading the graph again. I also checked the subtraction.

Do You Understand?

Show Me! Can you use the graph to tell how many stamps Ben and David have in all? Explain.

Guided Practice

Use the graph to write and solve problems.

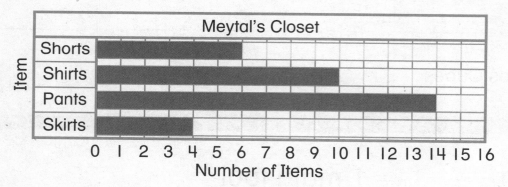

Meytal's Closet

Item: Shorts, Shirts, Pants, Skirts

Number of Items: 0 1 2 3 4 5 6 7 8 9 10 11 12 13 14 15 16

1. How many shirts and skirts are there in all?

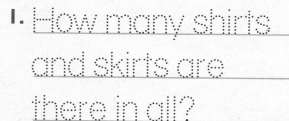

$10 \;(+)\; 4 = 14$

2.

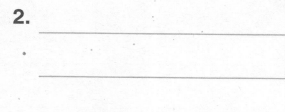

$\bigcirc \underline{} = \underline{}$

830 eight hundred thirty

Topic 15 | Lesson 6

Independent Practice

Use the bar graph to write and solve problems.

3. _____

_____

_____

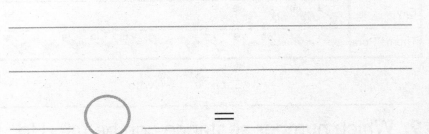

_____ ◯ _____ = _____

4. _____

_____

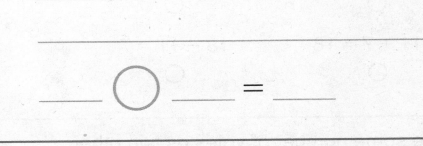

_____ ◯ _____ = _____

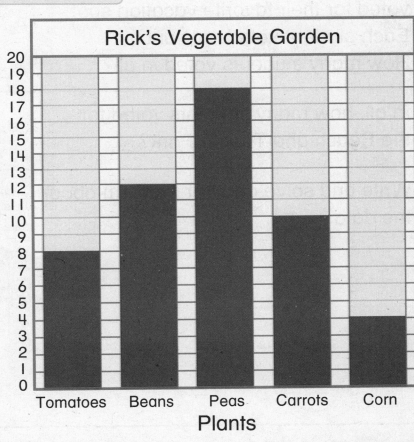

Rick's Vegetable Garden

Number of Plants

Tomatoes   Beans   Peas   Carrots   Corn

Plants

5. **Extend Your Thinking** Rick wants 20 of each type of plant in his garden.
How many more of each type of plant does Rick need?
How many new plants does Rick need in all?

Tomatoes _____   Beans _____   Peas _____   Carrots _____   Corn _____

Rick will add _____ new plants in all.

Problem Solving
Use the pictograph to solve the problems below.

6. This graph shows how many students voted for their favorite vacation spot. Each student voted only once. How many students voted in all? _____

7. In all, how many students voted for the Beach and Theme Park? _____

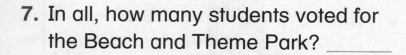

Favorite Vacation Spot	
Beach	✔✔✔✔✔✔✔✔✔✔✔
Mountains	✔✔✔✔✔✔✔
City	✔✔✔
Theme Park	✔✔✔✔✔✔✔✔✔✔✔✔

Each ✔ = 1 vote

8. Write and solve another problem about the data.

_____

_____

_____ ◯ _____ = _____

9. Which number sentence can be used to find how many more students voted for the Beach than the Mountains?

$7 + 7 = 14$ ◯

$11 - 7 = 4$ ◯

$11 + 7 = 18$ ◯

$18 - 11 = 7$ ◯

10. Extend Your Thinking One vacation spot has the same number of votes as two other vacation spots combined. Write the missing vacation spots below.

_____ has the same number of votes as _____ and _____ combined.

Explain how you solved the problem.

_____

Name _____

Another Look You can use the data to write and solve problems.

How many more votes did the Tigers get than the Lions?

🏠 **HOME CONNECTION**
Your child used bar graphs and pictographs to write and solve problems.

HOME ACTIVITY Look at the pictograph for team names together. Ask your child to find how many more votes there are for Wolves and Lions combined than there are for Tigers. Have your child explain how to find the answer.

Votes for Team Name	
Wolves	🧍🧍🧍🧍🧍
Tigers	🧍🧍🧍🧍🧍🧍🧍🧍🧍🧍
Lions	🧍🧍🧍🧍🧍🧍🧍🧍

Each 🧍 = I vote

Count the symbols for the votes for Tigers and Lions on the pictograph. Then subtract.

Tigers __10__   Lions __8__

__10__ − __8__ = __2__

The Tigers got __2__ more votes than the Lions.

Write and solve problems about the data in the pictograph above.

I. _____

_____

___ ◯ ___ = ___

2. _____

_____

___ ◯ ___ = ___

Use the bar graph to solve the problems.

Game Choices

Game	
Kickball	
Hide-and-Seek	
Tag	
T-ball	
Badminton	

0 1 2 3 4 5 6 7 8 9 10 11 12 13 14 15 16 17 18 19 20
Number of Students

3. How many more students chose Hide-and-Seek than Tag?

_____ students

4. How many students in all chose Kickball, Tag, and Badminton?

_____ students

5. ☆ How many fewer students chose Tag and Badminton combined than Hide-and-Seek?

   3
   ○

   4
   ○

   11
   ○

   12
   ○

6. ☆ Which two games were chosen by 28 students in all?

○ Kickball, Hide-and-Seek

○ Hide-and-Seek, Tag

○ Tag, T-ball

○ Badminton, Hide-and-Seek

7. Extend Your Thinking Use the data in the bar graph to write a problem about the students' game choices. Then solve your problem and explain your solution.

_____

_____

_____

Name _____

Build a necklace for a buddy! Then **make a graph** and **analyze** information about the beads.

1. Describe the shapes of the beads.

_____

_____

Draw the beads on the cord in any way you like.
Use 12 beads in all.

2. Write the shapes you used in the table. Write how many you used of each.

Shape of Bead	How Many

3. Show your bead data in a bar graph.

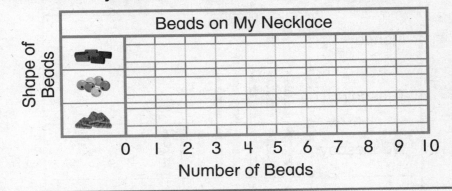

4. Sue will make a necklace to donate to charity. She will use two more of each bead shape than you used. How many beads will Sue use in all? Explain.

_____

_____

_____

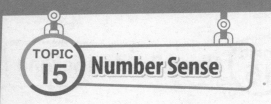

Data Sense

1. Kyle is learning Spanish.
   Each day he learns new words.
   The pictograph shows his progress so far.

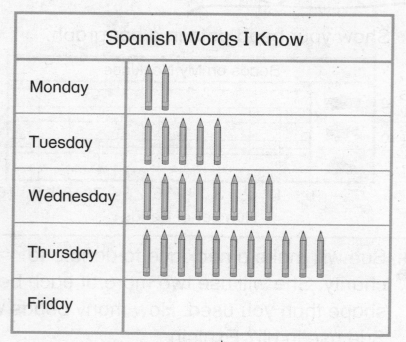

Spanish Words I Know	
Monday	✏️✏️
Tuesday	✏️✏️✏️✏️
Wednesday	✏️✏️✏️✏️✏️✏️
Thursday	✏️✏️✏️✏️✏️✏️✏️✏️
Friday	

Each ✏️ = 2 words

Predict how many words Kyle will know on Friday and Saturday.

Friday _____

Saturday _____

What's Wrong?

2. Look at Exercise 1. Tom says Kyle learned 7 new words on Tuesday. Is Tom correct? Explain.

Calendar Challenge

3. A calendar is a special type of table.

February						
Sun.	Mon.	Tu.	Wed.	Th.	Fri.	Sat.
1	2	3	4	5	6	7
8	9	10	11	12	13	14
15	16	17	18	19	20	21
22	23	24	25	26	27	28

Which two dates in one row have a sum of 27? _____

Which three dates in one row have a sum of 75? _____

Set A

You can make a bar graph to show data in a table.

Students voted for their favorite nut. The table shows the votes.

Favorite Nut	
Peanut	7
Almond	4
Cashew	5

Color one space for each vote in the bar graph.
Then use the graph to solve the problem.

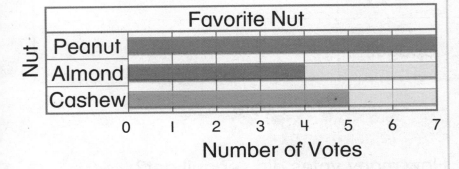

How many votes did almond get? 4

Use the table to complete the bar graph.
Then use the graph to solve the problems.

Favorite Yogurt	
Strawberry	3
Vanilla	7
Banana	6

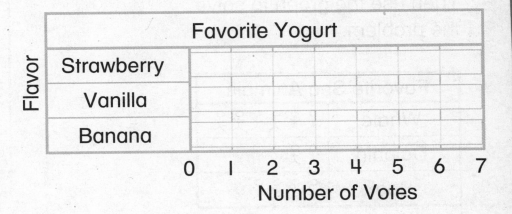

1. How many students voted for banana?

_____

2. Which flavor had the most votes?

_____

You can use a tally chart to show data in a pictograph.

Favorite Sea Animals	
Whale	|||||	
Dolphin	||
Seal	||||

Show the number of symbols in the pictograph.

Each ♀ stands for 1 vote.

Then use the graph to solve the problem.

Favorite Sea Animals	
Whale	♀♀♀♀♀♀
Dolphin	♀♀
Seal	♀♀♀♀

♀ = 1 vote

Which sea animal had the fewest votes?

dolphin

Use the tally chart to complete the pictograph.
Then use the pictograph to solve the problems.

Favorite Birds	
Blue Jay	|||||
Robin	||||| |||
Seagull	||||| |||||

Favorite Birds	
Blue Jay	
Robin	
Seagull	

🐦 = 1 vote

3. How many votes did seagull get?

_____

4. Which bird had the fewest votes?

_____

Set C _____

You can draw conclusions by looking at data in a graph.

The bar for tomato soup is taller than the bar for bean soup.

__More__ students voted for tomato soup than bean soup.

There are __more__ votes for tomato soup.

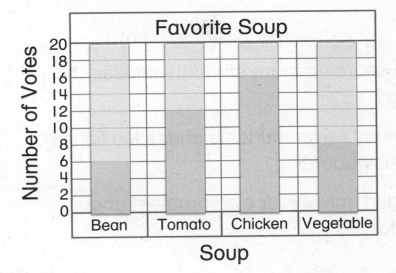

Did more people choose tomato soup or chicken soup? __chicken__

Which soup got fewer votes than vegetable soup? __bean__

Use the pictograph to solve the problems.

Trees in the Orchard	
Apple	🌳🌳🌳
Pear	🌳🌳
Peach	🌳🌳🌳🌳🌳
Cherry	🌳🌳🌳🌳

Each 🌳 = 10 trees

5. How many peach trees are there? _____

6. How many pear trees are there? _____

7. Are there more apple trees or cherry trees?

_____

8. The orchard has the fewest number of which kind of tree? _____

You can use the data in a graph to write and solve problems.

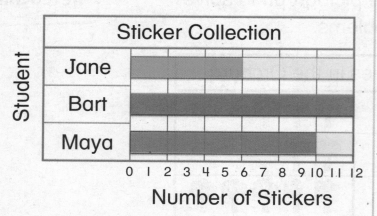

Sticker Collection

Student: Jane, Bart, Maya

Number of Stickers: 0 1 2 3 4 5 6 7 8 9 10 11 12

How many more stickers does Bart have than Jane?

Bart has __12__ stickers.

Jane has __6__ stickers.

__12__ – __6__ = __6__

Bart has __6__ more stickers than Jane.

Use the pictograph to solve the problems.

Favorite Winter Sport	
Skiing	❄❄❄❄❄❄❄
Snowboarding	❄❄❄❄❄❄❄❄❄
Skating	❄❄❄❄❄❄❄❄
Ice Fishing	❄❄❄❄

Each ❄ = 1 vote

9. Which sport did more students choose than skating? _____

10. How many fewer students chose ice fishing than snowboarding? _____

11. Write and solve your own problem about the data.

_____

_____

____ ◯ ____ = ____

Name _____

1. How many coins are in Pam's collection?

○ 9

○ 10

○ 11

○ 12

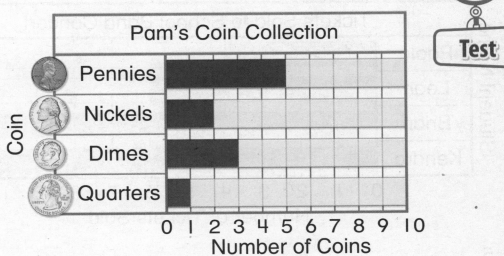

2. Which sentence about the pictograph is correct?

Favorite Sport	
Soccer	👤 👤
Baseball	👤 👤 👤 👤
Swimming	👤

Each 👤 = 2 votes

○ More students voted for Soccer than Baseball.

○ More students voted for Baseball than Soccer.

○ Fewer students voted for Baseball than Swimming.

○ Fewer students voted for Soccer than Swimming.

3. How many more tickets did Kendra sell than Leon?

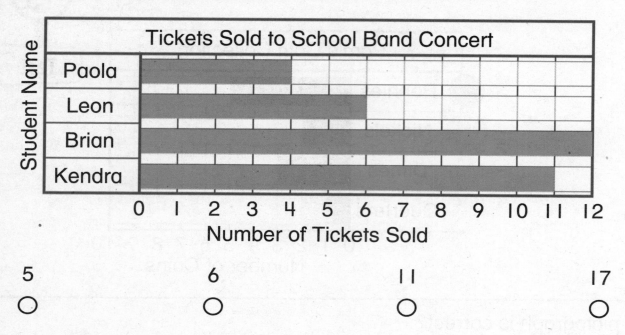

5 ⚪

6 ⚪

11 ⚪

17 ⚪

---

4. How many campers chose Swimming as their favorite activity?

⚪ 5

⚪ 10

⚪ 25

⚪ 50

Favorite Camp Activity	
Crafts	🧍🧍🧍
Swimming	🧍🧍🧍🧍🧍
Archery	🧍🧍
Tennis	🧍🧍🧍🧍🧍🧍

Each 🧍 = 5 campers

5. Scott is making a pictograph from the tally chart.
How many symbols should he draw in the bottom row?

Favorite Fruit	
Apple	IIII
Banana	⧍⧍⧍⧍ I
Pear	I
Orange	⧍⧍⧍⧍

Favorite Fruit	
Apple	☺ ☺ ☺ ☺
Banana	☺ ☺ ☺ ☺ ☺ ☺
Pear	☺
Orange	

Each ☺ = I student

3   4   5   6
○   ○   ○   ○

6. Marisol gets new stamps every month.
This graph shows the total number of stamps in
Marisol's collection for four months.
Which is the *best* prediction for how many
new stamps Marisol will get in August?

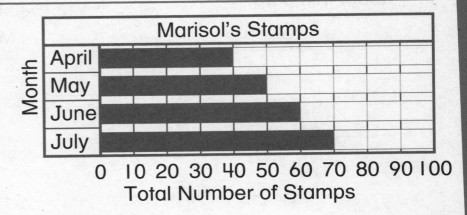

10   30   40   80
○   ○   ○   ○

7. Use the tally chart to complete the pictograph.
Then use the pictograph to solve the problems.

Favorite Flower	
Rose	ⅢⅢ I
Daisy	III
Tulip	ⅢⅢ
Lily	ⅢⅢ III

Favorite Flower	
Rose	
Daisy	
Tulip	
Lily	

Each 🌹 = 1 vote

How many students voted for Lily? _____

Which flower is the least favorite? _____

8. Write and solve your own problem about this data.

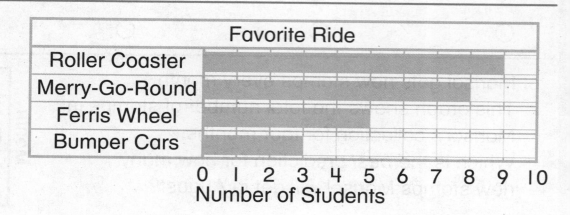

_____

_____

_____

_____ ◯ _____ = _____

Topic 15

Personal Financial Literacy

Essential Question: What are ways to use money?

This dog is drinking the water it needs.

Water is one of the things animals and plants need to live and grow.

Wow! Let's do this project and learn more.

Math and Science Project: Basic Needs

Find Out Talk to friends and relatives about their pets or plants. Find out how the pets or plants get what they need. Think about how much this might cost.

Journal: Make a Book Show what you found out in your book. In your book, also:

• List the parts of the plants or animals that help them get what they need.

• Make up and solve math stories about spending money to look after a pet.

Name _____

Review What You Know

Vocabulary

1. Circle the **dollar** sign.

¢   ÷ $(ⓢ)

2. Circle the **cent** sign.

(ⓒ) $ ×

3. Circle to show who has **more** money.

Tim has 85¢.   Joe has (97¢.)

Multiplication and Division

4. Complete each sentence.

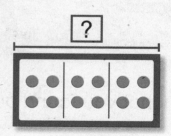

$4 + 4 + 4 =$ _____

$3 × 4 =$ _____

5. Mike has 6 apples.
He eats 2 apples each day.
How many days can he eat 2 apples until they are all gone?

_____ days

Money

6. Ryan has these coins.
How much money does Ryan have?

61

My Word Cards

Study the words on the front of the card.
Complete the activity on the back.

A-Z

spend

save

lend

borrow

responsible

irresponsible

My Word Cards

When you give someone money or an item that will be returned, you

_____

something to that person.

If you

_____

your money, you will have more money.

If you

_____

your money, you will have less money.

When you are given something to use for a certain amount of time and you do not return it, you are being

_____

When you are given something to use for a certain amount of time and you return it when you are done, you are being

_____.

When you

_____

money or an item, it needs to be returned when you are done.

My Word Cards

Study the words on the front of the card.
Complete the activity on the back.

A-Z

deposit

withdrawal

producer

The Vase Company

producer

consumer

consumer

My Word Cards

Use what you know to complete the sentences.
Extend learning by writing your own sentence using each word.

When you make something to sell, you are a

_____.

When you take money out of a bank, you are making a

_____.

When you put money into a bank, you are making a

_____.

When you buy something, you are a

_____.

Name _____

Solve & Share

How are these activities alike?
How are they different?
Sort the activities into two groups.
Explain how you sorted them.

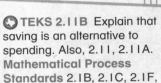

TEKS 2.11B Explain that saving is an alternative to spending. Also, 2.11, 2.11A. Mathematical Process Standards 2.1B, 2.1C, 2.1F, 2.1G.

TICKET BOOTH

LEMONADE

$ Bank $

I won't play that game. I'll keep my dollar.

When you get money, you can **spend** it or **save** it.

 Or

If you spend money, you will have less money.

I had 40¢. I spent 20¢ for a bottle of juice. Now I have 20¢ left.

$$40¢ - 20¢ = 20¢$$

If you save money, you will have more money.

I had 25¢. I earned 25¢ for walking a dog. I saved this money. Now I have 50¢!

$$25¢ + 25¢ = 50¢$$

If you save money for a long time, you will have a greater amount of money.

I saved $1 each week for 5 weeks. $1 + $1 + $1 + $1 + $1 = $5 Now I have $5!

Do You Understand?

Show Me! Steve had $5. Then he spent some money on lunch. Does Steve have more than $5 or less than $5 now? Explain.

☆ Guided Practice ☆

Circle **spend** or **save** for each picture.

1.

spend (save)

2.

spend   save

852 eight hundred fifty-two

Topic 16 | Lesson 1

Name _____

Read each problem. Circle **spend** or **save**.
Then solve the problem.

3. Tyler had 13¢.
Now he has 20¢.
Did Tyler spend or save?
How much did he spend or save?

spend   (**save**)

_____ ¢

4. Luz had $50.
Now she has $15.
Did Luz spend or save?
How much did she spend or save?

spend   **save**

$ _____

5. Linda had 74¢.
Now she has 50¢.
Did Linda spend or save?
How much did she spend or save?

spend   **save**

_____ ¢

6. Manuel had $29.
Now he has $46.
Did Manuel spend or save?
How much did he spend or save?

spend   **save**

$ _____

7. Extend Your Thinking Solve the problem.
Write or draw a picture to show how you solved it.

Debbie saved a dime each week for 4 weeks.
Gary saved a nickel each week for 7 weeks.
Who saved more money? How much more?

_____ saved more money.   _____ ¢ more

Problem Solving Solve each problem.

8. Michael saved 58¢ in April.
He saved 32¢ in May.
How much money did Michael save
in both months?

_____

9. Donna had 84¢.
Now she has 50¢.
Did Donna spend or save?
How much did Donna spend or save?

Saved 34¢ ○   Spent 34¢ ○

Saved 44¢ ○   Spent 44¢ ○

10. Extend Your Thinking Abby had 34¢. She spent 13¢ on a pencil. Then Abby earned 65¢.
She decided to save it. Write a number sentence to show how much money Abby has now.

_____ ¢ − _____ ¢ + _____ ¢ = _____ ¢

11. Extend Your Thinking Write or draw a picture to show an example of spending money.
Write or draw a picture to show an example of saving money.

Spend Money   Save Money

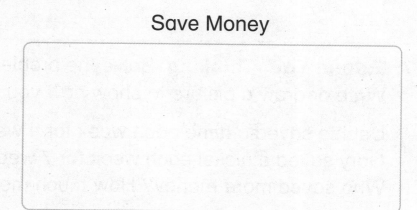

Name _____

Another Look You can save or spend money.

Sarah had 40¢. Now she has 60¢.
Did Sarah spend or save?
How much did Sarah spend or save?

Sarah has more money now. Sarah saved money!

🏠 **HOME CONNECTION**
Your child solved problems about saving and spending money.

HOME ACTIVITY Ask your child to solve this problem: Cindy had 20¢. Then she earned 45¢ and decided to save it. How much money does Cindy have now? You can use coins to solve the problem.

<u>40¢</u> + <u>20¢</u> = <u>60¢</u>

Sarah <u>saved 20</u> ¢.

Read each problem. Circle **spend** or **save**.
Then solve the problem.

1. Ruth had 25¢.
   Now she has 75¢.
   Did Ruth spend or save?
   How much did she spend or save?

   spend   **save**

   _____ ¢

2. Paco had $33.
   Now he has $15.
   Did Paco spend or save?
   How much did he spend or save?

   spend   **save**

   $ _____

Solve each problem.

3. Libby earned $12 mowing lawns. She saved part of the money and spent part of the money. The amounts that she saved and spent were the same.

How much did Libby save?

$ _____

How much did Libby spend?

$ _____

4. Manuel spent $10 for three lunches. One of his lunches cost $4. The other two lunches cost the same amount. How much did each of the other lunches cost?

$6 ○ $4 ○

$3 ○ $2 ○

5. Karen saved $14 less than Phillip. Karen saved $51. How much did Phillip save?

$37 ○ $51 ○

$55 ○ $65 ○

6. **Extend Your Thinking** Paul took the money from his two pockets and put it in his bank. He saved a total of 75¢. Paul had these coins in one pocket.

Draw the coins Paul could have had in his other pocket.

Name _____

Solve & Share

Anna saved 12¢ in Week 1, 8¢ in Week 2, 26¢ in Week 3, and 10¢ in Week 4.
How much did she save in all 4 weeks?
Show how you found your answer.

⭐ TEKS 2.11A Calculate how money saved can accumulate into a larger amount over time. Also, 2.10C, 2.11. Mathematical Process Standards 2.1B, 2.1D, 2.1E.

Digital Resources at SavvasTexas.com

Solve Learn Glossary Check Tools Games

_____ ¢

Jorge made a bar graph to show the money he saved for 6 months.

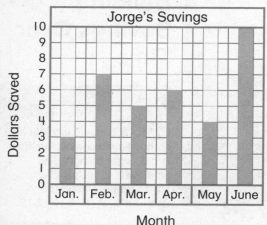

Jorge's Savings

How much money did Jorge save in 6 months?

Add the first 3 months. Then add the next 3 months.

$3 + $7 + $5 = $15
January February March

$6 + $4 + $10 = $20
April   May   June

$15 + $20 = $35

Add the totals. He saved $35 in 6 months!

How much more money does Jorge have at the end of June than at the end of January?

Subtract the amount he saved in January from the total amount he saved in all 6 months.

$35 − $3 = $32
Jorge has $32 more at the end of June.

Guided Practice

Use the bar graph above to solve each problem.

Do You Understand?

Show Me! Why was the total amount of Jorge's savings greater by June than by February?

1. In which month did Jorge save the greatest amount of money?

    June

   In which month did Jorge save the least amount of money?

   _____

2. How much more money did Jorge save in June than in January?
   Write a number sentence to solve.

   $_____ − $_____ = $_____

   $_____ more

Topic 16 | Lesson 2

Independent Practice

Use the bar graph to solve each problem.

3. How much money did Sharon save in all 6 months? Show your work.

$ _____

Sharon's Savings

Month		Dollars Saved
July		(bar to 9)
Aug.		(bar to 8)
Sept.		(bar to 10)
Oct.		(bar to 2)
Nov.		(bar to 12)
Dec.		(bar to 9)

0 1 2 3 4 5 6 7 8 9 10 11 12

Dollars Saved

4. How much more did Sharon save in November than in July? Write a number sentence to solve.

$_____ – $_____ = $_____

$_____ more

5. How much money did Sharon save in all during July and August? Write a number sentence to solve.

$_____ + $_____ = $_____

$_____ in all

6. Extend Your Thinking How much more were Sharon's total savings in July, August, and September than her total savings in October, November, and December? Show your work.

$_____ more

Problem Solving Solve each problem.

7. Joe saved $23 by walking dogs. Rosa saved $15 by raking leaves.
How much more money did Joe save than Rosa?

$_____ more

8. Adam saved money for three months. During the first two months, he saved $14. After three months, he had saved $23. How much money did Adam save in the third month?

$7 ⭕ $9 ⭕ $10 ⭕ $14 ⭕

9. Felipe saved $25.
Felipe saved $12 more than Katie.
How much money did Katie save?

Katie saved $_____ .

Think: Do I add or subtract the amount?

10. **Extend Your Thinking** Judy saved $8 each week for 3 weeks. Moe saved $4 each week for 6 weeks. Who saved more money? Explain.

_____

_____

_____

_____

Name _____

Another Look You can use a table to show saving money over time.

Jaime used this table to show the amount of money he saved in each of 5 weeks.
He saved 10¢ more in Week 5 than in Week 4.
How much money did Jaime save in Week 5?

Write a number sentence to solve the problem.

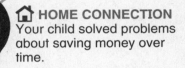

🏠 **HOME CONNECTION**
Your child solved problems about saving money over time.

HOME ACTIVITY Ask your child to solve this problem: Devon saved $12 in January and $8 in February. How much did he save in both months?

Week	Amount Saved
1	23¢
2	14¢
3	30¢
4	12¢
5	22¢

12¢ + 10¢ = 22 ¢

Jaime saved 22 ¢ in Week 5.

Use the table above to solve each problem.

1. In which week did Jaime save the greatest amount of money?

   Week _____

   In which week did he save the least amount of money?

   Week _____

2. How much money did Jaime save in all during Weeks 1 and 2?
   Write a number sentence to solve.

   _____¢ + _____¢ = _____¢

   _____¢ in all

3. Trevor saved money in May and June.
He saved $14 in June.
He has a total of $20 saved.
How much money did Trevor save in May?

$_____

4. Samantha wants to buy a bike for $60.
She has already saved $42.
Samantha saves $6 each week. In how many weeks will she be able to buy the bike?

6 weeks ○   5 weeks ○

4 weeks ○   3 weeks ○

5. Julio saved $15 during three months.
He saved the same amount of money each month.
Fill in the table to show the amount of money Julio saved in each of the three months.

Month	Amount Saved
June	$_____
July	$_____
August	$_____

6. Extend Your Thinking On Monday, Samantha saved these coins in her piggy bank.

On Tuesday, Samantha saved the same amount of money in her bank. She used 6 coins. Draw the coins that Samantha could have put in her bank on Tuesday.

Name _____

Solve & Share

The pictures in each column show different situations. Draw a line to match each situation in Column 1 with one that is similar in Column 2.

Explain how you made your matches.

⊕ TEKS 2.11E Identify examples of lending and use concepts of benefits and costs to evaluate lending decisions. Also, 2.11. **Mathematical Process Standards** 2.1A, 2.1D, 2.1F, 2.1G.

Digital Resources at SavvasTexas.com

Solve Learn Glossary Check Tools Games

Column 1

Column 2

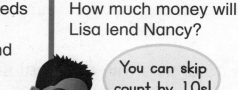

When you give someone money or an object that will be returned, you **lend** something to that person.

Lisa has 70¢. She needs 35¢ to buy a pen. Lisa also wants to lend Nancy money to buy 3 bookmarks.

10¢

How much money will Lisa lend Nancy?

You can skip count by 10s!

10¢   20¢   30¢

Lisa will lend Nancy 30¢.

Lisa started with 70¢, and she lent Nancy 30¢. Lisa has 40¢ left.

Lisa helped Nancy and Lisa still has enough money to buy a pen. Lending money was a good idea for Lisa.

Do You Understand?

Show Me! Deanna had $2 to pay for her lunch. She lent Lila $2 to buy a notebook. Do you think that it was a good idea for Deanna to lend Lila money? Explain.

⭐ **Guided Practice** ⭐ Draw a circle around the picture that shows lending. Draw an **X** over the picture that does not show lending.

I.

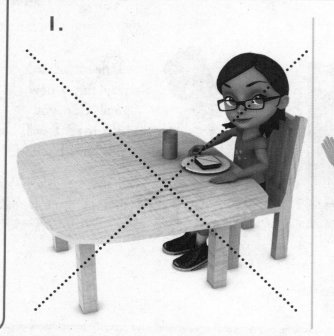

2.

I need a marker. Do you have one that I could use?

You can use this marker. Can you give it back to me tomorrow?

Name _____

Solve each problem.

3. Shawn lent his sister 15¢ on Saturday and 25¢ on Sunday.
What is the total amount that Shawn lent his sister on both days?

_____ ¢

4. Paco lent Mary 1 half-dollar, 1 quarter, and 2 dimes.
How much money did Paco lend Mary?

_____ ¢

5. Jason had 85¢.
Then he lent Gary 37¢ to buy milk.
How much money does Jason have left?

_____ ¢

6. Debbie lent Sally 50¢.
She gave her 4 coins.
One of the coins was a quarter.
What were the other 3 coins?

_____

Extend Your Thinking Give an example of a situation in which it is a good idea to lend something.

7. Describe the situation.

_____

_____

8. Tell why the situation in Exercise 7 is a good idea.

_____

_____

Solve each problem.

9. Maria lent her friend 56¢. Circle the coins that she could have lent.

10. Jin had 95¢ on Monday.
He lent Sam 27¢ on Tuesday.
How much did Jin have left?

_____ ¢

11. Jennifer lent a total of 75¢ to two of her friends.
She lent one friend 5¢ more than the other friend.
How much did Jennifer lend her friends?

30¢ and 35¢ ○   35¢ and 35¢ ○

30¢ and 45¢ ○   35¢ and 40¢ ○

12. Extend Your Thinking Describe a situation in which you think it would be a bad idea to lend money or an object to someone.

_____

_____

_____

Name _____

Another Look You can use coins to solve problems about lending money.

Keisha lent Joel just enough money to buy a folder and a pencil.
How much money did Keisha lend to Joel?

Use coins to show the price of each item.
Then count on to find the total cost.

School Supply Store

Folder: 10¢
Pencil: 12¢
Pen: 25¢
Eraser: 5¢

🏠 HOME CONNECTION
Your child solved problems about lending money.

HOME ACTIVITY Ask your child to draw pictures to show you the coins he or she could use to lend someone 40¢.

<u>10</u> <u>20</u> <u>21</u> <u>22</u>

<u>22</u>

Put the coins in order from greatest value to least value.

Keisha lent Joel <u>22</u> ¢.

Use coins and the chart above to solve each problem.

1. Sandy lent Mary just enough money to buy 3 pens.
How much money did Sandy lend to Mary?

_____ ¢

2. Linda lent Jim just enough money to buy 2 folders and 2 erasers.
How much money did Linda lend to Jim?

_____ ¢

3. Kiana had these coins. Then she lent her sister 15¢.

How much money does Kiana have left?

_____ ¢

4. Tammy lent her brother 45¢. She lent her sister 28¢. How much more money did she lend to her brother?

73¢ ○   27¢ ○

25¢ ○   17¢ ○

5. Dave lent Sarah 15¢ less than he lent Tim. Dave lent Sarah 50¢. How much money did Dave lend Tim?

35¢ ○   40¢ ○

65¢ ○   75¢ ○

6. Extend Your Thinking Sue lent a classmate her favorite stuffed animal for 6 months. Do you think this was a good idea? Explain.

_____

_____

_____

_____

868 eight hundred sixty-eight

Name ____________________

Solve & Share

In the first box, draw or write about a time when you used something that belonged to someone else.

In the second box, draw or write about a time when you let someone else use something that belonged to you.

Lesson 16-4
Borrowing Money

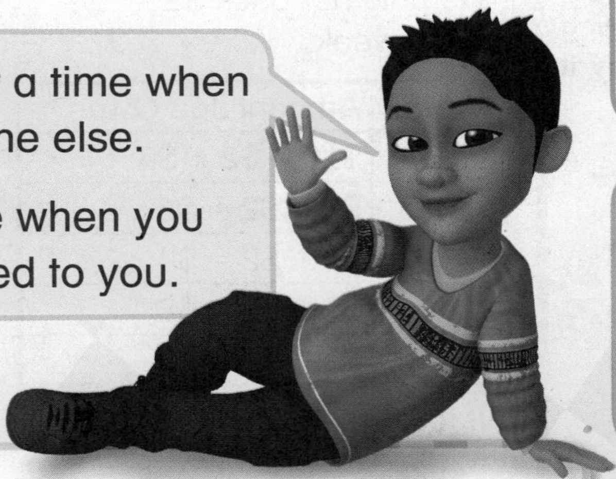

TEKS 2.11D Identify examples of borrowing and distinguish between responsible and irresponsible borrowing. Also, 2.11. **Mathematical Process Standards** 2.1C, 2.1F, 2.1G.

Digital Resources at SavvasTexas.com

Solve | Learn | Glossary | Check | Tools | Games

When you borrow money or an object, you are being responsible when you pay it back or return it.

Joe borrowed $10 from Mia. He paid her back $2 each week.

Week	Amount Joe Owes
1	$10 − $2 = $8
2	$8 − $2 = $6
3	$6 − $2 = $4
4	$4 − $2 = $2
5	$2 − $2 = $0

It took Joe 5 weeks to pay Mia back.

When you borrow money or an object, you are being irresponsible if you do not pay it back or return it.

Tara borrowed $10 from Lamar. She said she would pay back $2 each week.

Week	Amount Tara Owes
1	$10 − $1 = $9
2	$9 − $0 = $9
3	$9 − $2 = $7
4	$7 − $0 = $7
5	$7 − $1 = $6

After 5 weeks, Tara still owes Lamar $6.

Do You Understand?

Show Me! What is the difference between borrowing an object and getting a gift?

⭐ **Guided Practice** ⭐ Draw a circle around the picture that shows borrowing. Draw an **X** over the picture that does not show borrowing.

1.

Can I have $1 to buy a book? I will pay you back tomorrow.

Here is $1.

2.

Name _____

☆ **Independent** ☆ **Practice**   Solve each problem.

3. Tina borrowed 1 quarter, 2 dimes, and a nickel from Louis.
How much money did Tina borrow?

_____ ¢

4. Amanda borrowed $15 from Kim. She has paid back $6. How much money does Amanda still owe Kim?

_____

5. Dylan borrowed 25¢ on Wednesday and 40¢ on Thursday.
How much did Dylan borrow on both days?

_____ ¢

6. Raul borrowed 4 coins from his brother. One of the coins is a half-dollar. He borrowed a total of 86¢. What other coins did Raul borrow?

_____

Extend Your Thinking Tell whether each situation describes responsible or irresponsible borrowing. Circle **responsible** or **irresponsible**. Explain.

7. Dustin borrows a book from the library. He returns the book two days early.

responsible   **irresponsible**

_____

_____

8. Sharon borrows a book from the library. She returns the book five days late.

responsible   **irresponsible**

_____

_____

Topic 16 | Lesson 4   eight hundred seventy-one **871**

Problem Solving Solve each problem.

9. Doug had these coins. Then his sister paid him back 45¢ that she had borrowed.

Doug now has _____ ¢

10. Michelle borrowed 50¢ from Ryan. She paid him back equal amounts on Friday and Saturday. But Michelle still owes Ryan 20¢. How much did Michelle pay Ryan back on Friday?

30¢ ○   25¢ ○   15¢ ○   10¢ ○

Extend Your Thinking Andy and Ali borrowed some money. They both said they would pay the money back in 3 months. Complete each table.

11. Andy borrowed $15 from Connie.

Month	Amount Andy Owes	
April	$15 − $5	= $____
May	$____ − $5	= $____
June	$____ − $____	= $0

12. Do you think Andy was a **responsible** or an **irresponsible** borrower? Explain.

_____

_____

13. Ali borrowed $20 from Michael.

Month	Amount Ali Owes	
April	$20 − $4	= $____
May	$____ − $0	= $____
June	$____ − $____	= $14

14. Do you think Ali was a **responsible** or an **irresponsible** borrower? Explain.

_____

_____

872 eight hundred seventy-two

Topic 16 | Lesson 4

Name _____

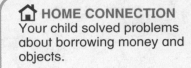
Another Look You can use coins to solve problems about borrowing money.

Ray borrowed 25¢ to buy an apple and 30¢ to buy a granola bar. How much money did Ray borrow in all?

Show each amount that Ray borrowed using coins.
Then count on to show the total amount that Ray borrowed.

25 ¢   50 ¢   55 ¢

Ray borrowed a total of 55 ¢.

> Ray will pay back the money that he borrowed.

🏠 **HOME CONNECTION**
Your child solved problems about borrowing money and objects.

HOME ACTIVITY Ask your child to tell you how much money someone would still owe if he or she had borrowed $20 and then paid back $12.

> Use coins to solve each problem.

1. Nadine borrowed 45¢ to buy breakfast on Monday. She borrowed 35¢ to buy juice on Tuesday.
How much money did Nadine borrow in all on both days?

_____ ¢

2. Terry borrowed 1 quarter and 3 dimes from Grace. The next day, Terry paid back 20¢ to Grace.
How much money does Terry still owe Grace?

_____ ¢

3. Joyce borrowed 75¢ from Patrick. Circle the coins that Joyce could have borrowed from Patrick.

4. Mickey borrowed equal amounts of money for milk on Wednesday, Thursday, and Friday. He borrowed 60¢ in all. How much money did Mickey borrow each day?

10¢ ○

20¢ ○

30¢ ○

40¢ ○

Extend Your Thinking Solve each problem.

5. Describe a situation in which you think a person is being **responsible** when borrowing money or an object.

_____

_____

_____

_____

6. Describe a situation in which you think a person is being **irresponsible** when borrowing money or an object.

_____

_____

_____

_____

Name _____

Solve & Share

Jane had $123 in the bank.
She went back to the bank and now she has $131 in the bank.

What did Jane do at the bank? Show how you know.

TEKS 2.11C Distinguish between a deposit and a withdrawal. **Mathematical Process Standards** 2.1A, 2.1F, 2.1G.

Digital Resources at SavvasTexas.com

Solve   Learn   Glossary   Check   Tools   Games

Jane's Money

When you put money into a bank, it is called a deposit. When you take money out of a bank, it is called a withdrawal.

Malinda had $189 in the bank.
Now she has $164 in the bank.

Did Malinda make a deposit or a withdrawal?
By how much did her amount of money change?

$189 − $164 = $25

Malinda has $25 less now.
She made a withdrawal.

Al had $157 in the bank.
Now he has $168 in the bank.

Did Al make a deposit or a withdrawal?
By how much did his amount of money change?

$157 + $11 = $168

Al has $11 more now. He made a deposit.

Do You Understand?

Show Me! Do you have more or less money in a bank after making a withdrawal?

Do you have more or less money after making a deposit?

Guided Practice

Write a number sentence to solve each problem. Then circle **deposit** or **withdrawal**.

1. Sasha had $58 in the bank.
She went to the bank and put in $24.
How much money does Sasha have in the bank now?

$58 + $24 = $82

$82

(**deposit**)

Sasha made a _____ .

withdrawal

2. Matt had $75 in the bank.
He went to the bank and took out $21.
How much money does Matt have in the bank now?

$____ − $____ = $____

$____

deposit

Matt made a _____ .

withdrawal

Independent Practice

Write a number sentence to solve each problem.
Then circle **deposit** or **withdrawal**.

3. Ricardo had $150 in the bank.
Now he has $132 in the bank.
By how much did his amount of
money change?

$_____ ◯ $_____ = $_____

Ricardo's amount of money changed
by $_____.
deposit

Ricardo made a _____.
withdrawal

4. Patty had $114 in the bank.
Now she has $159 in the bank.
By how much did her amount
of money change?

$_____ ◯ $_____ = $_____

Patty's amount of money changed
by $_____.
deposit

Patty made a _____.
withdrawal

5. **Extend Your Thinking** Solve the problem.
Show how you solved it.

Carmen had $112 in the bank. Then she
made a deposit of $53.
A day later, she made a withdrawal of $25.
How much money does Carmen have in
the bank now?

$_____

Problem Solving Solve each problem.

6. Caitlin made a withdrawal from the bank on Saturday that was $20 more than the withdrawal she made on Friday. Caitlin made a withdrawal of $35 on Saturday. What was the amount of Caitlin's withdrawal on Friday?

$_____

7. Kevin made a deposit of $120 on Wednesday and a deposit of $53 on Thursday.
How much larger was his deposit on Wednesday than on Thursday?

$67 $73 $106 $173
○   ○   ○   ○

8. Lucy had $73 in the bank. Then she made two deposits of $20 each.
How much money does she have in the bank now?
Write a number sentence to solve.

$_____ + $_____ = $_____

$_____

The next day, Lucy made a withdrawal of $25.
How much money does she have in the bank now?
Write a number sentence to solve.

$_____ − $_____ = $_____

$_____

9. Extend Your Thinking Write and solve a problem about making a deposit or a withdrawal at a bank.

Decide how much money you have at first.

Name _____

Another Look You can use addition and subtraction to solve problems about **deposits** and **withdrawals**.

Regroup if you need to!

Sophie had $57 in the bank.
She made a deposit of $29.
How much money does she
have in the bank now?

$57
+ $29
$86

$86

Bart had $92 in the bank.
He made a withdrawal of $27.
How much money does he
have in the bank now?

8 12
$92
- $27
$65

$65

🏠 **HOME CONNECTION**
Your child solved problems
about making deposits and
withdrawals at a bank.

HOME ACTIVITY Ask your
child to solve this problem:
Christopher had $49 in the
bank. Then he made a deposit
of $30. How much money
does Christopher have in the
bank now?

Add or subtract to solve each problem.
Show how you solved it.

1. Jenny had $105 in the
   bank. She made a deposit
   of $66.
   How much money does
   she have in the bank now?

   $_____

2. Luke had $137 in
   the bank. He made a
   withdrawal of $45.
   How much money does
   he have in the bank now?

   $_____

3. Dave made a $60 deposit on Tuesday. He deposited $15 more on Tuesday than he did on Monday. How much did Dave deposit on Monday?

$_____

4. ⭐ Lily had $83 in the bank. Then she made two deposits of the same amount. Lily now has $103 in the bank. How much was each deposit?

$20	$15	$10	$5
○	○	○	○

5. Extend Your Thinking Keisha had $139 in the bank. Then she made the deposits and withdrawals shown in the table. Complete the table.

Day	Deposit or Withdrawal	Amount of Money in Bank
Monday	Deposit of $14	$139 + $14 = $____
Tuesday	Deposit of $25	$____ + $____ = $____
Wednesday	Withdrawal of $30	$____ − $____ = $____
Thursday	Deposit of $55	$____ + $____ = $____
Friday	Withdrawal of $20	$____ − $____ = $____

How much more money did Keisha have in the bank on Friday than she had on Tuesday?
Write a number sentence to solve.

$_____ − $_____ = $_____

$_____ more

Check the amounts in the table above.

Name _____

Solve & Share

Look at each pair of pictures.
Write a story about each pair.
How is something being made? How is something being used? Explain.

TOY FACTORY

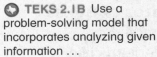

🌐 **TEKS 2.1B** Use a problem-solving model that incorporates analyzing given information . . .
TEKS 2.11F Differentiate between producers and consumers and calculate the cost to produce . . .
Mathematical Process Standards 2.1A, 2.1C, 2.1E, 2.1G.

Digital Resources at SavvasTexas.com

Solve   Learn   Glossary   Check   Tools   Games

Analyze

Raul makes and sells gift boxes.

Tina wants to buy a large box with ribbon and beads.

How much will it cost Raul to make this box for Tina?

Gift Box Materials

Sizes of Boxes	Decorations
Small: 5¢	Ribbon: 15¢ each
Medium: 15¢	Package of Stickers: 10¢
Large: 25¢	Package of Beads: 5¢

When you make something, you are a producer. When you buy or use something, you are a consumer.

Plan and Solve

Add together the costs of the items Raul will use.

25¢ + 15¢ + 5¢ = 45¢

It will cost Raul 45¢ to make the large box.

The prices for all of the materials are included in the total cost!

Justify and Evaluate

Raul made the box. Raul is a producer.

Tina bought the box. Tina is a consumer.

Raul is also a consumer because he bought materials!

Do You Understand?

Show Me! Name something that you could use as a consumer. Name something that you could make as a producer.

☆ Guided Practice ☆

Draw a circle around the picture that shows a **producer**. Underline the picture that shows a **consumer**.

1.

The Vase Company

2.

Name _____

Independent Practice

Write a number sentence to solve each problem. Then circle the word that tells whether the problem describes a **producer** or a **consumer**.

3. Stanley bought a cup of soup for 75¢ and a slice of bread for 20¢. How much did he spend in all?

_____¢ ◯ _____¢ = _____¢

_____¢

Stanley is a **producer** **consumer** .

4. Maria grew 32 daisies and 15 tulips in her garden. How many more daisies did she grow than tulips?

_____ ◯ _____ = _____

_____ more daisies

Maria is a **producer** **consumer** .

5. Tony is decorating a card. He spent 52¢ on glue and 29¢ on beads. How much did he spend in all?

_____¢ ◯ _____¢ = _____¢

Tony spent _____¢ in all.

Tony is a **producer** **consumer** .

6. Extend Your Thinking Betty Ann is painting a picture. Explain how she is both a **producer** and a **consumer**.

_____

_____

_____

_____

_____

_____

Problem Solving
Solve the problems below.

7. Ray made some toy cars.
The wheels cost $30. The paint costs $14.
The other materials cost $25.
How much did Ray spend to make the toy cars?

$_____

8. Kayla is knitting scarves for presents.
She spent the same amount on blue yarn as she spent on purple yarn.
Kayla spent $16 in all.
How much did she spend on purple yarn?

$4 ○ $12 ○

$8 ○ $16 ○

Extend Your Thinking Write an addition or subtraction problem for each situation.
Ask a friend to solve each problem.

9. Write a problem about someone using something or being a **consumer**.

_____

_____

_____

10. Write a problem about someone making something or being a **producer**.

_____

_____

_____

Another Look You can find examples of **producers** and **consumers**.

Jane is making some bracelets. She spent $17 on beads and $10 on string.
What is the total cost for Jane to make the bracelets?

Write a number sentence to solve the problem.

$ _17_ + $ _10_ = $ _27_

$ _27_

> Jane made bracelets, so she is a producer. Jane bought materials to make the bracelets, so she is also a consumer.

> Solve the problems.
> Then circle the problem that shows a producer.

1. Mary has $75.
   She spends $28 to buy a hat.
   How much money does Mary have left?

   $_____ − $_____ = $_____

   $_____

2. Robert is making a poster. He spent 35¢ for a poster board. He spent 27¢ for a marker to write on the poster.
   How much did Robert spend to make the poster?

   _____ ¢ + _____ ¢ = _____ ¢

   _____ ¢

3. Lindy had 87¢. Then she bought paper to make cards. Now Lindy has 51¢. How much did she spend on paper?

_____ ¢

4. ⭐ Derrick is making a toy airplane. He spent 55¢ on paint. He spent 10¢ less on paint than on glue. How much did Derrick spend on glue?

○ 65¢   ○ 55¢   ○ 45¢   ○ 35¢

Enrique's class is making and selling picture frames. Use the lists to solve each problem.

Size of Frames	Decorations
Small: 20¢	Piece of Yarn: 3¢
Large: 30¢	Package of Buttons: 10¢
	Bows: 5¢ each

5. Janet made a large picture frame. She used a package of buttons and 2 pieces of yarn to decorate her frame. How much did it cost to make Janet's picture frame? _____ ¢

6. Dean has 50¢. He wants to make a small picture frame and decorate it with 3 bows and 2 packages of buttons. Does Dean have enough money? Explain.

_____

_____

7. **Extend Your Thinking** Write your own problem about making a picture frame. Ask a friend to solve your problem.

_____

_____

Name _____

Think about how you can **connect** problems about money to things you learned earlier this year.

I. The pictograph shows Mila's first three deposits in the bank.

Explain how saving is different than spending. Then, show how much Mila deposited in December.

_____

_____

_____

Mila's Savings	
October	$ $ $ $
November	$ $ $ $ $ $
December	$ $ $ $

Each $ = 5 dollars

2. Describe a situation in which it would be a good idea for Mila to lend money. Explain.

_____

_____

_____

_____

3. Circle the situation that shows Allison borrowing money from Krista.

Krista gave Allison $2 as a gift.

Krista and Allison saved $2 each week for 4 weeks.

Allison asked for and got $2 from Krista. Allison will pay back 50¢ each week.

What Number Am I?

1. Solve each number puzzle.
   Write the letter for the number
   to spell a word.

   K = 1,200   T = 1,000   N = 900

   B = 950   A = 1,100   E = 1,050

   I am a 3-digit number.
   All my digits are different. _____

   I have the same tens and ones.
   I am 100 more than T. _____

   I have the same tens and ones.
   I am 100 less than T. _____

   You can make me with
   1,000 + 100 + 100. _____

   Write the letters in order to
   spell the word. _____

What's Wrong?

2. Mara says these are all examples of
   lending. Circle the examples of lending.
   Put an X on the examples where Mara is
   wrong.

   Ben let Julie use his umbrella for the
   afternoon.

   Tom bought his mom a gift for $10.

   Maria gave Bill $5 to be paid back by
   Monday.

   Chris shared his pizza with Pat.

3. Which lending example involves money?

   _____

   _____

Name _____

Set A

Reteaching

You can use a table to keep track of your money.

Day	Amount Saved
1	15¢
2	12¢
3	21¢
4	19¢

How much did you save in all on Day 1 and Day 2?

_15_ ¢ + _12_ ¢ = _27_ ¢

On Day _2_ you saved the
least amount of money.

Use the table to solve the problems.

Week	Amount Saved
1	11¢
2	19¢
3	26¢
4	9¢

1. How much money did you save in all in Week 3 and Week 4?

_____ ¢ ◯ _____ ¢ = _____ ¢

2. In which week did you save the greatest amount of money?
Week _____

Set B

When you _lend_ money to someone, that person should pay you back.

Lending money is a good idea when they pay you back. You help someone and get your money back.

Solve the problem on another piece of paper.

3. Make up your own story about when it would be a bad idea to lend someone something. Tell what was lent and why it was a bad idea.

Topic 16

eight hundred eighty-nine **889**

You can be ___responsible___ by returning an item you borrowed.

It is ___irresponsible___ to return an item late or not return an item at all.

Jo borrows Tom's bat. When the game ends, Jo gives the bat back to Tom.

Circle: (responsible)   irresponsible

Dan borrowed 50¢ from Zoe.
Later, Dan gave Zoe 20¢.
How much does Dan still owe Zoe?

___50___ ¢ − ___20___ ¢ = ___30___ ¢

Circle **responsible** or **irresponsible**.
Write a number sentence and solve.

4. Sam wanted to buy a headband and asked to borrow 75¢ from Vicky. Sam forgot to pay Vicky back.

Circle: responsible   irresponsible

5. Jon borrowed 71¢ from Kim.
Two days later, Jon borrowed 19¢ more.
How much did Jon borrow in all?

_____ ¢ ◯ _____ ¢ = _____ ¢

When you add money to the bank, you make a ___deposit___.

When you take money out of the bank, you make a ___withdrawal___.

Tori had $39 in the bank.
Now she has $101 in the bank.

Circle: (deposit)   withdrawal

By how much did her amount change?

$___101___ − $___39___ = $___62___

Circle **deposit** or **withdrawal**. Write a number sentence to solve.

6. Matthew had $193 in the bank.
Now he has $91 in the bank.

Circle: deposit   withdrawal

By how much did Matthew's amount of money change?

$_____ ◯ $_____ = $_____

Name _____

1. On Friday, Nathaniel had 63¢.
   On Monday, he had 48¢.
   Did Nathaniel spend or save?
   How much did he spend or save?

Saved 18¢ ○   Spent 18¢ ○

Saved 15¢ ○   Spent 15¢ ○

Use the bar graph to solve the problems.

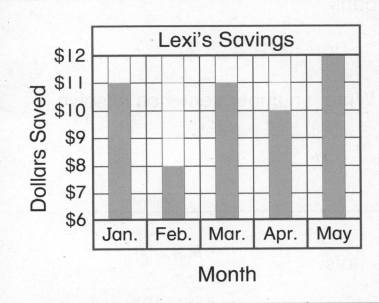

Lexi's Savings

Dollars Saved / Month

2. In which month did Lexi save the greatest amount of money?

May ○   April ○   March ○   February ○

---

3. How much money did Lexi save in all during January and February?

$7 ○ $14 ○ $19 ○ $20 ○

---

4. Which is an example of lending?

○ Suzie let Luke use her pencil.

○ Amari's mom fixed his breakfast.

○ John bought milk after school.

○ Maria gave Jamie a game.

5. Maggie lent two of her friends the same amount of money. She lent them a total of 90¢. How much money did Maggie lend to each friend?

25¢ ○   45¢ ○   35¢ ○   55¢ ○

6. Which is an example of **responsible** borrowing?

○ Jamie borrowed $2 from Shane to buy a game. Six months later, Jamie remembered that she had to pay Shane back.

○ Noel borrowed $6 from Kathy and paid her back $1 each day for six days.

○ Jose borrowed $4 from Lisa on Tuesday. On Wednesday, Jose borrowed 3 more dollars.

○ Rob borrowed $8 from Jim. After two months, Rob has not paid Jim any money back.

---

7. Angelica had $168 in the bank. Now she has $71 in the bank.
Did Angelica make a deposit or a withdrawal?

deposit   **withdrawal**

By how much did Angelica's amount of money change? Write a number sentence to solve.

$_____ ◯ $_____ = $_____

Angelica's amount of money changed by $_____.

---

8. Cher is knitting and selling hats for a craft fair.
She buys blue yarn and two knitting needles to make the hats.
How much did Cher spend to make the hats? _____
Is Cher a producer or a consumer? Explain your thinking.

Materials
Blue yarn 12¢
Yellow yarn 12¢
Red yarn 12¢
Knitting needle 40¢

_____

_____

_____

Here's a preview of next year. These lessons help you step up to Grade 3.

Step Up to Grade 3

Lessons

TEKS 3.2A Compose and decompose numbers up to 100,000 as a sum of so many ten thousands, so many thousands, so many hundreds, so many tens, and so many ones using objects, pictorial models, and numbers, including expanded notation as appropriate.

TEKS 3.2D Compare and order whole numbers up to 100,000 and represent comparisons using the symbols >, <, or =.

TEKS 3.3A Represent fractions greater than zero and less than or equal to one with denominators of 2, 3, 4, 6, and 8 using concrete objects and pictorial models, including strip diagrams and number lines.

TEKS 3.3C Explain that the unit fraction $\frac{1}{b}$ represents the quantity formed by one part of a whole that has been partitioned into b equal parts where b is a non-zero whole number.

TEKS 3.4A Solve with fluency one-step and two-step problems involving addition and subtraction within 1,000 using strategies based on place value, properties of operations, and the relationship between addition and subtraction.

The following Grade 3 TEKS are introduced in the Step-Up Lessons.

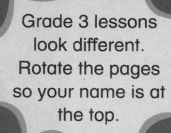

Grade 3 lessons look different. Rotate the pages so your name is at the top.

Lesson 1
Representing Numbers

TEKS 3.2A Compose and decompose numbers up to 100,000 as a sum of so many ten thousands, so many thousands, so many hundreds, so many tens, and so many ones using objects, pictorial models, and numbers, including expanded notation as appropriate. Also, 3.2. Mathematical Process Standards 3.1B, 3.1C, 3.1D, 3.1E

Digital Resources at SavvasTexas.com

Solve · Learn · Glossary · Tools · Games

Name _____

Solve & Share

Use place-value blocks to show 274.
Then, record three different ways you can write 274.

You can create and use representations. You can represent 274 many ways. *Show your work in the space below!*

Look Back!

Tools What other tools could you use to show 274?

A

All numbers are made from the digits 0, 1, 2, 3, 4, 5, 6, 7, 8, and 9.

Place value is the value of the place a digit has in a number.

This camel weighs 1,350 pounds.

Did you know a two-humped camel weighs between 1,000 and 1,450 pounds?

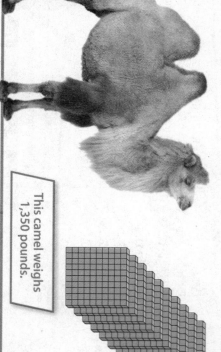

=

B

You can show 1,350 in different ways.

You can use place-value blocks.

1 thousand   3 hundreds   5 tens   0 ones

C

A number written in a way that shows only its digits is in **standard form**.

Write a comma between the thousands and the hundreds.

1,350

A number written as the sum of the values of its digits is in **expanded form**.

1,000 + 300 + 50

A number written in words is in **word form**.

one thousand, three hundred fifty

Do You Understand?

Convince Me! John said, "The numbers and pictures below show the number 3,247." Is John correct? Explain.

three hundred + 40 + 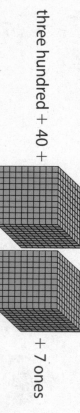 + 7 ones

Name _____

Another Example

How can you show 1,350 on a place-value chart?

thousands	hundreds	tens	ones
1,	3	5	0

The value of the 1 is 1 thousand, or 1,000.

The value of the 3 is 3 hundreds, or 300.

The value of the 5 is 5 tens, or 50.

The value of the 0 is 0 ones, or 0.

☆ Guided Practice ☆

In **1** and **2**, write each number in standard form.

1.

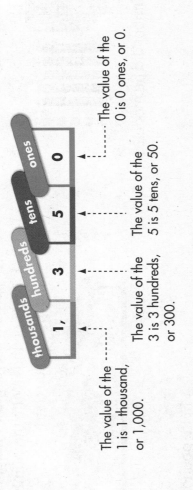

2. **Tools** Write a 4-digit number that has a tens digit of 7, a hundreds digit of 1, and 6 for each of the other digits. Use place-value blocks to help you.

☆ Independent Practice ☆

For **3** and **4**, write each number in standard form.

3.

4.

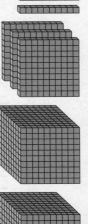

For **5** and **6**, write each number in expanded form and word form.

5. 526 _____

6. 2,157 _____

Problem Solving

7. Luis modeled a number using these place-value blocks.

Which number did he model?

A 4,450

B 3,470

C 454

D 355

8. Represent One of the largest pumpkins ever grown weighed 1,685 pounds. Write this number in the place-value chart.

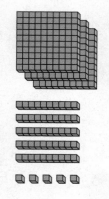

A 1,685-pound pumpkin weighs almost 1 ton! One ton is 2,000 pounds.

thousands	hundreds	tens	ones

9. Analyze Information Layla sent two thousand, five hundred twenty-three text messages last summer. Ryan sent 100 more text messages. Write the number of text messages Ryan sent in expanded form.

10. The number 3,507 written in word form is three thousand, five hundred seven. How do you write the number in expanded form?

A 3,000 + 500 + 10 + 7

B 3,000 + 500 + 70

C 3,000 + 500 + 7

D 3,000 + 50 + 7

11. Leo has 4 toothpicks. He places them as shown. What shape can Leo make if he adds two more toothpicks?

12. Extend Your Thinking Mario used place-value blocks to show the number 4,235. Then, he added two more thousands blocks. What was the new number? Explain.

Lesson 2
Greater Numbers

⊘ TEKS 3.2A Compose and decompose numbers up to 100,000 as a sum of so many ten thousands, so many thousands, so many hundreds, so many tens, and so many ones using objects, pictorial models, and numbers, including expanded notation as appropriate. Also, 3.2B. Mathematical Process Standards 3.1B, 3.1C, 3.1D, 3.1E, 3.1G

Digital Resources at SavvasTexas.com

 Solve
 Learn
 A-Z Glossary
 Tools
 Games

Name _____

Solve & Share

The news reported 95,687 people watched the parade. Record 95,687 in the place-value chart below. Use the place-value chart to help write the number in word and expanded forms.

You can create and use representations. You can represent 95,687 many ways.

thousands period | ones period

hundred thousands | ten thousands | one thousands | hundreds | tens | ones

Word form _____

Expanded form _____

Look Back!

Tools How does a place-value chart help you write a number in word form?

A

Great Sand Dunes National Park and Preserve in Colorado covers 85,932 acres of land.

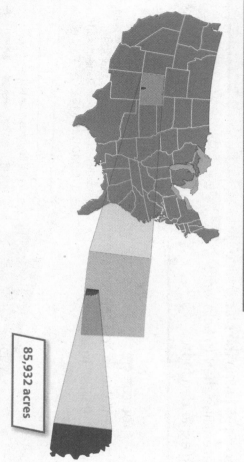

85,932 acres

B

How can you read, write, and name 85,932 in different ways?

> A **period** is a group of 3 digits in a number, starting from the right.

place-value chart:

thousands period			ones period		
hundred thousands	ten thousands	one thousands	hundreds	tens	ones
8	5,	9	3	2	

Two periods are separated by a comma.

C

standard form:
85,932

expanded form:
80,000 + 5,000 + 900 + 30 + 2

word form:
eighty-five thousand, nine hundred thirty-two

Do You Understand?

Convince Me! What number is shown below? Write the number in standard form. Use a place-value chart to help.

six hundred + 3 ones + 8 thousand + 70 + forty thousand

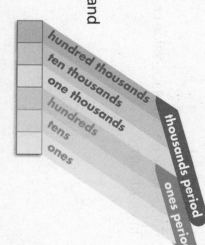

thousands period			ones period		
hundred thousands	ten thousands	one thousands	hundreds	tens	ones

Another Example

You can name 800,000 in different ways.

800,000 is 8 hundred thousands.

800,000 is 80 ten thousands.

800,000 is 800 thousands.

800,000 is 8,000 hundreds.

800,000 is 80,000 tens.

800,000 is 800,000 ones.

☆ Guided Practice ☆

In **1** through **4**, write each number in standard form.

1. thirty-two thousand, five hundred seven

2. seventy-eight thousand, two hundred thirty

3. $50,000 + 600 + 80 + 4$

4. $90,000 + 8,000 + 800 + 70 + 2$

5. Check for Reasonableness Marcus says the value of the digit 5 in 56,420 is 5,000. Do you agree? Why or why not?

6. Explain Describe how 50,434 and 45,304 are alike and how they are different.

☆ Independent Practice ☆

7. Write this number in standard form.

sixty-seven thousand, five hundred fifty

8. Write this number in expanded form.

57,374

9. Find the missing number.

$70,000 + \underline{\hspace{1cm}} + 500 + 8 = 74,508$

10. Find the missing number.

$60,000 + 2,000 + \underline{\hspace{1cm}} + 20 + 1 = 62,921$

11. Find the missing numbers.

$90,000 + \underline{\hspace{1cm}} + \underline{\hspace{1cm}} = 92,300$

12. Find the missing numbers.

$\underline{\hspace{1cm}} + 800 + \underline{\hspace{1cm}} = 50,812$

Problem Solving

13. Analyze Information Write the population of each city in the table in expanded form and word form.

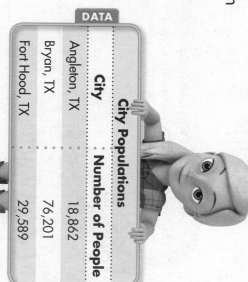

City Populations	
City	**Number of People**
Angleton, TX	18,862
Bryan, TX	76,201
Fort Hood, TX	29,589

14. Tools What is the time that is halfway between the two times shown on the clocks?

15. Communicate How many faces, edges, and vertices does a cube have?

16. Which is the word form of the number 68,049?

  A six thousand, forty-nine

  B six thousand, eight hundred forty-nine

  C sixty-eight thousand, four hundred nine

  D sixty-eight thousand, forty-nine

17. Extend Your Thinking Mount Everest is the tallest mountain in the world. It is 29,035 feet high. Write the height of Mount Everest in word form. Give the value of each digit.

Lesson 3
Comparing Numbers

TEKS 3.2D Compare and order whole numbers up to 100,000 and represent comparisons using the symbols >, <, or =. Also, 3.2. Mathematical Process Standards 3.1B, 3.1C, 3.1D, 3.1F, 3.1G

Digital Resources at SavvasTexas.com

 Solve   Learn   A-Z Glossary   Tools   Games

Solve & Share

The school store has 345 red pens and 380 blue pens. Are there more red or more blue pens?

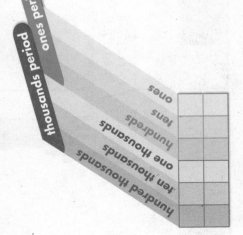

hundred thousands	ten thousands	one thousands	hundreds	tens	ones

thousands period   ones period

You can analyze relationships. You can analyze the relationship between place values with place-value blocks or a place-value chart.

Look Back!

Tools How do place-value blocks and place-value charts help you compare two different numbers?

How Do You Compare Numbers?

A

Which is taller, the Statue of Liberty or its base?

When you compare two numbers you find which number is greater and which number is less.

You can use symbols to compare numbers.

< is less than
> is greater than
= is equal to

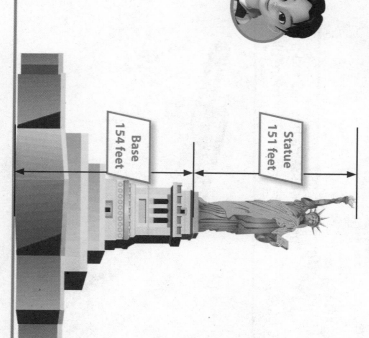

Statue
151 feet

Base
154 feet

B

You can compare 151 and 154 with place value.

same
same

154 > 151

4 > 1

The place-value blocks also show 151 is **less than** 154.

151 < 154

C

On the number line, 151 is to the left of 154. So, 151 is **less than** 154.

151 < 154

150   151   152   153   154   155

So, the base is taller than the statue!

Do You Understand?

Convince Me! Write one of the numbers below on each line to make true statements. Can you do it a different way? Explain.

2,314   2,413   1,234   4,321

_____ > _____   _____ < _____

Name _____

Another Example

To compare 23,456 and 23,482 on a place-value chart, line up the digits by place value. Compare the digits starting from the left.

	thousands period			ones period		
	hundred thousands	ten thousands	one thousands	hundreds	tens	ones
2	3,	4	5	6
2	3,	4	8	2

Both numbers have a 2 in the ten-thousands place, a 3 in the thousands place, and a 4 in the hundreds place. 23,456 has 5 tens while 23,482 has 8 tens.

23,456 < 23,482

☆ Guided Practice

For **1** through **4**, compare the numbers. Use <, >, or =.

1.
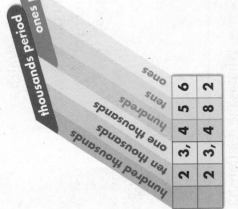

133 ◯ 67

2.

243 ◯ 252

3. 5,450 ◯ 5,045   4. 42,899 ◯ 42,989

5. **Check for Reasonableness** Kiara says since 5 is greater than 2, the number 596 is greater than the number 2,041. Do you agree? Why or why not?

6. Draw a number line to compare the numbers.

4,247 ◯ 4,742

☆ Independent Practice ☆

Leveled Practice In **7** and **8**, compare the numbers. Use <, >, or =.

7.

120 ◯ 93

8.

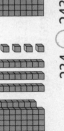

234 ◯ 243

Problem Solving ☆

9. Communicate Which is shorter, the Washington Monument or the Great Pyramid in Egypt? How do you know?

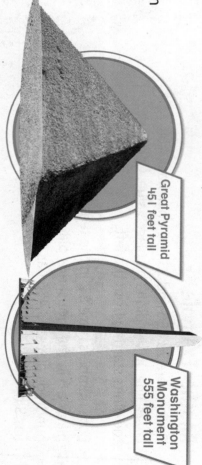

Great Pyramid
451 feet tall

Washington Monument
555 feet tall

10. Number Sense What is the relationship between the 6s in the number 66,247?

11. Reason Tony is thinking of a 4-digit number. Dari is thinking of a 5-digit number. Whose number is greater? How do you know?

In **12** and **13**, use the table at the right.

12. Math and Science Gemma recorded the temperatures at noon in Dallas, Texas, for five days. Write a comparison between the highest and lowest temperatures.

13. On which days was the temperature at noon less than 90°F?

14. Which number sentence is true if the number 1,573 replaces the box?

A 1,456 > ☐
B ☐ = 1,256
C 1,598 < ☐
D ☐ > 1,357

< means less than.
> means greater than.

DATA

Temperatures in Dallas, Texas

Day	Temperature (°F)
Monday	88°F
Tuesday	92°F
Wednesday	90°F
Thursday	86°F
Friday	89°F

15. Extend Your Thinking Suppose you are comparing 32,648 and 32,489. Do you need to compare the tens digits? Which number would be farther to the right on the number line? Explain.

Lesson 4

Adding with an Expanded Algorithm

TEKS 3.4A Solve with fluency one-step ... problems involving addition ... within 1,000 using strategies based on place value.... Also, 3.4.
Mathematical Process Standards 3.1B, 3.1C, 3.1D, 3.1E, 3.1F, 3.1G

Digital Resources at SavvasTexas.com

Solve

Learn

A-Z
Glossary

Tools

Games

Name _____

Solve & Share

Find the sum of 327 + 241. Think about place value. **Solve this problem any way you choose.**

You can formulate a plan. Part of your plan for solving this problem could be to show each of the numbers in expanded form. **Show your work in the space below!**

Look Back!

Connect How can using place value help you solve this 3-digit addition problem?

How Can You Break Large Addition Problems into Smaller Ones?

Find the sum of 243 + 179. Each digit in the numbers can be modeled with place-value blocks.

You can use place value to add the numbers.

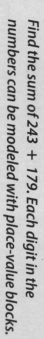

243

179

B

Step 1

Break 243 + 179 into smaller problems. Think about the place values of each number.

Hundreds	Tens	Ones
200	40	3
+ 100	+ 70	+ 9
300	110	12

C

Step 2

Then, add the sums of all the places.

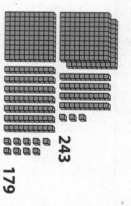

```
  300
  110
+  12
  422
```

So, 243 + 179 = 422.

Do You Understand?

Convince Me! Lexi says, "To solve 243 + 179, I can just count on with place-value blocks to find the answer: 100, 200, 300, another hundred from the 11 tens is 400, one more ten and 12 ones is 422!" How is Lexi's way like Steps 1 and 2 above?

908

☆ Guided Practice ☆

In **1**, use place value to find the sum.

1.

Find 354 + 431.

Hundreds	Tens	Ones	Total
300	50	4	
+ 400	+ 30	+ 1	

2. **Communicate** Suppose you were adding 824 + 106. What would the tens problem be? Why?

3. Write the smaller problems you could use to find 512 + 362. What is the sum?

☆ Independent Practice ☆

Leveled Practice In **4** through **11**, find each sum.

4.

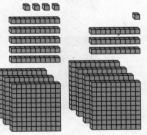

348 + 131

Hundreds	Tens	Ones	Total
300	40	8	
+ 100	+ 30	+ 1	

5.

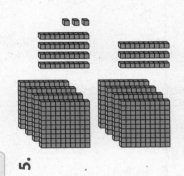

443 + 430

Hundreds	Tens	Ones	Total
400	40	3	
+ 400	+ 30	+ 0	

6. 264 + 524

7. 541 + 276

8. 249 + 180

9. 342 + 168

10. 191 + 502

11. 473 + 405

12. Represent Jan read a book with 288 pages. Lara read a book with 416 pages. How many pages did Jan and Lara read? Draw a strip diagram to model and solve the problem.

13. Explain Explain how the solids shown in Group A and Group B could have been sorted.

Group A   **Group B**

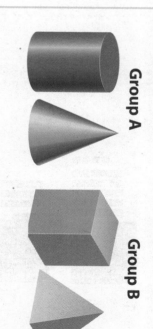

14. Cody wants to add 482 + 315 using place value. He begins by breaking the problem into smaller problems. He writes $(400 + 300) + (80 + 10) + (2 + 5)$. Which shows the sum of the hundreds, tens, and ones?

A 700 + 90 + 5

B 700 + 90 + 7

C 800 + 80 + 5

D 800 + 60 + 7

15. Formulate a Plan Bill needs to find 325 + 133. Into what three smaller problems can Bill break this addition? What is the sum?

You can use place value to add.

16. Construct Arguments Henry believes the sum of 345 + 124 is 479. Is Henry correct? Explain.

345	124

?

17. Extend Your Thinking A school cafeteria sold 215 lunches on Monday, 104 lunches on Tuesday, and 262 lunches on Wednesday. Did the cafeteria sell more lunches on Monday and Tuesday or on Tuesday and Wednesday? Explain.

Lesson 5
Models for Adding 3-Digit Numbers

TEKS 3.4A Solve with fluency one-step and two-step problems involving addition ... within 1,000 using strategies based on place value.... Also, 3.5A. Mathematical Process Standards 3.1C, 3.1D, 3.1E, 3.1F, 3.1G

Digital Resources at SavvasTexas.com

Solve

Learn

Glossary

Tools

Games

Name _____

Solve & Share

Find the sum of 146 + 247. *Solve this problem any way you choose.*

You can communicate. Using place-value blocks and drawing pictures of the blocks can show how you found the sum. *Show your work!*

Look Back!

Number Sense When you add numbers, how do you know if you need to regroup?

How Can You Add 3-Digit Numbers with Place-Value Blocks?

A

Find 143 + 285.

You can add whole numbers by using place value to break them apart.

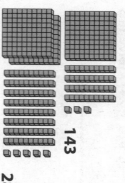

143

285

B

Add the ones, tens, and hundreds.

143

285

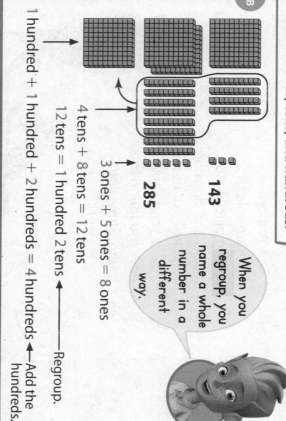

When you regroup, you name a whole number in a different way.

3 ones + 5 ones = 8 ones

4 tens + 8 tens = 12 tens

12 tens = 1 hundred 2 tens ——Regroup.

1 hundred + 1 hundred + 2 hundreds = 4 hundreds ——Add the hundreds.

C

4 hundreds   2 tens   8 ones

428

143 + 285 = 428

Do You Understand?

Convince Me! Mr. Wu drove 224 miles yesterday. He drove 175 miles today. Use place-value blocks or draw pictures of blocks to find how many miles Mr. Wu drove.

Name _____

Another Example

You may have to regroup twice when you add. Find 148 + 276.

Step 1

Add the ones.

8 ones + 6 ones = 14 ones

Regroup.

14 ones = 1 ten 4 ones

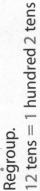

Step 2

Add the tens.

1 ten + 4 tens + 7 tens = 12 tens

Regroup.

12 tens = 1 hundred 2 tens

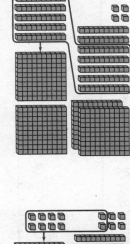

Step 3

Add the hundreds.

1 hundred + 1 hundred + 2 hundreds = 4 hundreds

So, 148 + 276 = 424.

☆ Guided Practice ☆

In **1**, use the model to write the problem and find the sum.

1.

2. **Connect** How do you know when you need to regroup?

3. **Tools** Use place-value blocks to find 136 + 279.

☆ Independent Practice ☆

In **4** through **6**, write the problem and find the sum.

4.

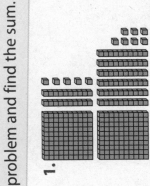

5.

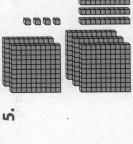

6.

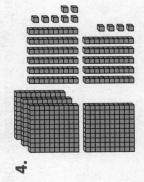

7. Draw a Picture Juan wants to use place-value blocks to show $148 + 256$. Draw a picture of the blocks Juan should use. What is the sum?

8. Represent Manuel plays basketball and scores 15 points in game one, 8 points in game two, and 17 points in game three. How many points did Manuel score? Use the number line to model and solve the problem.

0 10 20 30 40 50

9. Which number sentence do the place-value blocks show?

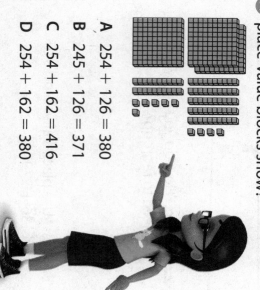

A $254 + 126 = 380$

B $245 + 126 = 371$

C $254 + 162 = 416$

D $254 + 162 = 380$

10. Represent Mrs. Samuels bought a $526 plane ticket in May and a $194 plane ticket in June. Use place-value blocks or draw pictures to find out how much Mrs. Samuels spent on both of the plane tickets.

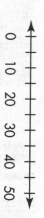

11. Extend Your Thinking Paula is saving money to buy a new computer that costs $680. Last month she saved $415, and this month she saved $298. Does Paula have enough money saved to buy the computer? Use place-value blocks to help you solve the problem. Explain.

12. Explain Al and Mark were playing a computer game. Al scored 265 points in the first round and 354 points in the second round. Mark scored 352 points in the first round and 237 points in the second round. Who scored more points and won the game? Explain.

Lesson 6

Subtracting with an Expanded Algorithm

 TEKS 3.4A Solve with fluency one-step and two-step problems involving … subtraction within 1,000 using strategies based on place value.… Also, 3.4. Mathematical Process Standards 3.1B, 3.1C, 3.1D, 3.1G

Digital Resources at SavvasTexas.com

 Solve

 Learn

 A-Z Glossary

 Tools

Games

Name _____

Solve & Share

Find the difference of 534 − 108. Think about place value. *Solve this problem any way you choose.*

You can reason. How could you break this problem into smaller subtraction problems? *Show your work in the space below!*

Look Back!

Number Sense How can using place value help you solve this subtraction problem?

How Can You Break Large Subtraction Problems into Smaller Ones?

A

At the end of the fourth round of a game of Digit Derby, Marco's score was 462 points. During the fifth round of the game, Marco loses points. What is Marco's score at the end of the fifth round?

Find 462 − 181.

Place value can help you break a subtraction problem into smaller problems.

End of Round 4

Marco has 462 points.

End of Round 5

Marco loses 181 points.

B

Step 1

Start with 462.

Subtract the **hundreds.**

$462 − 100 = 362$

So far, 100 has been subtracted.

C

Step 2

Next, start with 362.

Subtract the **tens.**

You need to subtract 8 tens, but there are not enough tens. So, subtract the 6 tens.

$362 − 60 = 302$

Then, subtract the 2 tens that are left.

$302 − 20 = 282$

So far, $100 + 60 + 20 = 180$ has been subtracted.

D

Step 3

That leaves just 1 to subtract.

Subtract the **ones.**

$282 − 1 = 281$

$100 + 60 + 20 + 1 = 181$ has been subtracted.

At the end of the fifth round, Marco's score is 281 points.

Do You Understand?

Convince Me! Find 453 − 262. Use place value to help break the problem into smaller problems. Show your work.

☆ Guided Practice ☆

In **1** and **2**, use place value to help break the problem into smaller problems.

1. Find 564 − 346.

564 − 300 = _____

264 − 40 = _____

224 − 4 = _____

220 − 2 = _____

2. Find 769 − 375.

769 − 300 = _____

469 − 60 = _____

409 − 10 = _____

399 − 5 = _____

3. Explain Why do you need to record the numbers you subtract at each step?

4. Reason Carmella is trying to find 784 − 310. She decides to start by subtracting 10 from 784. Do you agree with Carmella? Explain.

☆ Independent Practice ☆

Leveled Practice In **5** through **10**, follow the steps to find each difference. Show your work.

5. 728 − 413

First, subtract 400.

_____ − _____ = 328

Then, subtract 10.

_____ − _____ = _____

Then, subtract 3.

_____ − 3 = _____

6. 936 − 524

First, subtract 500.

936 − _____ = _____

Then, subtract 20.

_____ − 20 = _____

Then, subtract 4.

_____ − _____ = _____

7. 854 − 235

First, subtract 200.

_____ − 200 = _____

Then, subtract 30.

_____ − 30 = _____

Then, subtract 4.

_____ − 4 = _____

Then, subtract 1.

_____ − 1 = _____

8. 955 − 283

9. 946 − 507

10. 984 − 356

Problem Solving

11. Karl's book has 416 pages. He read 50 pages last week. He read another 31 pages this week. How many more pages does Karl have left to read?

A 125

B 335

C 345

D 245

> You can use estimation to remove two answer choices.

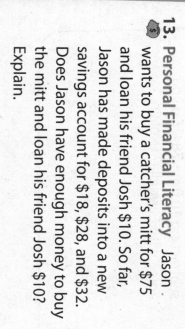

12. Analyze Information There are 96 boys and 83 girls in the school lunchroom. Near the end of lunch, 127 students leave. How many students are left in the lunchroom? Show how you can break part of the problem into smaller problems.

13. Personal Financial Literacy Jason wants to buy a catcher's mitt for $75 and loan his friend Josh $10. So far, Jason has made deposits into a new savings account for $18, $28, and $32. Does Jason have enough money to buy the mitt and loan his friend Josh $10? Explain.

14. Tools Write the time shown on the clock in 2 different ways.

15. Use a Strip Diagram Yuki had a necklace with 131 beads. The string broke, and she lost 43 beads. How many beads does Yuki have left?

131 beads

43	?

43 beads lost →   ? beads left →

16. Extend Your Thinking Which weighs more, two adult male Basset Hounds or one adult male Great Dane? Show the difference in pounds between the two Basset Hounds and the Great Dane. Draw strip diagrams to represent and help you solve the problem.

145 pounds

Great Dane

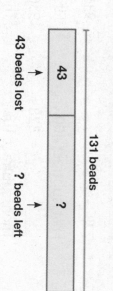

66 pounds

Basset Hound

Lesson 7

Models for Subtracting 3-Digit Numbers

TEKS 3.4A Solve with fluency one-step and two-step problems involving … subtraction within 1,000 using strategies based on place value.… Also, 3.5A. Mathematical Process Standards 3.1B, 3.1C, 3.1D, 3.1E, 3.1G

Digital Resources at SavvasTexas.com

Solve

Learn

Glossary

A-Z

Tools

Games

Solve & Share

Find the difference of 246 − 153. *Solve this problem any way you choose.*

Name _____

You can create and use representations. Drawing pictures of place-value blocks is one way to represent this problem and help you solve it. *Show your work in the space below!*

Look Back!

Check for Reasonableness How can you check to see if the difference you found for 246 − 153 is reasonable?

How Can You Subtract 3-Digit Numbers with Place-Value Blocks?

A

Fish caught near the Hawaiian Islands can be very large. How many more pounds does a broadbill swordfish weigh than a blue marlin?

Find 237 − 165.

Wild Hawaiian Fish Weights	
Type of Fish	**Weight (in lb)**
Blue Marlin	165
Broadbill Swordfish	237

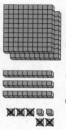

Use place value to subtract the ones first, the tens next, and then the hundreds.

Show 237 with place-value blocks.

B

Subtract the ones.

7 ones > 5 ones, so no regrouping.

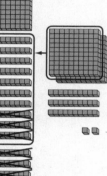

7 ones − 5 ones = 2 ones

```
  237
− 165
────
    2
```

C

Subtract the tens.

3 tens < 6 tens, so regroup.

1 hundred = 10 tens

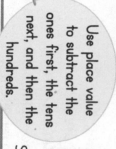

13 tens − 6 tens = 7 tens

```
   1 13
  2̷3̷7
− 1 6 5
──────
    7 2
```

D

Subtract the hundreds.

1 hundred − 1 hundred = 0 hundreds

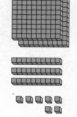

```
   1 13
  2̷3̷7
− 1 6 5
──────
    7 2
```

So, 237 − 165 = 72. A broadbill swordfish weighs 72 more pounds than a blue marlin.

Do You Understand?

Convince Me! Anderson needs $231 to buy a new bike. He saved $144 from his summer job. How much more does Anderson need to save to buy the bike? Write a subtraction sentence that models the problem. Use place-value blocks to help you solve the problem using the same steps shown above.

Name _____

☆ Guided Practice ☆

In **1** through **8**, use place-value blocks or draw pictures to subtract.

1.
```
  859
- 768
```

2.
```
  361
- 124
```

3.
```
  285
-  49
```

4.
```
  684
- 482
```

5. 384 − 358

6. 352 − 214

7. 512 − 101

8. 999 − 889

9. Communicate In the example on page 920, for 237 − 165, why do you need to regroup 1 hundred into 10 tens?

10. Represent Gary saved $287 doing jobs in his neighborhood. He bought a computer printer for $183. How much money did Gary have left? Draw a picture of place-value blocks to help you subtract.

☆ Independent Practice ☆

In **11** through **26**, use place-value blocks or draw pictures to subtract.

You can draw squares to show hundreds, lines to show tens, and dots to show ones. This picture shows 123.

□ | | ⋯

11.
```
  651
- 543
```

12.
```
  492
- 138
```

13.
```
  690
- 481
```

14.
```
  508
- 137
```

15.
```
  168
-  39
```

16.
```
  618
- 476
```

17.
```
  419
-  59
```

18.
```
  192
- 108
```

19.
```
  573
- 468
```

20.
```
  596
- 128
```

21.
```
  819
- 124
```

22.
```
  438
- 283
```

23.
```
  349
-  78
```

24.
```
  562
- 472
```

25.
```
  185
- 149
```

26.
```
  603
- 492
```

Problem Solving

For **27** and **28**, use the table at the right.

27. Tools How many more miles is it from Cleveland to Chicago than from Cincinnati to Cleveland?

28. Reason Mr. Sousa is driving from Washington, D.C. to Cleveland and then to Cincinnati. He has traveled 182 miles. How many miles are left in his trip?

DATA

Trip Distances

Trip	Miles
Cleveland to Chicago	346
Cincinnati to Cleveland	249
Washington, D.C. to Cleveland	372

29. It is 239 miles from Dallas to Houston and 275 miles from Dallas to San Antonio. How many fewer miles is it from Dallas to Houston than from Dallas to San Antonio?

30. An amusement park ride can hold 120 people. There are already 90 people on the ride and 58 people waiting in line. Which number sentence can be used to find how many people need to wait for the next ride?

A $90 + 58 = 138$

B $90 - 30 = 60$

C $58 - 30 = 28$

D $90 - 58 = 32$

31. Use a Strip Diagram Kendra got $20 for her birthday. She earned $62 babysitting. Then she earned $148 shoveling snow. How much money does Kendra have?

$20	$62	$148

?

32. Extend Your Thinking Kim needs to find $437 - 258$. Will she need to regroup to find the answer? If so, explain how she will need to regroup. What will Kim's answer be?

33. Analyze Information Claudia and Jasmine each ran for Junior High student council president. Which girl got more votes? How many more votes did that girl get?

DATA

Student Council President Votes

	7th Grade Votes	8th Grade Votes
Claudia	183	157
Jasmine	162	156

Lesson 8
Fractions and Regions

⊕ TEKS 3.3C Explain that the unit fraction $\frac{1}{b}$ represents the quantity formed by one part of a whole that has been partitioned into b equal parts where b is a non-zero whole number. Also, 3.3, 3.3A. Mathematical Process Standards 3.1B, 3.1C, 3.1D, 3.1E, 3.1G

Digital Resources at SavvasTexas.com

 Solve   Learn   A-Z Glossary   Tools   Games

Name

☆ Solve & Share ☆

Pat made a garden in the shape of a rectangle and divided it into 4 same-size parts. She planted flowers in one of the parts. Draw a picture of what Pat's garden might look like.

You can formulate a plan. Use information from the problem to plan your drawing of Pat's garden.

Look Back!

Number Sense How many parts of Pat's garden do **NOT** have flowers? Explain.

A

Mr. Peters served part of a pan of enchilada casserole to a friend. What does each part of the whole pan of casserole represent? What part was served? What part is left?

A fraction is a symbol that names equal parts of a whole. A unit fraction represents one part of a whole that has been divided into equal parts. A unit fraction always has a numerator of 1.

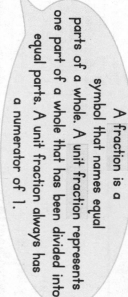

B

What You Think

There are 6 equal pieces in the whole, so each piece is $\frac{1}{6}$.

There is 1 piece missing, so one $\frac{1}{6}$-piece was served.

There are 5 pieces left, so five $\frac{1}{6}$-pieces are left.

The numerator shows how many equal parts are described. The denominator shows the total number of equal parts in a whole.

C

What You Write

$\frac{1}{6}$ ← numerator
  ← denominator

$\frac{1}{6}$ of the pan of enchilada casserole was served.

$\frac{5}{6}$ of the pan of enchilada casserole is left.

Do You Understand?

Convince Me! Below is a picture of a pie pan. Draw lines and use shading to show that five $\frac{1}{8}$-pieces are still in the pan, and that three $\frac{1}{8}$-pieces were eaten. Remember to draw same-size parts.

924

☆ Guided Practice ☆

In **1** through **4**, use the figure below.

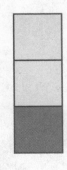

1. Write the unit fraction that represents each part of the whole.

2. How many $\frac{1}{3}$-parts are yellow?

3. What fraction of the whole is yellow?

4. What fraction names *all* of the parts in the whole?

5. In the problem in Box A on page 924, what fraction names all of the pieces in the casserole?

6. **Represent** Mrs. Rao made a cake. What fraction of the whole cake does each piece represent?

7. In the picture in Exercise 6, how many $\frac{1}{8}$-pieces were eaten? What fraction of the whole cake was eaten?

☆ Independent Practice ☆

In **8** through **11**, write the unit fraction that represents each part of the whole. Then write the number of blue parts and the fraction of the whole that is blue.

8.

9.

10.

11.

12. Draw a rectangle that shows 6 equal parts. Then shade $\frac{3}{6}$ of the rectangle. Explain how you know you shaded $\frac{3}{6}$ of the rectangle.

☆ Problem Solving ☆

In **13** through **15**, use the chart to the right.

13. Kiko and some friends bought a medium party tray. They ate 5 sections of the tray. Which of the following shows the unit fraction, and the fraction of the tray that was left?

A $\frac{1}{8}, \frac{3}{8}$

B $\frac{1}{6}, \frac{4}{6}$

C $\frac{8}{8}, \frac{2}{8}$

D $\frac{1}{6}, \frac{1}{6}$

14. **Explain** Jesse and his friends ordered a large party tray. Which unit fraction does each section of the tray represent? How do you know?

15. **Number Sense** Which costs more, 4 small party trays or 2 large party trays? Show your comparison using dollar amounts and the > symbol.

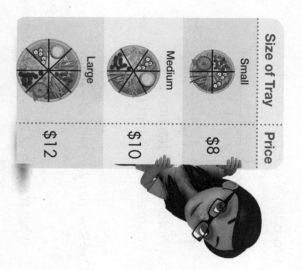

Size of Tray	Price
Small	$8
Medium	$10
Large	$12

16. **Use a Strip Diagram** Janice has 2 scarves. Carla has 3 times as many scarves as Janice. How many scarves does Carla have? Use the strip diagram to write and solve an equation.

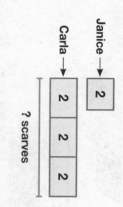

Janice → | 2 |

Carla → | 2 | 2 | 2 |

? scarves

17. **Extend Your Thinking** Draw a circle that shows 6 equal parts. Shade more than $\frac{3}{6}$ of the circle, but less than $\frac{5}{6}$ of the circle. What fraction have you modeled?

18. **Number Sense** What is the distance around the baseball card? Write a number sentence to help you solve the problem.

6 cm

8 cm

926

Copyright © Savvas Learning Company LLC. All Rights Reserved.

Name

☆ Solve & Share

Use two-color counters to show the fraction $\frac{5}{8}$. Draw a picture of the counters you used. Can you find more than one way to show the fraction $\frac{5}{8}$? Explain.

Lesson 9
Fractions and Sets

⊙ TEKS 3.3A Represent fractions greater than zero and less than or equal to one with denominators of 2, 3, 4, 6, and 8 using concrete objects and pictorial models ... . Also, 3.3, 3.3C.
Mathematical Process Standards 3.1A, 3.1B, 3.1C, 3.1D, 3.1E, 3.1G

Digital Resources at SavvasTexas.com

Solve   Learn   Glossary   Tools   Games

You can create and use representations. How will the two colors of the counters help you model the fraction? *Show your work.*

Look Back!

Reason How can you show $\frac{8}{8}$ using counters?

Digital Resources at SavvasTexas.com

A

An animal shelter in San Antonio has kittens up for adoption. A group of 8 kittens arrives on Monday. What fraction of the group of kittens is orange? What fraction of the kittens is **NOT** orange?

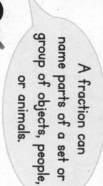

A fraction can name parts of a set or group of objects, people, or animals.

The unit fraction $\frac{1}{8}$ represents one kitten in the set of 8 kittens.

B

What You Write

You can use counters to show the kittens.

$\frac{6}{8}$ ←—Number of orange kittens
←—Total number of kittens

$\frac{2}{8}$ ←—Number of kittens that are **NOT** orange
←—Total number of kittens

C

What You Say

Six eighths of the kittens are orange.

Two eighths of the kittens are not orange.

Do You Understand?

Convince Me! In the example above, why is the denominator the same for the part of the group of kittens that is orange, and for the part of the group that is not orange? Why are the numerators different?

Name _____

☆ Guided Practice

In **1** and **2**, write the unit fraction that represents one counter in the set. Then, write the fraction of counters that are red.

1.

2.

In **3**, use counters or draw a picture to show the fraction.

3. $\frac{3}{4}$

4. Marcia has 8 counters. $\frac{5}{8}$ of the counters are red. What fraction of the counters are **NOT** red?

5. **Connect** A group of 5 students is waiting for a train. Three of them are wearing sweaters. What unit fraction represents one student in the group? What fraction of the students in the group are wearing sweaters?

☆ Independent Practice ☆

Leveled Practice In **6** through **8**, write the unit fraction that represents one counter in the set. Then, write the fraction of counters that are yellow.

6.

7.

8.

In **9** through **11**, use counters or draw a picture of the set described.

9. 3 shapes, $\frac{2}{3}$ of the shapes are circles

10. 5 shapes, $\frac{3}{5}$ of the shapes are triangles

11. 4 shapes, $\frac{2}{4}$ of the shapes are squares

12. Melissa has these marbles. What fraction of Melissa's marbles are pink?

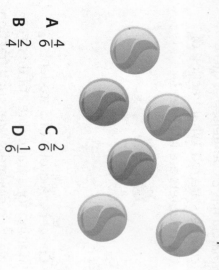

A $\frac{4}{6}$ C $\frac{2}{6}$

B $\frac{2}{4}$ D $\frac{1}{6}$

13. Zach read 112 pages of a book over the weekend. Pedro read 143 pages. How many pages did they read in all? Complete the strip diagram to find the answer.

112	

14. Darren has 3 brown poodles, one black poodle, and 2 orange tabby cats. What unit fraction represents one poodle in the set of poodles? What fraction of Darren's poodles is brown?

15. Mental Math Rodney wants to use mental math to find the product of 7×50. Explain how he can do this.

16. Draw a Picture Draw a picture to show a set of 6 apples. Color the picture to show that $\frac{4}{6}$ of the apples are green.

You can model fractions using pictures.

17. Represent In 3 years, Beth will be 12 years old. Draw a strip diagram and write and solve an equation to find how many years old Beth is now.

18. Extend Your Thinking Cut flowers usually lose some of their petals within a week. What fraction of the flower petals have **NOT** fallen off the flower?

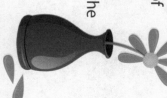

Name _____

Solve & Share

The strip shown below represents 1 whole. Show and label $\frac{3}{4}$ of the length of the strip. Show and label $\frac{7}{8}$ of the length of the same strip.

Lesson 10
Fractions and Length

 TEKS 3.3A Represent fractions … with denominators of 2, 3, 4, 6, and 8 using concrete objects and pictorial models, including strip diagrams …. Also, 3.3C, 3.3D. Mathematical Process Standards 3.1B, 3.1C, 3.1D, 3.1E, 3.1G

Digital Resources at SavvasTexas.com

Solve

Learn

A-Z
Glossary

Tools

Games

You can check for reasonableness. How can you be sure that the lengths you showed for $\frac{3}{4}$ and $\frac{7}{8}$ are accurate? *Show your work.*

Look Back!

Justify Can $\frac{3}{4}$ the length of the whole strip be shown using $\frac{1}{4}$ parts of the strip? Can $\frac{7}{8}$ of the length of the whole strip be shown using $\frac{1}{8}$ parts of the strip? Explain.

A

Haley made a bracelet using 8 red beads. Some of the beads have letters that spell her name. What fraction of the length of Haley's bracelet has beads with letters? What fraction of the length of the bracelet does **NOT** have letters?

A fraction can name part of a length.

$\frac{1}{8}$	$\frac{1}{8}$	$\frac{1}{8}$	$\frac{1}{8}$	$\frac{1}{8}$	$\frac{1}{8}$	$\frac{1}{8}$	$\frac{1}{8}$
	H	A	L	E	Y		

B

What You Write

Five of the $\frac{1}{8}$ parts of the length have letters.

$\frac{5}{8} = \frac{1}{8} + \frac{1}{8} + \frac{1}{8} + \frac{1}{8} + \frac{1}{8}$

$\frac{5}{8}$ ← Number of parts of the length that have letters
   ← Total number of parts in the bracelet length

Three of the $\frac{1}{8}$ parts of the length do **NOT** have letters.

$\frac{3}{8} = \frac{1}{8} + \frac{1}{8} + \frac{1}{8}$

$\frac{3}{8}$ ← Number of parts of the length that do not have letters
   ← Total number of parts in the bracelet length

C

What You Say

Five eighths of the bracelet length has letters.

Three eighths of the bracelet length does **NOT** have letters.

Eight eighths of the bracelet length is red.

Do You Understand?

Convince Me! What fraction of the length of ribbon below is pink? What fraction of the ribbon is **NOT** pink? Express the fraction of the length that is pink as a sum of unit fractions.

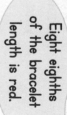

$\frac{1}{4}$	$\frac{1}{4}$	$\frac{1}{4}$

Name _____

☆ Guided Practice ☆

In **1** and **2**, write the unit fraction that represents each part of the length. What fraction of the length is shown?

1.

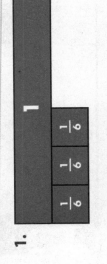

2.

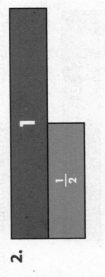

3. Represent Show the whole (1) for each of the fraction strips below by drawing additional $\frac{1}{3}$ strips and $\frac{1}{4}$ strips.

$\frac{1}{3}$

$\frac{1}{4}$

4. Represent Draw $\frac{1}{8}$ strips to show $\frac{7}{8}$ of the whole.

1

☆ Independent Practice ☆

In **5** through **8**, write the unit fraction that represents each part of the length. What fraction of the length is shown?

5.

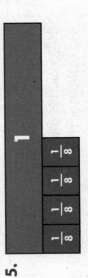

6.

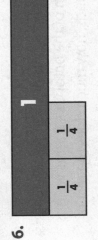

7.

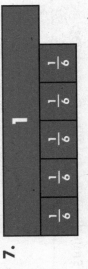

8.

9. Suppose there were 3 fewer $\frac{1}{8}$ strips in the diagram shown in Exercise 8. What fraction of the length would be shown? How do you know? Express this length as a sum of unit fractions.

10. Reason Hanna ran $\frac{5}{8}$ of the distance around a track. Then, she walked until she had gone the whole distance around the track 1 time. What fraction of the distance around the track did Hanna walk? Use the diagram to help.

The whole shows the distance around the track.

1				
$\frac{1}{8}$	$\frac{1}{8}$	$\frac{1}{8}$	$\frac{1}{8}$	$\frac{1}{8}$

11. Erika is using multi-colored yarn. What fraction of the length of the yarn is red?

$\frac{1}{6}$	$\frac{1}{6}$

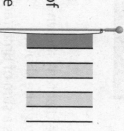

A $\frac{1}{6}$

B $\frac{1}{4}$

C $\frac{2}{6}$

D $\frac{4}{6}$

12. Communicate Write a problem that can be modeled with this diagram. Then, solve your problem.

1	
$\frac{1}{4}$	$\frac{1}{4}$

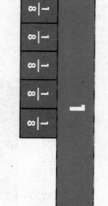

13. Explain An octopus weighs 42 pounds. If each of the octopus's 8 arms weighs 3 pounds, how much does the rest of the octopus weigh? Explain how you found your answer.

14. Estimation Kyle wants to buy a pair of roller skates and a tennis racket. He estimates that the total cost of the items will be $140. The roller skates cost $48. What is a reasonable estimate for the price of the tennis racket?

15. Represent Dean colors $\frac{1}{6}$ of the flag green and $\frac{2}{6}$ of the flag yellow. Color the rest of the flag red, and then tell what fraction of the flag is red.

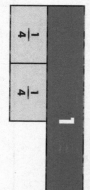

16. Extend Your Thinking Ariana paints $\frac{2}{6}$ of a windowsill. Her sister paints the rest of the windowsill. What fraction of the windowsill does Ariana's sister paint? Draw fraction strips to model the problem.

Glossary

add

When you add, you join groups together.

$$3 + 4 = 7$$

addend

the numbers you add together to find the whole

$$2 + 5 = 7$$

↑ ↑

addends

addition sentence

plus

$$3 + 2 = 5$$

↑ ↑ ↑

addend addend sum

after

424 comes after 423.

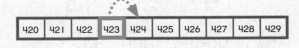

| 420 | 421 | 422 | 423 | 424 | 425 | 426 | 427 | 428 | 429 |

a.m.

7:10 AM

The half of the day from midnight to midday can be described as a.m.

area

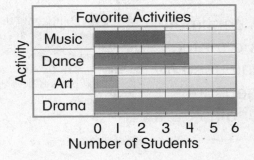 = 6 square units

The area is the measure of the space inside a plane shape.

bar graph

A bar graph uses bars to show data.

Favorite Activities

Activity: Music, Dance, Art, Drama

Number of Students: 0 1 2 3 4 5 6

before

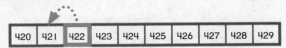

| 420 | 421 | 422 | 423 | 424 | 425 | 426 | 427 | 428 | 429 |

421 comes before 422.

borrow

When you borrow money or an item, it needs to be returned when you are done.

cents

1 cent (¢)   10 cents (¢)

centimeter (cm)

A centimeter is a metric unit used to measure length.

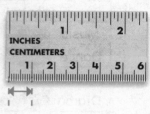

coins

1¢   5¢   10¢   25¢   50¢ $1.00

column

1	2	3	4	5
11	12	13	14	15
21	22	23	24	25
31	32	33	34	35

↑
column

compare

When you compare numbers, you find out if a number is greater than, less than, or equal to another number.

147 143

147 is greater than 143.

cone

A cone is a solid figure with a circle as its base and a curved surface that meets at a point.

consumer

When you use or buy something, you are a consumer.

cube

A cube is a solid figure with six faces that are matching squares.

cylinder

A cylinder is a solid figure with two matching circles as bases.

data

Favorite Fruit	
Apple	7
Peach	4
Orange	5

Data are information you collect.

decagon

A decagon is a polygon that has 10 sides.

decimal point

A decimal point separates dollars from cents.

$1.25

decimal point

decrease

$$600 \longrightarrow 550$$

600 decreased by 50 is 550.

deposit

When you put money into a bank, you are making a deposit.

difference

the answer in a subtraction sentence

$$14 - 6 = 8$$

8 is the difference.

digits

Numbers have 1 or more digits. 43 has 2 digits.

dime

10 cents or 10¢

divide

You divide to separate a number of items into groups of equal size.

$$12 \div 3 = 4$$

divided by

$$18 \div 3 = 6$$

divided by

division sentence

$$4 \div 2 = 2$$

4 divided by 2 equals 2.

dodecagon

A dodecagon is a polygon that has 12 sides.

dollar

$1.00 or 100¢

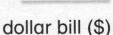

dollar bill ($)   dollar coin

dollar sign

The dollar sign is the symbol that is placed before the numbers when you are writing an amount of money.

$375

dollar sign

doubles

A doubles fact has two addends that are the same.

$$4 + 4 = 8$$

addend   addend   sum

edge

An edge is where two flat surfaces of a solid figure meet.

edge

eighths

When 1 whole is separated into 8 equal parts, the parts are called eighths.

equal parts

parts of a whole that are the same size.

All 4 parts are equal.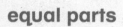

equal share

2   2   2

An equal share is the same amount in each group.

equal to (=)

$$36 = 36$$

36 is equal to 36.

estimate

When you estimate, you make a good guess.

This table is about 3 feet long.

even

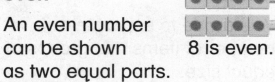

An even number can be shown as two equal parts.

8 is even.

expanded form

Expanded form shows the place value of each digit.

$$400 + 60 + 3 = 463$$

face

The flat surface of a solid figure that does not roll is called a face.

faces

fact family

a group of related addition and subtraction facts

$$2 + 4 = 6$$
$$4 + 2 = 6$$
$$6 - 2 = 4$$
$$6 - 4 = 2$$

flat surface

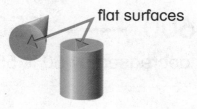

flat surfaces

foot (ft)

A foot is 12 inches.

fourths

When 1 whole is separated into 4 equal parts, the parts are called fourths.

fraction

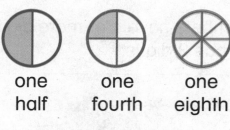

one half   one fourth   one eighth

A fraction names part of a whole or part of a set.

greater than (>)

5 is greater than 1.

$$5 > 1$$

greatest

the number or group with the greatest value

35 47 58 61

greatest

greatest value

The coin that has the greatest value is the one that is worth the most.

The quarter has the greatest value.

half-dollar

50 cents or 50¢

half past

Half past is 30 minutes past the hour.

It is half past 9.

halves

When 1 whole is separated into 2 equal parts, the parts are called halves.

height

Height is how tall something is.

hendecagon

A hendecagon is a polygon that has 11 sides.

heptagon

A heptagon is a polygon that has 7 sides.

hexagon

A hexagon is a polygon that has 6 sides.

hour

An hour is 60 minutes.

hundred

10 tens make 1 hundred.

inch (in.)

An inch is a standard unit used to measure length.

increase

550 ⟶ 600

550 increased by 50 is 600.

input

The input is the number that you start with.

Input	Output
3	5
4	6
5	7

irresponsible

When you are given something to use for a certain amount of time and you do not return it, you are being irresponsible.

join

To join means to put together.

3 and 3 is 6 in all.

least

the number or group with the smallest value

35 47 58 61

← least

least value

The dime has the least value.

lend

When you give someone money or an item that will be returned, you lend something to that person.

length

Length is the distance from one end to the other end of an object.

The length of the bat is about 1 yard.

less than (<)

2 is less than 6.

$$2 < 6$$

mental math

Mental math is math you do in your head.

Start at 23. Count on 33, 43.

$$23 + 20 = 43$$

meter (m)

A long step is about a meter. A meter is about 100 centimeters.

minute

There are 60 minutes in 1 hour.

multiplication sentence

$$4 \times 2 = 8$$

4 times 2 equals 8.

multiply

$$3 \times 2 = 6$$
$$2 + 2 + 2 = 6$$

To multiply 3×2 means to add 2 three times.

near doubles

An addition fact with near doubles has an addend that is one more than the other addend.

$$4 + 5 = 9$$

addend   addend

nearest centimeter

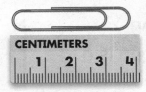

The closest centimeter to the measure is the nearest centimeter.

nearest inch

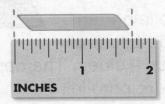

The closest inch to the measure is the nearest inch.

next ten

the following ten after a number

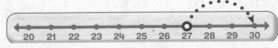

30 is the next ten after 27.

nickel

5 cents or 5¢

nonagon

A nonagon is a polygon that has 9 sides.

number line

A number line is a line that shows numbers in order from left to right.

number sentence

A number sentence has an operation symbol (+ or −) and an equal sign (=).

$$3 + 2 = 5$$

$$\begin{array}{r} 9 \\ -2 \\ \hline 7 \end{array}$$

This is a horizontal number sentence.

This is a vertical number sentence.

number word

A number word shows a number using words. The number word for 23 is twenty-three.

octagon

An octagon is a polygon that has 8 sides.

odd

An odd number cannot be divided into two equal parts.

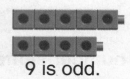

9 is odd.

order

Numbers can be put in counting order from least to greatest or from greatest to least.

27 72 107 117 **171**

least   greatest

output

The output is the number you get after using the rule with an input.

Input	Output
3	5
4	6
5	7

parallelogram

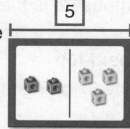

A parallelogram is a quadrilateral that has 4 sides. The opposite sides are parallel.

part

A part is a piece of a whole.

2 and 3 are parts of 5.

 5

penny

I cent or I¢

pentagon

A pentagon is a polygon with 5 sides and 5 vertices.

pictograph

A pictograph uses pictures to show data.

Favorite Ball Games	
Baseball	♀ ♀
Soccer	♀ ♀ ♀ ♀ ♀ ♀ ♀
Tennis	♀ ♀ ♀ ♀

Each ♀ = I student

plane shape

A plane shape is a flat shape.

circle   rectangle   square   triangle

p.m.

The half of the day from midday to midnight can be described as p.m.

7:10 PM

polygon

A polygon is a plane shape with 3 or more sides.

predict

When you predict, you say what you think will happen.

There is a pattern in this cube train.

You can predict that the next two cubes will be green and yellow.

producer

When you make something to sell, you are a producer.

product

The answer to a multiplication sentence is called the product.

$$4 \times 2 = 8$$

↑ product

pyramid

A pyramid is a solid figure with a base that is a polygon and faces that are triangles that meet in a point.

quadrilateral

A quadrilateral is a polygon with 4 sides.

quarter

25 cents or 25¢

quarter past

15 minutes after the hour.

It is quarter past 4.

quarter to

15 minutes before the hour.

It is quarter to 4.

rectangular prism

A rectangular prism is a solid figure with bases that are rectangles.

regroup

10 ones can be regrouped as 1 ten.

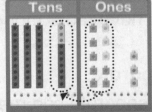

related

Addition facts and subtraction facts are related if they have the same numbers.

$$2 + 3 = 5$$
$$5 - 2 = 3$$

responsible

When you are given something to use for a certain amount of time and you return it when you are done, you are being responsible.

row

1	2	3	4	5
11	12	13	14	15
21	22	23	24	25
31	32	33	34	35

← row

save

If you save your money, you will have more money.

separate

To separate can mean to subtract, or to take something apart into two or more parts.

$$5 - 2 = 3$$

side

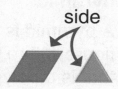

side

A side is a line segment that makes one part of a plane shape.

solid figures

Solid figures have length, width, and height.

These are all solid figures.

spend

If you spend your money, you will have less money.

sphere

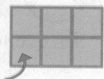

A sphere is a solid figure that looks like a ball.

square units

The area of the rectangle is 6 square units.

square unit

standard form

The standard form is a way to write a number using only digits.

436

subtract

When you subtract, you find out how many are left or which group has more.

$$5 - 3 = 2$$

subtraction sentence

$$12 - 4 = 8$$

difference

minus

sum

$$3 + 4 = 7$$

$$
\begin{array}{r}
4 \\
+ 3 \\
\hline
7
\end{array}
$$

sum →

symbol

A character or picture used to represent something is called a symbol.

The symbol will be ⚲. Each ⚲ represents 1 student.

tally mark

We use tally marks to keep track of information in an organized list.

Ways to Show 30¢			
Quarter	Dime	Nickel	Total
I		I	30¢
	III		30¢
	II	II	30¢
	I	IIII	30¢
		ЖІ I	30¢

tens digit

how many groups of ten are in a number

238

tens digit

thousand

10 hundreds make 1 thousand.

times

Another word for multiply is times.

times

$$7 \times 3 = 21$$

factor factor product

trapezoid

A trapezoid is a plane shape with 4 sides, 4 angles, and 4 vertices. One pair of sides are parallel.

triangular prism

A triangular prism has two faces that are triangles and three other faces that are rectangles.

unequal

Unequal parts are parts that are not equal.

5 unequal parts

unit

You can use different units to measure objects.

About 12 inches.
About 1 foot.

vertex

A vertex is a point where 2 sides or 3 or more edges meet. A cone also has a vertex.

vertex

whole

The two halves make one whole circle.

width

Width is the distance across an object.

withdrawal

When you take money out of the bank, you are making a withdrawal.

yard

A baseball bat is about a yard long.

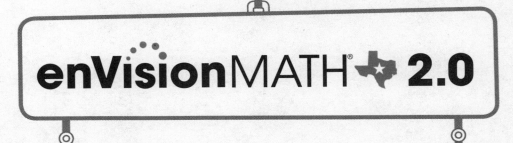

Photographs

Photo locators denoted as follows: Top (T), Center (C), Bottom (B), Left (L), Right (R), Background (Bkgd)

001 Peshkova/Fotolia;**041** Rich Carey/Shutterstock;**087** Adisa/Shutterstock;**133** Graph/Shutterstock;**181** Peter Wollinga/Shutterstock;**239** Nancy Gill/Shutterstock;**297** Bonita R. Cheshier/Shutterstock;**363** Sergey Uryadnikov/Shutterstock

435 Juriah Mosin/Shutterstock;**483** HamsterMan/Shutterstock;**525L** Galyna Andrushko/Shutterstock;**525R** Alexey Stiop/Shutterstock;**571** Marek Velechovsky/Shutterstock;**627** O Driscoll Imaging/Shutterstock;**699** Ant Clausen/Fotolia;**795** James Insogna/Fotolia;**845** Carola Schubbel/Fotolia